LINCOLN CHRISTIAN COLLEGE AND SE
P9-CRQ-783

MARKETING TO
women

How to
Increase Your Share
of the
World's Largest
Market

SECOND EDITION
MARTI BARLETTA

Dearborn™
Trade Publishing
A **Kaplan Professional** Company

This publication is designed to provide accurate and authoritative information in regard to the subject matter covered. It is sold with the understanding that the publisher is not engaged in rendering legal, accounting, or other professional service. If legal advice or other expert assistance is required, the services of a competent professional person should be sought.

Vice President and Publisher: Cynthia A. Zigmund
Senior Acquisitions Editor: Michael Cunningham
Production Editor: Caitlin Ostrow
Interior Design: Lucy Jenkins
Cover Design: Jody Billert, Design Literate
Typesetting: Elizabeth Pitts

© 2006 by Martha Barletta

Published by Dearborn Trade Publishing
A Kaplan Professional Company

All rights reserved. The text of this publication, or any part thereof, may not be reproduced in any manner whatsoever without written permission from the publisher.

Printed in the United States of America

06 07 08 10 9 8 7 6 5 4 3 2 1

Library of Congress Cataloging-in-Publication Data

Barletta, Marti.
    Marketing to women : how to increase your share of the world's largest market / Marti Barletta.—2nd ed.
       p. cm.
    Includes bibliographical references and index.
    ISBN 1-4195-2019-9 (alk. paper)
    1. Women consumers. 2. Marketing. I. Title.
    HC79.C6B337 2005
    658.8′ 04—dc22

                                   2005021741

Dearborn Trade books are available at special quantity discounts to use for sales promotions, employee premiums, or educational purposes. Please call our Special Sales Department to order or for more information at 800-621-9621, ext. 4444, e-mail trade@dearborn.com, or write to Dearborn Trade Publishing, 30 South Wacker Drive, Suite 2500, Chicago, IL 60606-7481.

"If your competition learns before you do what Marti Barletta knows about marketing to women—you won't be the alpha anything. Read this book on the way home from the bookstore. And don't spend another nickel on marketing until you've finished it."
—Mickey Brazeal, Associate Director, Marketing Communication Program, Stuart Graduate School of Business, Illinois Institute of Technology

"If you're looking for a way to increase sales for your business, you need to read this book. *Marketing to Women* is an engaging, insightful road map to marketing success with women—full of practical advice you can implement today."
—Heidi L. Steiger, Executive Vice President, Neuberger Berman, and founder of The Women's Partnership

"Martha Barletta's insights on marketing to women are plenty, often both surprising and self-evident. They are well documented, served with clarity, and quite often with a delightful sense of humor. I urge you to grasp, learn, and become inspired."
—Hans-Olov Olsson, Senior Vice President and Chief Marketing Officer, Ford Motor Company (formerly President and CEO, Volvo)

"*Marketing to Women* reveals important insights for successfully marketing products and services to the growing women's market. When businesses understand and meet the complex needs of women, they can successfully grow their market share. In this book, Martha Barletta provides the tools that enable businesses to do just that."
—Jocelyn Carter-Miller, Executive Vice President and Chief Marketing Officer, Office Depot, Inc.

"I see the forest! *Marketing to Women* unveils an incredible market potential that can be leveraged by almost any business today. This stuff should be standard reading for every business executive."
—Janet Seese Disbrow, Vice President, National Sales and Marketing,
SBC Directory Operations

"Ignore this book and you could be leaving half the money on the table. Half of my customers are fundamentally different from the other half. This book shows marketers and salespeople what women want! Well-researched and very readable, the book lays out some fascinating findings about gender differences and then illustrates how to translate them into savvy strategy and actionable tactics. Barletta brings real-world experience to her ideas and backs them up with countless examples. Any marketer—male or female—trying to sell to women has got to get this book!"
—Paul Iaffaldano, Chief Revenue Officer, The Weather Channel
Interactive

DEDICATION

To my daughter, Sarah, whom I admire for her fiery, independent spirit and tenacious intellect; to my son, Nick, who has astonished us since age three with his wisdom and wit; and to my husband, Van, whose many insights have often enlightened me and whose unflagging support in all matters business and personal has so greatly enhanced my success.

CONTENTS

PART IV The Bigger Picture

When I saw Marti's book *Marketing to Women,* I was immediately transported back in time. December 1996. Boston. I attended a meeting with 30 women business owners, women authors, women entrepreneurs. And I was abruptly introduced to the Women's Opportunity.

Looking back, I'm not just amazed by how much I didn't know. I'm stunned by how *I didn't know what I didn't know.* Stunned by the enormous opportunity. Bottom line: This "Women's Thing" is . . . unmistakably, in my opinion . . . ECONOMIC OPPORTUNITY NO. 1.

(And there's no close second.)

Statistics overwhelm: Women are responsible for 83 percent of all consumer purchases. Home furnishings . . . 94 percent. Vacations . . . 92 percent. Houses . . . 91 percent. Consumer electronics . . . 55 percent. Cars . . . make 60 percent of purchases, significantly influence 90 percent. Services are the same story: Choice of a new bank account by women . . . 89 percent of the time. Health care . . . 80 percent of decisions, over two-thirds of all health care spending.

Add in women's role as "purchasing officer" for consumer goods for their families and their significant role as professional purchasing officer for corporations and agencies, and, in effect, you have an American Women's Economy that accounts for over half of the U.S. GDP . . . about $7 trillion. Translation: Earth's largest economy . . . American Women.

American women by themselves are, in effect, the largest "national" economy on earth, larger than the entire (!) Japanese economy. The opportunity I've just described amounts to trillions of $$$$$$ in the United States, trillions and trillions more around the world.

"This" is even bigger than the Internet. *I have never before tripped over an opportunity this size.*

And what makes this an opportunity? (1) The plain fact that men and women are different. *Dramatically* different. (2) At the moment, almost no one "gets it."

Men and women *are* equal, to be sure. (Or at least should be!) But I am an unabashed "difference feminist," as it's labeled. There is no doubt—I think, beyond a shadow of a doubt—that men and women are *different.* And different in a way that is oh, so relevant to business—from product development to marketing to distribution strategies.

Try the following and see if you in any way disagree: "Men always move faster through a store's aisles. Men spend less time looking. They usually don't like asking where things are. You'll see a man move impatiently through a store to the section he wants, pick something up, and then, almost abruptly, he's ready to buy . . . For a man, ignoring the price tag is almost a sign of virility." It's amusing. Its implications: enormous. Source: the meticulous research Paco Underhill has performed for the most prestigious clients over the last few decades.

Or take women and financial advisors: Women want a carefully considered plan, want to be listened to, want to be taken seriously. Want to read the material, want to think about it. Women do *not* want . . . an in-your-face sales pitch.

Every time I launch a discussion about all this, I still hear the echoes of that December 1996 meeting. I still hear those Very Powerful Women . . . without exception . . . telling me the degree to which they have been ignored, dismissed, treated as brainless by bankers and doctors and car salesmen and computer salesmen.

A smartly turned-out, six-figure-income financial services executive approached me after one of my riffs on women's treatment in the marketplace. Over lunch a few days before, she'd gone to a Mercedes dealership with every intention of buying a car. All three salesmen were in their cubicles, eating their sandwiches. As she wandered the showroom floor, none bothered to wander in her direction. Finally, some guy finished off his peanut butter and jelly, or whatever, and came over to her. First words out of his mouth: "Honey, are you sure you have the kind of money to be looking at a car like this?"

Some of the men who read this remark will say, "Bull. She's making it up, or at least she's exaggerating." *None* of the women who read this will have that reaction. (None!) This is something that, after years of listening and studying, I . . . *know.* I've got, literally, dozens upon dozens upon dozens of stories like this . . . from financial services companies and hospitals and hotels and computer companies, as well as those forever-dim car companies . . . to back me up.

Bottom line: *Financial services* companies don't get it. *Hospitality* companies don't get it. *Health services* companies don't get it, even though two-thirds of health care employees are women. God alone knows, *automobile* companies, with a half-trillion dollars a year in retail sales in the United States alone, don't get it.

This idea is enormous. It is simple. It is subtle. It is obvious. It is the (economic) world's . . . BEST KEPT SECRET. *Until now.*

Finally . . . we have a book that tells how to do it.

Marti Barletta *gets* the Women's Opportunity. She *gets* women and knows how to bring them to your brand—and keep them there. She brings to us readers years of practical experience across all marketing disciplines: advertising, direct marketing, promotion, event marketing, and more. This is why I named her MVP/BizGuru for 2004: "Marti is the most vociferous and accomplished spokesperson-presenter in the mega-opportunity world of Marketing to Women." She backs up all the talk about gender differences with careful research. And, most important, she shows how to leverage these differences to create a real "women's strategy"—cost-effective and practical—that will drive your sales skyward and pull your profits right along with them.

The numbers are unequivocal. The gender differences are undeniable. The opportunity is inarguable. The market is enormous. The competitive advantage is inevitable. The opportunity—trillions of dollars in the United States alone—is waiting.

Near the end of the book, Marti provides some summary advice to CEOs. At the top of the list: "All this" is not about a "specialty marketing group" for women's stuff or some sort of "women's initiative." *"All this"* is *about a struggle for the very soul of the company and the essence of the brand itself*—for computer and financial service firms at least as much as for consumer goods marketers.

In short, boldness and wholesale commitment alone will lasso this matchless opportunity.

Good luck. Remember, you have a rare opportunity to lead the parade!

ACKNOWLEDGMENTS

Top Ten Reasons This Book Exists

1. *Changes since the first edition.* Since the release of this book's first edition in 2003, I have been excited and delighted to note the number of new participants in the marketing to women "space." In 2003, there were three books published in the last decade of the 20th century. Mine was the first of the 21st century, and it was soon followed by a respectable number of excellent entries. In 2003, I could count my competitors on one hand—and now I'd need three hands. And the most exciting development has been the very recent surge in major companies' in-market enthusiasm for marketing to women.

   When I started my consultancy six years ago, there was no more than a dawning awareness that women might warrant some marketing attention, and it was seen very much in the context of an "emerging" or niche market. Yes, health care had long known women were their primary customers, and there were feeble signs of life within the financial services arena. But to tell you the truth, those signs were few and far between, and it was occasionally quite the challenge to come up with in-market examples of some of the principles in this book. An ad here, a promotion there, a sponsorship over in the corner somewhere . . .

   Then, suddenly, The Age of Enlightenment! Now there are flourishing initiatives not only in financial services but also in home improvement, home services, retail, consumer electronics, golf, and, yes, even in the automotive industry. So this new edition is fully loaded with a smorgasbord of live examples—case studies that clarify and ad samples that illuminate.

2. *An all new chapter: PrimeTime Women™.* Moreover, I've added a new chapter focused entirely on what I call the target marketer's

golden bull's-eye: PrimeTime Women™. That's what I call that vital, active, involved, high-spending band of women between the ages of 50 and 70 years old. They're unlike any previous generation of women in history—more educated, engaged, and energetic—and will set the pattern for all the generations of women to follow them. Because they're in their highest earning years, at a point where their households command their maximum asset levels, they've got a little more time and a *lot* more money than younger women, and they're determined to put it to good use.

And what do marketers call these peak prospects? "Middle-aged women," "mature women," "senior women" . . . Like it or not, these terms are rarely either intended or received as a compliment. Marketers already have plenty on their plates, and women of that description don't seem all that appealing as a great way to build sales and share.

And yet, they are! In fact, for many industries they may well be the sole source of growth for the next 15–20 years. So I figured I'd get out ahead of the pack and start figuring out what marketers can do to make the most of their money with this market.

This chapter is the first pass at the subject of my next book—the trend that isn't trendy (yet!) but that will be the really big money maker for companies who get it—*PrimeTime Women*™.

3. ***Robyn Hall.*** The godmother of the book, whose confident command of marketing, piercing creative insights, and prodigious project management talents make her an indispensable godsend.

4. ***Mike Slind.*** The former *Fast Company* editor whose help in capturing complex psychological dimensions with a wry wit and clever turn of phrase informed and illuminated the new Prime-Time Women™ chapter immensely.

5. ***Angel Gibson.*** The planning maven whose depth of consumer knowledge and unconventional thinking give this book a fresh perspective on what's new and happenin' in Marketing to Women. And ***Maris Gersh,*** the bright young newcomer to our team whose resourcefulness and analytical insights have amazed us from day one and already added so much.

6. The rest of *The TrendSight Group team: Betsy Westhoff*, the leader whose decisiveness, good judgment, and exceptional people abilities make her the perfect executive to build the company toward an ever brighter future; *Marcia Sutter*, whose creativity and strategic savvy qualify her as both marketing maven and chief guardian of our brand; *Jane Demakos*, whose strong business instincts, sense of purpose, and wicked wit have enlightened me and our consulting clients in every meaning of the word; *Tammy Murray*, who runs my life, thank heavens, and whose unfailingly even temper and cheerful spirit have saved me from many a cloudy day; and *Michaela Shaw*, our archivist and collective memory, whose labors preserve us from the chaos of information overload. The whole team's commitment and enthusiasm are phenomenal—more than I could have dared hope for, and I thank you for it with all my heart.

7. The *Dearborn Trade Publishing team*, whose talents, commitment, support, and enthusiasm go far above and beyond the publishing norm, and have contributed so incredibly much to the book's success: *Mary B. Good*, the original visionary editor who saw the potential in this book and brought it to reality; and *Michael Cunningham*, the editor now entrusted with guiding it further along the path to continued growth. I am also immensely grateful to the Marketing and Sales teams at Dearborn, including *Eileen Johnson*, VP, Business Development; *Leslie Banks*, Marketing and Publicity Director; *Courtney Goethals*, Senior Publicist; and *Agnes Banks*, International Sales and Rights Manager. And, most immediately, to the conscientious and skillful Production staff, including *Jack Kiburz*, Senior Managing Editor; and *Caitlin Ostrow*, Production Editor. Words can't convey my appreciation and admiration to each member of the team that stands behind this book, offering support, expertise, and energy toward its success.

8. *Jeff Kleinman*. A prince among men and a king among agents, whose savvy advice, confident guidance, and continuous involvement have significantly advanced the value and success of this book at every stage.

9. ***Elissa Polston.*** A dear friend and the sharpest marketing mind I've ever met, whose ability to see beyond boundaries reveals new paths for everyone, and whose flashing wit inspires delight in all who know her.

10. ***Dr. Jeanie Egmon.*** A friend indeed, whose three "thought interventions" genuinely changed my path dramatically: first, to find my calling, and then to crystallize my thinking into the Gender-Trends™ model that guides my work every day.

To all of you, my heartfelt thanks.

Unveiling the Market

Women's Wealth and
Purchasing Power

Back in the 1950s, when cars had tail fins and Saturday nights were spent at the drive-in, a car company stumbled upon the big idea of gender marketing. Knowing that women were buying cars in greater numbers than ever before, the company offered a new model for female customers: it had pink floral upholstery and a matching parasol. The model was a dismal failure. Women weren't buying it. Gender marketing didn't work.

Women are the world's most powerful consumers. They are the big spenders, whether you're talking about households, corporate purchasing, or small businesses. Would you believe that until the first edition of this book was published, *not a single book* addressed the nuts-and-bolts specifics of how to market to persons of the female persuasion? Even today, there are only a handful of other books on gender-based marketing. Yet there are plenty of books that focus on much smaller markets with a lot less money—kids' marketing, Gen X marketing, and ethnic marketing, to name a few.

Why is that, when women make up *just over half* the population and, more important, control *well over half* of the spending? It's time for a book that presents the business case, identifies the operating insights, and details specific marketing tactics for the consumer group marketers need most: *women.* This is that book.

What's the first rule of marketing? *Understand your market.* The second rule? *Understand your consumer.*

What Makes Women a Worthwhile Market?

Packaged goods companies and retailers have long recognized that women form the core of their market. However, until very recently, the big-ticket industries—automotive, financial services, computers, consumer electronics, home improvement, and travel, for example—appear to have overlooked female customers almost entirely. Despite the fact that women represent a significant percentage of the buyers in most of these categories—usually 40 to 60 percent—we still see almost exclusively male-targeted advertising.

Somebody's not watching the "buy-o-meter" carefully enough. By not understanding their markets, these companies are leaving money on the table. Women consumers who could be converts if approached with the right marketing message are instead choosing to go over to the competition. Present and future profits are slipping through these marketers' fingers like sand—very expensive sand!

What is worse—and makes this missed opportunity a devastating sales drain—is the multiplier effect each female consumer sets into motion. What women buy, women "sell"; when they're pleased with products and services, they talk about them to others—men and women alike. The resulting word of mouth is the most powerful marketing tool you could ask for. Not only is it free (not a bad benefit for the budget conscious), but it's more credible, effective, and persuasive than any paid marketing tactic. Every new woman customer you acquire creates a multiplier effect of sales referrals and extra business.

How could a market so huge and lucrative be overlooked?

> "It is a ridiculously rare corporation that takes advantage of the women's opportunity. What a costly mistake." —Tom Peters, *The Circle of Innovation*

Surely American business, with its highly honed ability to follow the dollar signs, couldn't fail to notice a consumer group whose spending power is greater than the entire economy of Japan?

> A reality TV show was doing an episode that involved leaving a $50 bill on the sidewalk and taping the reactions of people as they came along, spied the cash, and then responded in one way or another. Surprisingly, many people didn't pick up the money. When producers asked the passersby why they'd ignored the $50, most of the answers were similar: I figured the money couldn't possibly be real or someone would have picked it up already.

Sometimes, what looks like cash for the taking and money for the making really *is* just what it looks like. And just because your competitors aren't sharp enough to know a golden opportunity when it's right in front of them, there's no reason for you to pass up a profitable prospect.

The fact is that although the women's market has been skimming along below the radar for a number of years, it is *very real*—and it's moving at a velocity that will leave anyone who remains unconvinced behind in the marketing dust.

The statistics and research are unequivocal. Tom Peters, one of the top marketing gurus in the world, has been championing the women's market for years, calling it "Opportunity Number One for the foreseeable future." His 1999 book, *The Circle of Innovation,* devoted a full chapter to it, titled "It's a Woman's World." His booklet *Women Roar!* emphasizes the dangers of ceding the market to the competition. His most recent book, *Re-Imagine!,* dials up the message with a chapter titled "Trends Worth Trillion$$$ I: Women Roar." Ironic as it may seem, you could say that Tom Peters is the "*Father* of Marketing to Women."

Why Market Differently to Women?

The answer lies in Rule Two—understand your consumer. Up until now, we all assumed that men and women operated pretty much the same way when it came to buying decisions. We thought the marketing maxims developed and handed down by the founders of commercial communications were "normal" for all adults. Upon closer examination, it's turning out that they're normal for *men.* Women have a very different set of priorities, preferences, and attitudes. Their purchase decision process is radically different. And they respond differently to marketing media and messages, language, and visuals. Any marketer who wants to capture a substantial share of a woman's wallet has some gender learning to do in order to understand this previously over-looked consumer.

At this point, you may be asking yourself: *So what if men and women are different? A car is still a car, and a computer is a computer–right?*

Wrong question.

Never Mind the Product, It's the Prospect That Matters

Ford, Sprint, and IBM pitch their products to a number of different target audiences. And while the basic function and features of each of those products remains the same regardless of whether the user is a young girl, a grandmother, or a mom, most of us can quickly recognize the foolishness of using the same marketing approach for prospects of such varying ages and mindsets.

Similarly, men and women perceive, believe, and behave in ways unique to their gender. At times, their differing roles in life—different work, different play, different domestic responsibilities—generate dif-fering needs. Smart marketers know it's not the product and its fea-tures that should drive the marketing; it's the prospect and *her* needs. The communication connection—aligning your brand with your target audience's perceptions and preferences—is what will propel the success of your marketing programs.

Some of the gender differences we'll be looking into are pretty sur-prising. All of them will reveal insights on how to boost your business results by tailoring your marketing to the mindset of your target. The process itself will illuminate a remarkable number of new pathways to the competitive advantage you're looking for.

Men's Marketing Doesn't Work with Women

For personal or political reasons, some people are adamant that men and women are the same; others concede that gender differences exist but view them as immaterial to marketing decisions. People with these viewpoints would like to believe that their current marketing is as effective with women as it is with men. It's not.

Gender-based differences in perceptions, attitudes, and communication styles generate gender-differentiated responses in priorities, decision processes, and purchase outcomes. You can address these differences in your marketing to great advantage, or you can ignore them at your peril. But if you put on blinders, I have to warn you—you're going to be blindsided by your competition, and your share will suffer accordingly.

Women's Marketing Increases Customer Satisfaction among Men

Some marketers do recognize that men and women are different, but they worry that if they tailor their product or service in ways meaningful to women, it will undermine the product or service appeal to men. In fact, exactly the opposite is true. As you'll see, plenty of companies have made marketing and service improvements in order to increase brand appeal to women—and as a bonus, they've discovered that their male customers are happier, too.

The Eight Myths of Marketing to Women

There are plenty of misconceptions about how and why to market to this powerful consumer group. Some of the most prevalent are summarized below. Many advocates of women's marketing have encountered similar objections from skeptical senior management and wished they had convincing answers to these ill-informed assertions. By the time you finish reading this book, you'll be able to debunk each and every one of the eight myths of marketing to women.

But the women's market is real. The numbers are unequivocal. The gender differences are undeniable. The opportunity is inarguable, the market is enormous, *the competitive advantage is inevitable.*

So where are the marketers? Lost in the mists of "conventional wisdom," apparently. Let this book be your lighthouse. Once you see through the myths, your path is clear. The shortest distance between you and business success is *marketing to women.*

The Eight Myths and Myth Busters of Marketing to Women

Myth #1. Marketing to women may be appropriate because it supports diversity; but with our limited resources, we need to stay focused on the business.

Reality. Marketing to women is not about diversity—it's about sales, share, and profits.

Everyone knows the buying power of women consumers is increasing, but some of the numbers are astonishing: Women bring in half or more of the income in most U.S. households. They control 51.3 percent of U.S. private wealth. They handle 80 to 90 percent of spending and purchasing for the household, including unexpected areas like car repairs, tires, computers, and home improvements. Women-owned businesses employ one out of every seven people in the United States. Make no mistake—it's the money, honey. Your brand needs to figure out how to keep it all from flowing to your competitors.

Myth #2. We need to keep our marketing focus on our core customers—men.

Reality. If you're always looking back, how do you expect to move forward?

Many situation analyses look back at the past instead of forward to the future. As a result, a finding that the current customer base is 70 percent white males is typically followed by the inference, "Therefore, it is obvious that white males are our best target." This ignores the fact that most big-ticket companies, such as car manufacturers, computer makers, and tele-communications enterprises, have never gone after other markets with the kind of commitment it takes to make an impact. Don't let past practices limit your thinking and obscure your view of the opportunity.

Myth #3. Average income for women is lower than for men. It doesn't make sense to go after a low-income market.

Reality. Be careful to look beyond the averages.

The women's market is essentially bipolar. One of the most dramatic changes of the 20th century was the entry of women into the workforce beginning in the 1960s and 1970s. Consequently, younger women's incomes, attitudes, and decision-making styles vary significantly from those of their baby boom predecessors. Yet most marketers continue to look at averages for total women, which misleads them into overlooking a wealth of lucrative growth segments.

Myth #4. Marketing to women will require us to double our budget or, worse, split it in half.

Reality. Marketing to women takes the same budget and delivers more bang for the buck.

The secret? In many respects, women want all the same things as men—and then some. Accordingly, when you meet the higher expectations of women, you are more than fulfilling the demands of men. If you've got the guts to go for it, moving your money from an all-male audience to an all-female audience will boost your share and marketing ROI dramatically—particularly if you can sustain your commitment for at least three years. The female buyer base is not saturated with either product or communication; your marketing efforts flourish in an arena virtually uncontested by competitive clutter; your prospects control more spending and investing dollars than men do; and each new woman customer delivers a major multiplier effect through word of mouth and referral rates that far exceed men's. Is it any wonder you get more bang for your buck? Even if you have a fear of commitment and don't want to take the "radical" route described above, the same budget, directed to a dual audience instead of primarily to men, will yield significantly greater returns than you've seen from past marketing efforts.

Myth #5. With women, marketing is all about relationships.

Reality. Don't buy into the simplistic assertion that with women, it's all about relationships.

Although it's true that women put more emphasis on relationships—personal and corporate—than men do, their purchase decisions and responses to communications are affected by far more than "relationships." From word meaning to word-of-mouth referrals, product priorities to Internet usage patterns, women differ from men in many, many marketing dimensions. And to overlook their complexities would be to undermine the effectiveness of your company's programs.

Myth #6. The best way to focus on marketing to women is to undertake a dedicated initiative within our Emerging Markets group.

Reality. Don't single it out—build it in.

In many companies, the marketing-to-women initiative is undertaken by a group designated "Emerging Markets" or "Specialty Markets." With responsibility for African American, Hispanic, and Asian markets—and women—these groups typically have responsibility for 80 percent of the population, yet are allocated at most 10 to 20 percent of the budget!

Women are *not* a niche; at 51 percent of the population, they are the *majority*. Moreover, their buying power far outstrips their representation in the population. In a number of traditionally male categories, they are already the majority: 60+ percent of new cars, 66 percent of home computers, and 55 percent of consumer electronics are purchased by women. Women's preferences and priorities should be integrated into every marketing initiative in the company instead of marginalized as an outlying, solo program. At the strategic stage of planning, researchers, brand managers, sales management, marketing directors, advertising executives—*everyone* involved with consumer communications—should make sure their assumptions and strategic priorities do not overlook the consumers who offer the most opportunity to build sales, share, and the bottom line: *women*.

Myth #7. We believe in gender-neutral marketing—it's what women want.
Reality. Gender-neutral marketing is not how you put your sales into overdrive. Some companies are concerned that treating women differently will offend them—and it will, if it's not done right. (See Myth #8.) Some are adamant that men and women are the same and conclude that their current marketing is equally effective with women and men. It isn't. Hundreds of studies have shown dramatic gender-based differences in perceptions, attitudes, priorities, and communication styles—all the elements that drive brand awareness, preference, persuasion, and sales.

Many companies are trying to justify their reasons for not making changes, going on with business as usual. But it's a justification that's hard to sustain. Today's advances in customer relationship management are driven precisely by the recognition that treating all your customers the same is *not* the best way to make the most of your marketing dollar. You don't market to 'tweens the way you do to 20-somethings; Mona Lisa would respond to a very different pitch than Madonna. Refusing to acknowledge women buyers' different preferences and priorities won't make them go away—the preferences, that is. The women probably will.

Myth #8. I've heard of companies that did woman-specific advertising and nothing happened or it backfired. Gender-specific marketing doesn't work.
Reality. Bad gender-specific marketing doesn't work.

In 1996, Cadillac tried to reach out to women. It launched advertising for the new Catera on the Super Bowl broadcast featuring Cindy Crawford in a leather getup reminiscent of Xena, with copy that began, "Once upon a time, there was a princess . . ." Astonishingly, architects of the campaign asserted it was designed to appeal to women via its "fantasy empowerment" theme. Not astonishingly, it didn't work.

It would be fascinating to see the creative strategy for this TV spot. The people who wrote and approved it were probably under the impression that they knew what women wanted. Chances are it was either not tested with women or was tested with a segment of women not likely to be the best prospects for a luxury vehicle like a Cadillac (few of whom would find either Crawford or Xena aspirational!). The moral of the story: Just as with every other marketing initiative, if you want it to work, you've got to get it right.

How Do We Get Beyond Gender Generalities to Actionable Tactics?

My insights on marketing to women originate in the observation that men and women are different. Brilliant, yes? You may laugh, but the fact of the matter is that even though almost everybody would agree with that simple premise, nobody has translated it into marketing implications—until now. Why not?

The root of the problem is that most people who know a good deal about gender differences don't know much about marketing; and most people who know a good deal about marketing have only a rudimentary understanding of gender differences. Consequently, most articles on the topic offer generic platitudes and stop disappointingly short of concrete principles and tactical applications. General observations like "You have to understand the target"; "All women are not the same"; "Women are complex"; "Recognize her values and emotions"; and "Women are all about relationships" are undeniably true but don't go far enough to be actionable. The end result is that most marketing programs targeted to women fail to maximize the power and potential of this opportunity.

What you need is an approach that combines the perceptiveness of gender expertise and the practical punch of strategic marketing experience—a way to translate understanding into actionable tactics. In short, you need this book.

How This Book Will Boost Your Business

There is so much support proving the power and wealth of the female market that it seems downright odd that some companies still *resist the opportunity*. They look beyond, over, or straight through the female market as if it doesn't exist. This book aims to help you avoid such a costly oversight by answering the three key questions raised above:

1. What makes women a worthwhile market?
2. Why market differently to women?
3. How do we get beyond gender generalities to actionable tactics?

Once those questions are answered convincingly, resistance is futile. Companies that understand their market, understand their consumer, and understand how to translate insights into action will survive and thrive, as they build their share with the largest consumer market in the world. Companies that don't will die. No exaggeration, no histrionics— just simple fact.

Part I of this book begins by quantifying the magnitude of female spending power. Frankly, if you've been getting all your market information from the news media, I wouldn't blame you if you had the (mistaken) impression that there's no money in the women's market. *Au contraire, mon frère,* there's a lot of money out there—and the quick, concise, and convincing evidence in Chapter 1 is going to lay it out for you. Real news you can use for a change!

Chapter 2 will set forth the key findings on gender differences reported through a variety of scientific disciplines. Hundreds of studies spanning cultures across the world have revealed a myriad of significant and relevant variances between male and female. By reviewing some of the key research findings on the biological and behavioral differences between men and women, I'll lay the foundation for understanding and appreciating our differences and evolving a new, more effective way to communicate, motivate, and market.

As we move forward into Part II of the book, I'll assemble the *Gender-Trends™ Marketing Model*. Building on the scientific findings of the previous chapter, and drawing on my 20-plus years of hands-on marketing experience, the model first maps the female mindscape, then highlights differences in how women respond to the various elements of the marketing mix, and, finally, spells out the way a woman consumer's decision process differs from a man's. You'll see that it's more than a theoretical framework or a pretty graphic all dressed up with nowhere to go. The GenderTrends™ Marketing Model is a useful tool with practical applications that will give you the means for dramatically enhancing your marketing and sales effectiveness.

In Part III, I'll apply the GenderTrends model to each stage of the planning process most marketers use in developing their product programs and marketing initiatives. You'll learn ways to use your enhanced understanding of gender-specific tactics and communications to boost the effectiveness of every marketing and sales dollar in your budget, including:

- How to connect with your women consumers' real meanings, motivations, and communication keys
- How to select the marketing tactics that will tap their hot buttons
- How to create groundbreaking advertising platforms and creative executions
- How to follow through to the final frontier—face-to-face selling and service

In Part IV we'll take a step back from the detailed tactics to look at the big picture as well as at some groups I believe deserve a little extra focus. Not all women are the same, and Chapter 11 is devoted to one particular segment of women that warrants special attention (currently they are getting NONE!). I call this group PrimeTime Women™—a name that captures both the zest and buying power of women over 50—they hold the purse strings of the future.

The book closes with a chapter called "Notes to the CEO," which is addressed to the executive who signs off on your company's strategic focus and allocates its resources across the organization. The compelling business case, the convincing insights, and the conviction of the business director who leads the charge toward women's marketing cannot succeed without the commitment of top management and the budget for a comprehensive initiative. If your chief executive reads nothing else on the subject, make sure he or she takes a look at this summary of how and why marketing to women offers your company the best return on your marketing and sales dollar.

Who Am I to Say So?

As you read through *Marketing to Women*, you'll learn that differences in men's and women's attitudes, aptitudes, and abilities have developed through a combination of biological factors, like chromosomes and hormones, and behavioral causes, like evolutionary roles and cultural socialization. To these factual findings, I've added my own interpretations and marketing opinions to provide some concrete ideas for you to use in building your business.

My points of view on women's marketing have been shaped by a number of different elements, including my genetics, my upbringing, my career interests, and my business experience. Take my parents, for example. My father speaks French, Urdu, and Arabic and has penned two terrific mysteries and an epic novel. My mother, a published poet and Fulbright scholar who taught English at the University of Lima in Peru, speaks French and Spanish and has immersed herself in the study of Native American languages for the past 30 years. With genes like that, who wouldn't find herself fascinated with communications and languages? Because communications and languages are two key cornerstones of marketing in general and female gender culture in particular, apparently my parents blessed me with an interest in, and an aptitude for, the field before I was even born.

My natural propensities were nurtured by the environments I was raised in. Because my father was an economist in the Foreign Service of the State Department, I grew up all over the world. From my Moroccan *amah* to French first grade, through tours of duty in Beirut, Brussels, and Singapore, I had ample opportunity to immerse myself in different cultures, coming to understand and delight in the fact that different people have different ways of doing things. Similarly, men and women brought up in male and female gender cultures have different ways of doing things. And whereas I might have fallen into the trap of thinking that one way was better or worse than another, my travels have helped me to see that they are not—they are just different, that's all.

My choice of a marketing career grew out of this interest in people—who they are, what they want, and how they behave. I majored in economics at Carleton College and followed up with an MBA from Wharton, where my favorite classes were the ones oriented around consumer behavior. Four years in brand management honed my analytical skills and appreciation for how all the elements of the marketing mix interact with each other. Fifteen years working on blue-chip brands like Kraft and Kodak at leading advertising agencies like FCB and integrated marketing firm Frankel gave me hands-on experience with a whole spectrum of marketing disciplines, including strategy, positioning, promotion, event marketing, and others.

I always liked working on "new business," because each pitch was an opportunity to study an unfamiliar category and consider some innovative marketing ideas. During pitches for grocery products, personal care, and retail accounts, we knew from the start our target audience would be some segment of the women's market. What I found interesting, though, was the growing role of women buyers in the big-ticket categories historically purchased by men. From cars to computers, from home improvement to health care and high tech, women were rapidly raising themselves onto the radar screen in unprecedented numbers.

In addition, more and more of the marketing executives at my client and prospect companies were women. Yet many of the marketing principles we accepted and applied in our programs were rooted in an outlook and set of assumptions that were slightly foreign to the norms and practices of most women. And every year, a study would surface saying women felt marketers were doing a lousy job reaching them with messages they found appealing, let alone compelling. Something was out of alignment, and it seemed to me there could be a mighty big business opportunity in figuring out what it was and how to fix it. That's when I created my own informal PhD program in gender-specific marketing.

To me, the study of male and female gender cultures has become just flat-out fascinating. The original application of a lifetime of marketing learning to a new way of thinking about consumers is thought provoking and exciting. And the resulting marketing insights offer some amazingly fruitful and innovative ways to capture a competitive edge.

When I launched my company The TrendSight Group (http://
www.trendsight.com) in 1998, not much was going on in the marketing-to-women field. But over the past several years, interest in this category has surged, as evidenced by the number of books, articles, and
news reports on the topic as well as by my busy speaking and consulting calendar. I believe we have reached the "tipping point," as Mal-
colm Gladwell calls it, in marketing to women. Fortune 500 companies
and small business owners are getting it! Over the past five years I've
had the opportunity to work with dozens of companies who recognize
that improving their communication to women will increase their
share of the world's largest market segment. And although the products are diverse (financial services, retail, home improvement, golf,
wine, cameras, to name a few), the end results are remarkably similar—
increased sales, customer satisfaction, and retention—once companies
begin marketing to women.

Gender-savvy principles apply in the workplace as well. We're working with lots of companies who recognize that effective business-to-
business communications to women translate into more effective and
efficient ways to work in today's corporate world.

And the great thing is, marketing to women is not rocket science and
it doesn't take incremental marketing dollars. All it requires is looking
at your marketing plan from a different angle.

I truly believe that marketing effectively to women is *the most significant and profitable opportunity in marketing today.*

By this time next year, you could be harvesting the benefits of a busi-
ness-building initiative that boosts your share, customer loyalty, and
marketing return on investment by improving your communications to
women. As we move forward, you'll access the tools that will allow you
to make every element of your marketing plan not only more female
friendly but also more financially productive.

With that in mind, let's start by taking a look at the research and reality that defines today's market of female consumers. You may be surprised at what you find—who's got the money, where it's coming from,
and, most important, who controls America's checkbook.

Why Market to Women?

CHAPTER 1

The Power of the Purse

The first thing you notice when you open the proverbial purse is a good sign: there's a big fat wallet inside. While any given woman may not be toting a roll of bills, collectively "she" is. She's not only earning it today, either; she's powering up to earn more and more over the years ahead.

More important to marketers, as the primary purchaser for everything her household needs, she's *spending* it—along with her husband's paycheck. And her buying authority goes beyond traditionally female purchases like clothing, furnishings, and food. These days women are buying cars, computers, and carpeting, and shelling out the cash for insurance policies, investments, and improvements to the home as well.

What's most important to marketers is *who gets those dollars*—and I can tell you how to make sure it's you and your company. But first, let me fill you in on some of the less-known facts of the female market.

The "Silent Generation" Shakes the World

The big sea change started with women of the so-called silent generation, which is what many demographers call people born between

1925 and 1942. The irony is that the women of this generation weren't silent at all. They brought about one of the most sweeping upheavals ever seen in any society—and fundamentally altered the male/female equation.

Tremendous changes have occurred over the past 35 to 40 years, symptoms of a sociological explosion that has left virtually no field, no marketing group, and no person unaffected. The women of the silent generation may have gone to college initially for their "MRS" degree—but they went to college. They may have entered the workplace out of a sense of national duty, standing in while the men went to war; but once there, they found they could do the work and liked the feelings of contribution and accomplishment—not to mention the independence of a paycheck.

Their daughters, the baby boomers, shifted into higher gear in their workplace goals, fueled in part by the desire to have economic independence after seeing the effects of its absence on their mothers, particularly when their mothers' marriages ended. For the men's part, old worries about women taking jobs away from the men who needed them receded. In the late 1980s and early 1990s, many households were grateful for that second income—perhaps considered disposable before—when many husbands lost their jobs in massive layoffs. By the time the economy roared back to life later in the 1990s, employers were just grateful to have the human capital that women represented. The cumulative effect was that the workplace opened to women more fully than ever, and despite the occasional grumbling and resistance from hard-liners, the entire view of women's right to occupy the workplace—at any level—underwent a seismic shift.

Women Now: Advancing through Advanced Degrees

For the past 15 years, women have been taking home a substantial majority of college degrees—57 percent, as a matter of fact, or one-third more than men.[1] The occupational opportunities open to women will continue to grow as the job market continues to trend toward an information economy. An explosion of jobs available to the well educated will propel women's earning power upward at a geometric rate—maybe even fast enough to break through the glass ceiling they've been bumping up against until now.

GenderTrends Genius: Lisa Finn

Editor, Marketing to Women, *a monthly newsletter that covers research on women's attitudes and behavior, tracks marketing efforts aimed at women, and identifies and analyzes trends in the women's market.*

What's New about the Women's Market?

For years, women have been recognized as the "gatekeepers" for family products, and they continue to be primary decision makers for most household goods. Now marketers in industries ranging from automotive to financial services, luxury travel to electronics, are discovering that women not only hold the keys to household purchases but also are increasingly driving big-ticket expenditures for themselves and their families. In essence, women are multiple markets in one: They buy for themselves, they buy for their families, and, in increasing numbers, they buy for their businesses.

Forward-thinking companies are finding ways to capitalize on all three— by developing marketing plans that address women's multifaceted lifestyles and by evaluating and retraining existing sales and customer service forces to better serve women's needs and interests. (Continued on page 299)

Graduate degrees just take the opportunities up a notch; they open up jobs in the field in which the graduate work was done, yet also create access to related jobs that have even higher earning potential. For instance, women are earning 58 percent of master's degrees[2] and are expected to earn 47 percent of all doctoral degrees in 2005.[3] Fifty-two percent[4] of today's law school graduating classes are women. And a law degree provides access to far more than a career practicing law; it provides the track to partnerships, judicial careers, government posts, and more. Similarly, business schools are seeing greater numbers of female graduates: women now earn more MBAs than do men.[5] In another top-earning profession, 46 percent of the medical degrees are being awarded to women.[6]

Other occupations, from biotech to economics, accounting to auditing, and management to marketing, are all seeing women assuming larger roles.

As this change in the workplace continues, one obvious result is that women are building their current incomes. This in turn ratchets up the household income in dual-earner families—even as it fuels the demand for more consumer goods. The dual-worker family not only *has* more, it *needs* more: two cars, two computers, two 401(k) plans, and so on. And the dual-earner dynamic expands women's participation in the household's big purchases. It's her money, too, and she gets more say in how it's spent.

Another important consequence of women's growing earning power is that women are enabled to view marriage as a personal choice rather than an economic necessity. This in turn results in an increase in the total number of households: more houses, more accoutrements, more *spending.*

The simple fact is that *women are now deeply integrated into the workplace, are more educated on average than men,* and *often earn as much as or more than men.* The result is power: the power of the purse that comes from earning.

In short:

- Women *earn and own* more today than at any previous time in recorded history—and their financial power is accelerating.
- Independent of income or ownership, women *control most of the spending* in the household. The generally accepted estimate of women's buying power puts it at 80 percent of all household spending.

The Four Components of the Women's Market

There are four ways in which the women's market wields a big stick: the first two provide some perspective on how much women earn and own; the second two cast light on how women spend.

1. Earning Power: What's in Her Wallet?

On average, women are earning a whole lot more money than they used to. In fact, households across America can thank women's earning power for their steady growth in the standard of living. It's true now and will continue to be so. Over the next two decades we will see the immense assets of two generations become increasingly concentrated in the hands of baby boomer women. What that means is that

---

FIGURE 1.1 Wives Earning More Than Husbands[7]

- All women: 31%
- Women with MBAs: 60
- Women earning more than $100,000:   70

---

there's an existing market today and an even larger potential market that spans the next two decades.

Let's look at a few reasons for this change in both the current and future women's markets:

- *Soaring income.* Over the past three decades (1970–2002), men's median income has barely budged (+0.6 percent after adjusting for inflation), while women's has soared (+63 percent).[8]

- *Narrowing wage gap.* While it's true that on average, full-time, year-round working women earn only 78 cents on the dollar compared to their male counterparts, that wage gap is narrowing rapidly.[9] In 1998, women ages 25 to 34 earned 83 cents on the male dollar; and younger women ages 19 to 24 earned 89 cents.[10]

- *Earning more.* As of 2002, 31 percent of women outearned their husbands.[11] That was up from 25 percent in 1997 and 17 percent in 1987, so the trend seems to be rising rapidly.[12] High earnings correlate directly with higher education: Almost half (43 percent)[13] of working wives with graduate degrees earn more than their husbands, as do 60 percent of women with business degrees. (See Figure 1.1.)

- *Majority of household income in majority of households (HH).* Women bring in *half or more* of the HH income in the *majority* of U.S. households. Don't forget that 27 percent of U.S. households are headed by single women—and those women, of course, bring in *all* of their household income.

- *Higher-paying occupations.* Although most women still work in the traditionally female occupations of secretary, teacher, and nurse, a substantial and growing percentage work in nontraditional occupations that pay more.[14]

- *Financial acuity.* Between 1985 and 1995, women gained majority status as financial managers, accountants and auditors, and economists. So much for the stereotype of women not being good with numbers![15]

2. High-Net-Worth Women: The Ultimate Asset Holders

Most people are surprised to learn that affluent women *already* control the majority of financial assets in this country. For instance, check out these facts:

- *Bringing home the bacon.* Seventy percent of women earning more than $100,000 carn more than their husbands.[16]
- *Accumulating assets.* Forty-eight percent of estates worth more than $5 million are controlled by women compared to the 35 percent controlled by men.[17] Women constitute 47 percent of individuals with assets over $500,000.[18]
- *Women of wealth.* Women control 51.3 percent of the private wealth in the United States.[19]
- *Top dollar.* Among top wealth holders in 1995, the average net worth for women was $1.38 million, slightly higher than for male wealth holders, and the females carried less debt.[20]
- *Decision power increasing.* Men and women shared major financial decisions in *half* of the affluent households in 2000 versus 40 percent in 1995.[21]

This is just the tip of the iceberg. The largest wealth transfer in history is about to take place as baby boomers inherit from their parents. In turn, because women generally outlive their husbands, the family assets will become concentrated in the hands of boomer *women.* On average, these women will be widowed at age 67 and will most likely survive their husbands by 15 to 18 years.[22] (Although the difference in average life expectancy is only seven years, men still tend to marry women significantly younger than themselves.) During these years, women will have control of the household assets. What no one yet knows is what kinds of spending patterns will emerge from what is undoubtedly the youngest, healthiest, wealthiest, best-educated, and most ambitious group of retired women ever. (Learn more about these high-spending PrimeTime Women™ in Chapter 11.)

Retirement and estate planning providers, real estate and travel companies, and luxury car makers are among those realizing that these women are a critical consumer segment. Unless they reach out to them, they will see their customers walk out the door and go to the competition that does.

These impressive assets are only part of the story. Just as important, if not more so, is how, and how much, women spend.

3. Consumer Spending Power: Household Chief Purchasing Officer

Domestic products. Buying the "small stuff" has always been in the woman's domain. Part of her domestic duties as wife and mother has been to keep the family healthy, warm, and well nourished. From the family meal to the family doctor, from shirts for her husband to shoes for her kids, chances are those choices have always been hers. In fact, retailers and packaged goods companies have known for a long time that their primary purchaser was female. What many marketers haven't caught on to yet, though, is that women's spending power now extends far beyond shirts and shoelaces.

Big-ticket items. In the past, the big-ticket items like cars, insurance policies, and major appliances were historically bought by—and therefore marketed to—men. Things have changed! Nowadays, women drive the purchases even in historically male-driven categories:

- 53% of investment decisions[23]
- 55% of consumer electronics[24]
- 60% of home improvement buyers; 80% of home improvement decisions[25]
- 60+% of new cars[26]
- 66% of computers[27]

Women need their own cars, their own computers, their own cell phones, and their own investment accounts—among many other big-ticket items—and so manufacturers are facing a whole new market.

Single women. Get this: Single women head 27 percent of households in the United States. Did you register that? In more than *one out of four* U.S. households, women are the sole decision makers! And they're in the market for cars, computers, homes, financial services, and just about anything else you can think of.

Married women. Looking at married households (55 percent of U.S. HH), the fact of the matter is that the woman of the house spends not only her own paycheck but a good deal of her partner's as well. She still handles almost all the domestic spending. In fact, in 85 percent of U.S. families, women are the ones to take care of the checkbook and pay the bills.[28] And when it comes to the big-ticket items, not only is she buying her own products—like the single women above—but she also has a disproportionate say in the shared decisions, such as cars, investment accounts, and family vacations.

Chief financial decision makers. A *Health* magazine report found that women have greater control over financial decisions in their households than might have been popularly supposed. Eighty-six percent of women are either the main decision makers (32 percent) or joint decision makers (54 percent) of household financial matters. Eighty-two percent of women are actively investing, and 76 percent are comfortable making important financial decisions.[29]

One thing guaranteed to make me throw my copy of *BrandWeek* across the room is yet another mention of the "highly coveted demographic, 18 to 34-year-old men." They spend money, yes, but nothing like the money women spend. Let me repeat that—*nothing* like the money women spend. Articles appear in marketing magazines about a particular consumer subgroup, outlining the huge amounts of dollars at stake. It is time for all marketers to understand exactly how much bigger the women's market is than all of them combined. See Figure 1.2 for a chart that shows the straight dollar comparisons.

4. Women Mean Business: Controlling the Company Checkbook

Companies that market business to business also need to pay attention, because when it comes to business buying, women play a signifi-

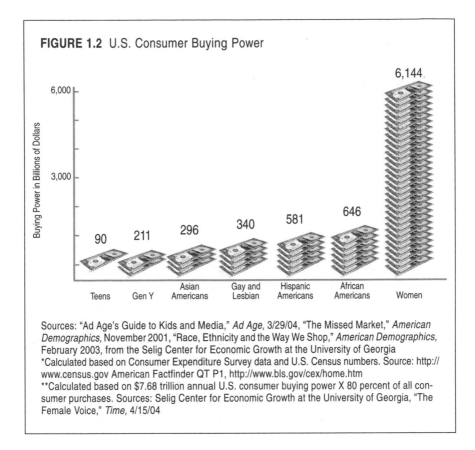

FIGURE 1.2 U.S. Consumer Buying Power

Sources: "Ad Age's Guide to Kids and Media," *Ad Age,* 3/29/04, "The Missed Market," *American Demographics,* November 2001, "Race, Ethnicity and the Way We Shop," *American Demographics,* February 2003, from the Selig Center for Economic Growth at the University of Georgia
*Calculated based on Consumer Expenditure Survey data and U.S. Census numbers. Source: http://www.census.gov American Factfinder QT P1, http://www.bls.gov/cex/home.htm
**Calculated based on $7.68 trillion annual U.S. consumer buying power X 80 percent of all consumer purchases. Sources: Selig Center for Economic Growth at the University of Georgia, "The Female Voice," *Time,* 4/15/04

cant role as well. Whether you target the corporate market or the small business market, there are compelling reasons to get smart about marketing and selling to women.

The big-business market: climbing the corporate ladder. Obviously, it is no longer unusual to see women in the corridors and conference rooms of today's corporate offices. In fact, today, 49 percent of all professional- and managerial-level workers are women.[30] Even more interesting to the businesses that sell materials to major companies is the fact that 53 percent of all purchasing managers and buyers and 58 percent of wholesale and retail buyers are women.[31]

Human resources executives, who play a key role in deciding on the financial services providers for their companies, are predominantly women. Office administrative managers, who choose the businesses that will provide their company's supplies and services, are mostly women. And business communication leaders, who buy the production and media services for their company's marketing, advertising, and PR, are very often women. If knowing your customer is the key to selling to her effectively, lots of business-to-business companies had better start learning how women buy.

The small business market: the new "entrepreneuse." Most people are unaware that women-owned businesses, defined by the Small Business Administration as businesses whose *ownership* is at least 51 percent female, constitute 40 percent of all companies in this country. (Looking at businesses whose ownership is at least 50 percent female brings that number up to 48 percent.) Women are literally creating the future of American business. Between 1997 and 2004, women-owned businesses grew at nearly twice the rate of all firms (17 percent vs. 9 percent) and added employees at twice the rate (24 percent vs. 12 percent). Would it surprise you to learn that women-owned businesses employ almost 10 percent of all Americans (19.1 million) and generate $2.5 trillion in annual sales?[32]

Companies targeting the small business market and looking to open new accounts need to focus in on the fact that women business owners accounted for a full 70 percent of all new business start-ups over the past decade! And lest you leave with the impression that women-owned businesses are fledgling enterprises uncertain to survive, know that women-owned employer firms have a three-year survival rate equal to that for all firms.[33] Women business owners also make a big impact in their communities, with a lot of influence beyond their own companies. They are philanthropically active: 70 percent volunteer at least once per month; 31 percent contribute $5,000 or more to charity annually; 15 percent give $10,000 or more.[34]

Clearly, marketers who sell to small business owners have every reason to focus on women. Increasingly, the buyer for small office/home office (SOHO) equipment, supplies, communication technology, travel, banking, and business services has a female face.

The four factors we've just discussed are powerful enough *alone* to sound the alert for marketers. However, there's more. Not only do women make up the majority of the market, but they are also more profitable.

Profitability in the Women's Market

Marketing to women will deliver more profit to your bottom line than will putting the same budget against an all-male target.

More Profitable Customers

Two dimensions of the women's buying process make them more profitable customers than men in the long term: loyalty and referrals. First, because women are more demanding in making the initial purchase in a category, they recoup their time investment by staying more loyal to the brand they've chosen in subsequent purchase cycles. Second, because word of mouth is more prevalent among women, they are more likely to recommend to others those brands or salespeople that impress them favorably—in essence, you're getting free marketing of the most powerful kind. How many marketing opportunities do you know that can deliver higher sales *and* higher profits at the same time?

Higher Customer Satisfaction—among Men, Too

Effectively targeting women generates higher customer satisfaction–among both women and men. Companies as diverse as BMW, Wyndham Hotels, and Merrill Lynch have found that marketing and service improvements designed to enhance brand appeal among women have resulted in greater customer satisfaction among men as well. The reason? In many respects, women want all the same things as men—and then some. Accordingly, when you meet the higher expectations of women, you are more than fulfilling the demands of men. You've got two satisfied customers for the price of one, so which market would *you* emphasize?

Better Return on Your Marketing Dollar

Marketing to women delivers a better return on your marketing dollar through both higher customer acquisition and greater customer retention. While in many categories the traditional male targets are saturated, the corresponding women's segments are untapped and virtually uncontested by competition. Furthermore, because women are more in-clined to long-term brand relationships, enhanced loyalty means every marketing dollar invested in acquiring women customers results in a higher overall retention rate. It just makes *sense* to put greater focus where you get more bang for your buck.

Gone are the days when father knew best, the days when a loving husband bought a new washing machine for his wife's birthday or brought home a new family car as a surprise. Marketers in big-ticket industries recognize the shift, but so far only a few of them are realiz-ing they need to get savvy about how women make decisions, what mo-tivates their purchases, and how they respond to marketing differently than men.

Whether you're an established market leader looking for new mar-kets or an innovative newcomer who thrives on new ideas, the women's market is the kind of big idea that can make a major difference to the bottom line (not to mention boosting your own visibility as a farsighted marketing leader!). And if anyone says to you, "Where's the incremen-tal market? Women are *already buying* most of the cars and computers, so how will marketing to women build our business?" here's your an-swer: "Sure, they're buying—but wouldn't you rather they bought *your* brand instead of your *competitor's?*"

The largest, fastest-growing market in the world is waiting. Through-out the world, women control consumer spending. They're accumulat-ing income and investable assets never before seen in history. And they're expanding their decision-making presence in corporations and small business.

The business is *there;* the real question is, where are *you?*

CHAPTER 2

The Differences That Make a Difference

Are women different? It's a fair question. During the 1960s, '70s, and '80s, women put a lot of energy into insisting that they were *not* different; that, with the exception of physical strength, women were identical to men. It was an understandable attempt to break out of the conventional wisdom of the day: men were the workers, the providers of family resources, while women were the nurturers, better fit to stay home. Gender differences hardened into gender stereotypes, and women noticed that in terms of occupational opportunities, the ones women were "obviously" suited for tended to be poorly paid and subordinate to men. Men made good doctors and women were good nurses; men were great managers and women were terrific secretaries.

When they asked why, the answer was that men and women were different. Men had certain skills and abilities that were necessary for the bigger jobs, and women didn't. If women wanted the perks and opportunities the men enjoyed, they had to have the same skills and abilities; they had to be the same.

Women of my mother's generation helped to create a new equality in the 1960s and 1970s, both at home and out in the larger world. They struggled to open doors for women by insisting that, except for brute physical strength and the cumulative effects of centuries of gender stereotyping (oh, is that all?), women were the same as men. Certainly, they knew—and taught others—that women were no less intelligent or able.

When I went to Wharton in the late '70s, it was still a mostly male bastion of business, and corporate life was more of the same. Like all my female colleagues, I wore my man-look suits, the ones with the little floppy ties and quarterback shoulder pads. We were trying to fit in, to look like the guys. Most of us were quick to absorb the rules of male culture, too, instinctively knowing to behave as much like the guys as possible. I might give in on issues like height and physical strength; it was pretty obvious that most men were taller and stronger. But like my mother before me, I was absolute and adamant: there were no differences between men and women that weren't the product of false gender stereotypes. To say I was skeptical of the concept of difference would be a gross understatement.

Differences Defined

Thirty years later, there have been literally thousands of studies, in fields as diverse as anthropology, biochemistry, neuroscience, human development, psychology, and sociolinguistics, many undertaken by women scientists and many by men. Former absolutes and adamant beliefs notwithstanding, we now have hard data that confirm there are *significant differences between men and women in every field just mentioned.* Each gender comes equipped with its own set of abilities, attitudes, priorities, preferences, and more. From a communications point of view, these differences have significant implications across the entire marketing spectrum.

Now, instead of unfounded conventional wisdom or instinctive emotional reactions to an outdated system, we have research to go on. Some of the findings are unexpected and eye-opening, and some confirm the old ways of thinking. Maybe that's not so surprising. After all, who among us hasn't observed—sometimes uncomfortably—the realities of differences in areas like child's play, where boys form armies and march to war, and girls form households and go to the store? Even without the data to prove these differences, most of us have noticed them. The hard data—and there's plenty of it—back up the observations.

While most people probably haven't tucked a ream of the research into a tote bag, sighing with pleasure at the thought of a little light beach reading, the research exists, and women are becoming increasingly aware of it. Interestingly, their attitudes have also changed to fit the new findings. A 1995 study by Grey Advertising reported that women not only acknowledge gender differences but also are proud of them.[1] Today's women see a lot of benefits to being female.

> ## What do I really mean when I say that men are like this and women are like that?
>
> I mean that the average for *men as a group* is statistically different from the average for *women as a group*. "On average, men are taller than women." What I *don't* mean is this:
>
> - There's no overlap. "All men are taller than all women."
> - The statement is true for any given individual. "John is a man, so John must be taller than Jane." The tendency is an absolute. "Jane is a woman, so she cannot be taller."
>
> So when I say, "On average, men are more aggressive and more competitive than women," I don't mean all men are aggressive, or women are never competitive, or women are not at all competitive.
>
> One more thing: For convenience, I often say "Men are like this and women are like that" when I mean, "On average, men tend to be like this and women tend to be like that." If you could just do a mental "find and replace" on those phrases throughout the book, I'd appreciate it. It'll save us all some time.
>
> Why this explanation of the obvious? You'd be surprised at the number of people who try to help me appreciate distinctions like this at my speeches and seminars.

From Fiction to Fact

There are two questions that often come up at this point: First, *are the differences between men and women real?* Are they truly inherent in the human being, or are they the result of cultural socialization and therefore specific to a particular country or generation? Second, *who comes out better—men or women?* Meaning . . . well, you know what they mean when they ask this—and shame on them!

Are the differences real? At heart, this question is asking about the time-honored nature versus nurture debate. And the reason people ask (besides curiosity) is that before anybody stakes a recommendation or a marketing program on the gender differences I'm talking about, they want to make sure the differences are still going to be around five or ten years from now—very reasonable.

Most of us have read that, without even realizing it, people treat babies wrapped in pink blankets different from the way they treat those wrapped in blue ones. And that's only the beginning. Throughout their life, boys and girls receive different messages about what's "normal" for them—at school, at play, and on the TV screen. The question is, Are boys and girls different because they're treated differently? Or are they treated differently because they *are* different?

The big news on nature versus nurture is that the more scientists learn, the more they are inclined to believe that *nature* has a lot more say about who we are than we previously realized. And *nurture* differences—shorthand for cultural socialization, parental practices, and community norms—don't seem to change the results. As we'll see in a moment, studies have found the same gender differences in cultures as divergent as a U.S. suburb and a hunter/gatherer tribe in Indonesia. Some studies have found gender differences consistent across *species* as different as monkeys, mice, and men. Talk about different cultures! Some gender differences are a matter of simple, physical fact; for instance, while doing the same mental task, men's brains light up the CAT scan in one area, women's in another. Other gender-specific responses correlate directly with the measurable amount of certain hormones in the bloodstream.

Brain function and hormones don't change by culture. Studies have recorded measurable gender differences in babies less than 24 hours old—a little young to have picked up much about the culture yet! It's starting to look as though a lot of gender differences are hardwired into the basic blueprint. So yes, the differences are real.

Gender judgments. If you recall, the second question was, Who really comes out better—men or women? One of the difficulties in developing gender-savvy principles—whether in marketing, management, or anything else—is that the idea of *gender culture* is unfamiliar and even counterintuitive to all of us at first. We approach the topic loaded with judgments we don't even recognize until someone points them out to us. And our initial inclination is to reject or dismiss the way the other gender behaves as a deviation from the norm—our own gender being the "normal" one or the "nicer" one or the "more logical" one, of course.

Most people are not aware of how the many differences in gender culture manifest themselves in everyday life. We think that because we grow up in the same neighborhoods, the same homes, as brother and sister, we basically have the same culture. We assume that a given action in a given context has pretty much the same meaning to all of us. So when gender A doesn't behave or react as gender B would under similar circumstances, it's plain to see that the other gender is "obviously" not doing things the "right" way. And that has to stem from either an *inability* to do it right or a *motivation* to do it wrong.

Not only do we jump to conclusions and make judgments; in point of fact, we also often harbor suspicions that the other gender is doing whatever it is they're doing—the behavior that is different—on *purpose* and most likely to aggravate us! *Is she just* pretending *she can't get the VCR to work? Is he just* acting *as though he doesn't hear me?* Don't tell me these queries have never crossed your mind—you know they have!

The concept of *gender culture* is very useful in helping people to divest themselves of some of the judgments we all start off with. In the United States, we take showers alone—most of the time—whereas in Japan, communal baths aren't at all uncommon. In France, it's common to kiss three times in greeting. We recognize these differences as the customs of other cultures, and we know not to interpret their meaning within the context of our own culture. In fact, if a business executive wants to do business in Japan or France, he or she would be mighty foolish not to take some time to learn the national customs and as much of the language as possible.

Similarly, in male gender culture, men don't share women's preference for multitasking or their penchant for exchanging compliments and personal stories. But if they want to do business with the locals in this highly lucrative market, the savvy among them will get acquainted with female gender culture—and fast.

Of Mice and Men

Are the differences between men and women truly significant enough to make it worth writing—or reading—a book about those differences as they relate to marketing? Let me give you an analogy: I'm sure you've heard that many of the new drugs and treatments in development to address various human disorders are tested on mice. The reason, I've read, is that mice and human beings share 95 percent of the same DNA. That's right, 95 percent! I guess it makes sense: both have two eyes, two ears, four limbs, a stomach, a heart, and so on. But I can't help thinking, boy, that last 5 percent sure makes a *big* difference—the size, the fur, the tail, the ears!

From that perspective, how different are men and women, really? In my mind, it's like the mice and men: women and men may be 95 percent the same, and only 5 percent different, but *boy*, does that last 5 percent make a big difference! Especially because much of that 5 percent is concentrated right at the heart of marketing: differences in perceptions, preferences, aptitudes, behaviors, communication patterns, and more. You wouldn't attempt to market to a mouse the same way you would to a human (if for some odd reason you found yourself in the marketing-to-mice business). For mice, you'd promise cheese, maybe, and you'd speak in the high, squeaky tones mice like to use. The differences between men and women are in some ways as profound as the differences between mice and men.

It can be tricky to talk about male/female differences in a way that nobody finds offensive. For lots of good reasons, it's still kind of a sore subject with a lot of people. That's why it's important to review the data. We need to sort out the truth from the tripe and be aware of the very real differences between men and women so that we can adapt appropriately. The findings are fascinating, and the applications are endless—in your home, in your workplace, and, of course, in your marketing and communication plans.

So let's get to it: How *are* women different from men?

The Real in Gender Reality: What Are the Differences?

What makes a woman a woman? Is it "sugar and spice and every-thing nice" with some maturity thrown in for good measure? Actually, it's more like chromosomes, hormones, and brains. In reality, the de-ciding factors are far more related to proven evolutionary and biolog-ical factors than they are to fairy tales, myths, or stereotypes.

Evolutionary Influences—Adam, Eve, and the First Case of Peer Pressure

When you get right down to it, every gender difference in this book traces straight back to sex and survival—and I'm not being glib. Men and women have two different survival instincts, or evolutionary strat-egies. The ultimate goal? Maximize the number of kids who survive you. Men's strategy: Make the maximum number of kids. Women's strategy: Help the kids you have survive.

Our male ancestors needed to climb the tribal ladder as fast as they could and, once they reached the penthouse, to enjoy the rewards, which often included more mating privileges. This required competi-tiveness, backed up by aggressiveness if need be. Hunting required the ability to focus on a target and strong spatial/navigation skills to get back to home base.

Meanwhile, for the females it was more a question of hanging in there through the rigors of raising kids and trying to make sure that the offspring made it to the point of procreation. With less testoster-one to push women toward aggressive behavior and with a passel of cave-kids to care for, women needed survival savvy, the ability to col-laborate with family members and neighbors in order to share resources, and a selfless drive to nurture the young. For a summary and more detailed understanding of these differences, see Figure 2.1.

Biological Influences—More Than Another Freshman Course Requirement

Now that we know each gender's survival strategies, let's take a look at how Mother Nature hardwired them into human biology. The three

FIGURE 2.1 Ultimate Goal: The One Who Dies with the Most Kids Wins

How to . . .	His Strategies	Her Strategies
STAY ALIVE	**Fight competitors for food, territory, and rank in the pack.** Higher-ranking males get the first sitting at all meals and the best female companionship.	**Stay alive as long as possible.** It's the best way to maximize the number of offspring born and to raise them to the point of self-sufficiency. **Don't pick a lot of fights.** You could get killed. (You don't have to fight for mates; don't worry, you'll have more suitors than you want.) **Do team up with other like-minded females.** Everyone gets more food and sometimes free baby-sitting.
MATE	**Fight off competitors (like most mammals).** In some species, only alphas get to mate or **win "female choice" awards (like most birds and reptiles).** Be sure to fluff your feathers and strut your stuff.	**Choose your mate carefully.** You can only have so many pregnancies, so you have to get really good at *reading nuances* to judge suitors' hardiness, genetic compatibility, and success as providers.
MAXIMIZE NUMBER OF SURVIVING OFFSPRING	**Mate often, with different females.** The proverbial "quickie" is the safest way to not get caught with your prehistoric pants down. The more one-night stands you have, the more shots you get at genetic immortality.	**Nurture offspring carefully.** Thanks to the biological setup, you don't get nearly as many chances as males to produce offspring. You have to make sure the ones you have make it. The *best maternal instincts and mothering skills* will pass on to the next generation.
FAVORITE SAYING	**"Survival of the fittest."**	**"It takes a village."**

basic components of the system are chromosomes, hormones, and brain structure. Each one interacts with the others so seamlessly that it's hard to tell their output apart sometimes. But let's take a crack at it.

Chromosomes—Why ask Y? It all starts with one little Y chromosome, a tiny piece of genetic material that boots up the whole system. Of the 46 chromosomes in normal human cells, this one little bit of information drives the gender program. The sex of the embryo is determined by the father's genetic contribution and by whether the egg's successful suitor is X-bearing (female) or Y-bearing (male). Both XX and XY fetuses are female at first. Then, about six weeks after conception, the little Y-guy triggers a prenatal testosterone "wash" that changes everything. Presto! The female fetus becomes a boy! (You realize what this means—rather than women being "Adam's rib," *men* are actually the derivative model!)

That's really all you *have* to know about chromosomes, but I can't resist passing along one more fun fact.

Intelligence

Headline: *"Brainy sons owe intelligence to their mothers."*[2] It turns out that the primary genes for intelligence, all eight of them, reside on the X chromosome. Men get one X chromosome from their mothers, whereas women get two Xs, one from Mom and one from Dad. So, while women's intelligence is a composite of both parents' "smarts," men get all their intelligence from their mother.

Because men get no matching chromosome from the father to "average out" the mother's, the male population's IQ distribution curve spreads out more toward the extreme edges of the bell curve, whereas the female population tends to cluster closer to the central "average." So although it has often been noted that there are more male geniuses, this explains why there are more male idiots as well.

Hormones—Gender chemistry. The gender culture game is certainly kicked off by chromosomes, but the more we know, the more we realize that hormones are the star players on the field.

The male hormone. Some scientists call *testosterone* "The Big T," and this bad boy is the main man when it comes to male-linked personality characteristics like aggressiveness, self-assertiveness, the drive for dominance, competitiveness, risk taking, and thrill seeking.[3]

Scientists have measured a direct correlation between testosterone and competitive people, as well as competitive circumstances. Both men *and women* in hard-driving, aggressive occupations such as trial law and athletics have higher T-levels (testosterone) than do people in nurturing, interpersonal occupations like teaching and counseling. Among men, testosterone increases before, during, and—for the winner only—after a competitive situation like a tennis match. Women's T-levels also respond to competitive situations, but here's an interesting twist: among women, after-the-match T-levels are more correlated to the feeling that she played well than to whether she won.

One study followed boys and girls whose mothers were prescribed testosterone during pregnancy as treatment for a related condition. It found the testosterone-dosed boys *and girls* tested higher than did their siblings on self-sufficiency, self-assuredness, independence, and individualism: girls tested 50 percent higher, whereas boys' scores soared 100 percent.[4] Conversely, when pregnant women took prenatal *female* hormones as treatment for a different disorder, girls *and boys* were found to prefer more group activity and showed more reliance on others than did their siblings—both considered female characteristics. These hormones are powerful stuff—a couple of squirts in the womb and they literally change your whole personality for life!

Like women, men have hormonal cycles. The Big T fluctuates daily (highest in the very early morning) and annually (highest in the autumn). I've heard it said there are a few people who are worried about having women in positions of political or military authority because of their monthly cycles. So given that testosterone is the hormone most closely correlated with aggression and men have ten times more than women, were they thinking we should ask the generals to start work after 9:00 AM and step down for a few months in September? Just wondering!

Although most people are well aware of testosterone's link with competitiveness, assertiveness, and self-reliance, fewer realize it is also a direct driver of a variety of aptitudes you would normally think of as being more learned or individual than biochemical. Tests on men and women measuring spatial, mechanical, and math abilities show that individuals of both genders get higher scores at times when their tes-

tosterone levels are higher. Again, our mousy relatives help to illustrate the point. If you inject female mice with testosterone, they are
able to run mazes as fast as their brethren. Conversely, if you restrict
the natural testosterone levels in males, they slow down and get lost a
lot. (And, of course, they wouldn't *dream* of asking for directions!)

The female hormones. Estrogen, the primary female hormone, has
two roles: (1) high levels of estrogen are associated with strong nesting
and nurturing feelings, giving a deep satisfaction from caring for
home and family members, and (2) the hormone also acts to suppress
the effects of the testosterone that women generate. When estrogen
levels are lower (and thus testosterone has more of a free rein), women
are more competitive, improve in math and spatial skills, and are more
prone to aggressive behaviors—just like men.[5] So beginning around
their middle 50s, women may be surprised to find their checkbooks
easier to balance and an increased confidence in their ability to program the VCR.

Progesterone, another female hormone, also promotes parental/care-
taking urges and is released when a woman sees a baby—any baby, not
just her own. In fact, when a woman sees *any* "releaser shape," something with short stubby arms and legs, a round plump torso, an over-
sized head, and large eyes (like a teddy bear, as opposed to a Pinocchio
puppet), progesterone is released, and the parenting instinct is triggered.[6] You can often tell the precise moment when this happens: it's
when all the women in the room croon "Awww, how cute!" at the exact
same time!

Oxytocin, a hormone that promotes a "sense of partnership and urge
to care for a child,"[7] floods the system during labor and delivery and
in one other crucial circumstance: when women are under stress.
Years ago, scientists identified adrenaline as the body's primary response to stress and termed its hyperenergetic effect the "fight or
flight" syndrome. Until recently, no one realized that among the respondents in all the studies, only about 25 percent had been women.
Now, new research has revealed that when women are stressed out,
they release more oxytocin than adrenaline, thus triggering an urge
for interpersonal interaction. It's proof of something we women have
always known: There's nothing like a girlfriend to talk to when you've
had a bad day. Scientists call this female response to stress the "tend

and befriend" syndrome and credit the stronger interpersonal support networks most women develop as part of the reason why women
have less heart disease and longer life spans than do men.[8]

In addition to estrogen, progesterone, and oxytocin, there's also *se-rotonin,* a hormone that is *inversely* correlated with risk-taking behavior. Women have more serotonin than men do and more serotonin
receptor sites in the brain, which damp down the thrill-seeking urges
and exhibitionist behavior probably originating in testosterone.[9] Men
have no such luck (or no such constraint, depending on how you look
at it), and that accounts for their higher susceptibility to boredom and
their greater desire for excitement and adventure, which in turn account for those perfectly natural drives to hurl themselves out of an
airplane with nothing but a backpack between them and death. By
contrast, women's higher serotonin levels act to suppress those urges—
it must be that "stay alive as long as possible" evolutionary drive at
work. But isn't it odd that when it comes to women's everyday behavior, everyone says "risk averse" like it's obviously a bad thing?

Brain structure/operation—redesigning the hard drive. Together, chromosomes (like the little Y-guy) and hormones (like the Big T) somehow inspire the male brain to reorganize itself differently from the
female original. Using PET scans and MRI scans, neuroscientists can
now view on-screen what areas of the brain are active when particular
tasks are being performed—and this means they can literally see the
differences in brain activity between men and women. Dozens of researchers are studying a broad range of brain functions, and a consistent pattern is emerging. They've found that men's brains are more
localized, specialized, and efficient at focusing; whereas women's are
more distributed, connected, and better at integrating.

Localization/Specialization. For example, when rhyming, only one
area on the left side of the brain shows activity in men, while two areas—
one in the left hemisphere, one in the right—show activity in women.
Similarly, men's emotional centers are concentrated in the right hemisphere, one in the front and one in the rear. Women's emotions are distributed throughout several areas in the brain, with "outposts" in both
the left and right hemispheres.[10] As further confirmation, scientists
have found that if a woman gets injured in one brain area, after a while

she often recovers some of the faculties associated with that area, whereas men do not, suggesting women have a "backup center" they can activate in an emergency.

Brain connectivity. Women's brains have more connections than men's. At the cellular level, they have more dendrites, which conduct the impulses between brain cells. And at the anatomical level, the tissues and fibers that connect the left and right hemispheres are larger and more developed. Scientists believe this may account for women's inclination to think holistically, preferring to view each element and interaction in context as part of a bigger picture. They also think this brain connectivity may account for the legendary women's intuition, allowing women to pull together more detail from disparate sources—sight, speech, emotional overtones—and emerge with a non-linear conclusion.

One lobe or two? As a rule, men seem to favor the right hemisphere of the brain; certainly they use the right hemisphere more efficiently than women. However, women are not left hemisphere oriented, as you might expect. Instead, brain scans show that women use *both* the right and left hemispheres *together.* (In my presentations, I'm always tempted to make a remark about how women use their whole brains, while men use half a brain, but I know that would be wrong.)

Women's Ways of Knowing—Senses and Sensitivity

Extrasensory perception. Would you believe that men and women *literally* see things differently? How apt is that? Men are better at focused, sharp vision (think "spotlight"), while women have better peripheral vision (think "floodlight").[11] For all four remaining senses, women's responses are more acute; they can detect more subtle levels of input. For hearing, women become uncomfortable with sounds about half as loud as men prefer.[12] With their more highly attuned sense of smell, women are much more sensitive to odor and fragrance; in fact, women can recognize their newborns by smell alone! Taste, too, differs in women, who have a greater ability than men to experience the four areas of taste: bitter, sweet, salty, and sour. Finally, the most dramatic gender differences show up in response to touch. In some tests, in fact, there is no overlap—the *most* sensitive guy can't feel skin contact and sensations as well as the *least* sensitive woman![13]

Emotional access. Obviously, women don't corner the market on strong emotion; if they did, how could we account for the powerful poetry, music, and other art created by men? Nonetheless, I bet we would find nearly universal agreement that women are the more emotional sex. Three key factors play into this: First, researchers believe that, on average, women actually *experience* the entire range of emotions with greater intensity and more volatility than men.[14] Second, in female gender culture, it's accepted—even expected—that women will *express* their emotions more often. In fact, men pride themselves on their self-control in *not* showing emotion. And third, because of women's greater brain connectivity, women can *articulate* emotions better, because there are more connections between the emotional and verbal centers of the brain.

Attention and focus. You know, it used to really irk me when I would hear people say that women are more detail oriented. Somehow, that expression always made me feel that they were *really* saying, "Men are good at big, important things, and women are good at the little things that don't matter very much." But it turns out that what's actually going on is that men notice or care about *only* the big important things, while women notice and care about the big important things *and* the details.

In study after study, women pick up on details and nuances better than men. In one study, when asked to recall as many objects as they could from a room where they had just been sitting for exactly two minutes, women's recall of the number and specificity of the objects they had seen significantly exceeded men's. Similarly, anyone who has ever talked to a couple after they've traveled together knows that after visiting a new city, college campus, or vacation spot, the woman will recall more details than the man.[15]

Part of this ability to notice and recall more may stem from a greater sensitivity to smaller nuances, a quality that Dr. Joan Meyers-Levy at the University of Chicago calls "bandwidth." In her research, she asked women and men to sort the same stack of cards into piles according to whatever similarities they perceived. What she found was that women tended to sort the cards by more finite distinctions, resulting in more stacks with fewer cards per stack, while men more often ended up with fewer stacks, each containing more cards. Conceptually, let's say the deck has 50 cards. Women are more likely to sort out 10 stacks with 5 cards each, while men are more likely to macrogroup them into 5 stacks of 10 cards each. To men, the smaller differentiating details either don't register or don't make as much difference as they do to the women.

On a related note, women are also more sensitive to interpersonal nuances—tone of voice, facial expression, and similar details. Dr. Judith Hall's survey of over 50 studies on the topic revealed that more than 80 percent of them found women to be better at this "social perception" than are men.[16]

So women are more detail oriented in that they notice, care about, and act on all the same things as men—and then some.

Contextual thinking. Psychologists report that women regularly think more contextually and holistically, placing the elements they see in relation to each other and integrating them into a bigger-picture "whole." For example, you may be familiar with the Rorschach test, in which subjects are shown a number of cards, each of which contains an inkblot of a varying shape. Subjects are asked to describe what they see when they look at each inkblot: a car, happiness, a bigmouth bass, or whatever else pops to mind. Researchers find that men talk about various elements of the inkblot separately, whereas women try to make sense of the image as a whole.

Conversely, women have a much more difficult time with the opposite task, called "disembedding," which involves discerning objects separate from their context or background. To simplify the point, one could legitimately say that men are the analysts (they take things apart), and women are the synthesizers (they put things together). This turns out to be one of the key points of female gender difference, as I'll discuss in Chapter 4.

People powered. Women are more person oriented than men are from the get-go. Baby girls only three days old sustain eye contact with adults twice as long as newborn boys. As early as four months, girls can

distinguish facial features and tell the difference between photos of
people they know and photos of strangers—while boys can't.[17] As we
get older, these tendencies remain in place. A study conducted among
teenagers used a stereoscopic headset to lash simultaneously a different image to each eye. One eye saw an object, the other a person; it
was up to the brain to decide what it had seen. Consistent with everything else we know about them, girls more frequently reported seeing
the *person,* while boys saw the *object.*[18]

This difference in orientation extends to the external, beyond perception and focus; it's behavioral as well. I think few of us would be
surprised to learn that when video cameras were placed in a college
cafeteria, researchers learned that college girls talked mostly about the
people in their life, while the boys were more likely to talk about
sports, politics, tests, and class work.[19]

Verbally inclined. It's generally accepted these days that women are
more verbally adept than men, so I'm not going to spend a lot of time
here to prove it. Suffice it to say that girls speak, read, and write earlier
than boys, and they have better grammar, spelling, and word generation skills.[20] Moreover, in school, twice as many girls are in the top-
scoring group in verbal skills, whereas twice as many boys are in the
lowest scoring group.[21]

That said, I would like to spend a moment on the role of conversation for women compared to men. Women use their verbal skills to
build bonds with other people. Whereas men get closer to other people by *doing stuff* together, women get closer by *talking* together. When
men want to spend some friendly time with a pal, they play ball, fish,
or go to a game.

Women, on the other hand, see the primary point in getting together as talking. There may or may not be some kind of background
activity involved—shopping, going to the park with the kids, or taking
a walk—but the *point* is to get in a good, long gab. In Chapter 4, we'll
come back to this—it's another key element in female gender culture.

The Minds of Men—Things and Theorems

Now, let's wrap up the chapter by talking about *men's* abilities and preferences for a change—and especially men's abilities in those areas where women are less adept and less interested. Why should we talk about these things? So that you can *stay away from them* in your marketing approaches! We've seen that men are evolutionarily less oriented toward all the "people stuff" that women focus on. What *men* find fascinating and important—not to mention much easier to do—are what one researcher summed up as "things and theorems." Under things, we're going to look at mechanical skill and spatial abilities; under theorems, we'll spend a moment on math aptitude and abstract principles.

Mathematical aptitude. Among math whizzes in the top 10 percent, the boy-to-girl ratio is 3:1; among the top 1 percent, the ratio goes up to 13:1.[22] Moving out of the extremes and into the mainline, although girls get better grades in math courses throughout the school years—researchers think it's due to better study habits—boys consistently do better on aptitude tests.[23] Researchers were surprised to learn (as was I) that girls are actually better with the numbers. In the United States, Thailand, China, and Japan, at least, girls' computation skills tested higher than boys'. What gave boys their aptitude advantages were their stronger talents at reasoning and problem solving.

Abstract principles. Researchers have found that men more often think according to abstract principles than do women. There are lots of different kinds of abstract principles, mind you, and some are pretty hard to measure. For an indicator of men's strategic strengths, we could look at the game of chess in Russia, a country where both men and women are encouraged to play: 450 men and only 6 women qualified as grand masters. A little closer to the communications area is this observation: Given a choice between the priorities of the law and the legitimate needs of an individual, men will tend to side with the law, a system of rules and abstractions, while women will more likely side with the person within the context of the specific situation. Psychologists say that when it comes to resolving complex interpersonal situations, women tend to base their thinking on examples and personal experience, while men's thoughts are more likely to concern ideals of right and wrong, justice, fair play, or duty.[24] Men say, "This is what's right. Here are the rules." Women say, "It depends."

Spatial acuity. One of the strongest, most unequivocal areas of male advantage is the ability to perceive, visualize, and act in three dimensions. Men's targeting skills, which involve judging distances, movement, and speed, as well as precise hand-eye coordination, are superb. On mental rotation tests gauging the ability to imagine what a complex shape would look like from a different angle, boys and men consistently—and substantially—outperform girls and women. Of the top scorers on maze puzzles, 92 percent are male. The average man is definitely more adept than the average woman at throwing a javelin, catching a baseball, or judging whether the car will squeeze past that double-parked truck.

In an interesting "real life" application, John and Ashley Sims were inspired by their observation that many women map readers physically turn a map to orient it to the direction in which they are heading. In 1998, they produced a male/female map of England. On one side, there was a conventional layout, with north at the top, east on the right, and so on. On the reverse side, they placed an upside-down map, with south at the top and all of the names flipped accordingly. As they had expected, the Simses only got a handful of orders from men. However, the map seems to prove the point on spatial differences: *there were 15,000 orders from women!*[25]

Mechanical ability. Most people hold the stereotype that men are better at mechanical challenges—and that makes most people right. Boys constituted the top three percent of scorers on mechanical aptitude tests; in fact, in that elite set, there were no girls at all.[26] There have been tremendous effort and support put into the recruitment of women to the spatial/mechanical professions. Despite that, inroads to these professions have not even remotely approached the advances women have made into law, business, and medicine. To this day, 80 percent of architects and 90 percent of engineers are men.[27]

To see mechanical aptitude in action, one Yale study tested college students' ability to program a VCR from a set of written instructions. An impressive 68 percent of the men were able to do it on the first try. Amazing! (Amazing to women, that is!) Among the female students, only 16 percent were able to meet the challenge.[28] It's nice to know I'm not the only one who finds the wretched things incomprehensible. If it weren't for my husband, it would always be 12:00 where I live—according to the VCR.

The key take-away here, gentlemen, is that it doesn't matter how cool you think the latest high-tech development is or how obviously easy it is to work the new gizmo you're launching. It doesn't matter how self-evident it is to you that "everyone" would want to see a blueprint of the car in the ad in order to appreciate the fine construction. It doesn't matter—because most women *really don't care* . . . and sometimes really don't like them.

Keep in mind, too, that in addition to the four areas we've just covered, there are probably others as well, where this general concept holds true. The critical point to remember is this: Before you move forward with a marketing approach or a communication campaign based on something *you* find hyperengaging, check it out against the principles of female gender culture to make sure you're aligned with your customer.

Different Folks, Different Strokes

There, now, don't you think that was interesting? But maybe you are wondering what it has to do with marketing. The answer is easy: *everything*. That's right, everything. As we move into Part II of the book, which introduces the GenderTrends™ Marketing Model, the relevance of every point you've just read will become clear.

We've just talked about a number of the differences that distinguish women from men. Now, we're going to embark on a crash course in female gender culture—a course that will equip you with the understanding you need to capture the attention and win the business of women consumers.

PART

The GenderTrends™ Marketing Model

Why and How Women
Reach Different Brand
Purchase Decisions

CHAPTER 3

The GenderTrends™ Marketing Model

The Big-Picture View

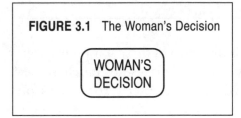

FIGURE 3.1 The Woman's Decision

WOMAN'S
DECISION

The ultimate goal of this book and the GenderTrends™ Marketing Model is to help you motivate more women consumers to buy your product or service. Along the way, we're going to be doing a lot of learning, strategizing, and specific application, but it's all aimed at influencing just one thing: your woman consumer's decision (see Figure 3.1).

The Star

After reading Chapter 2, you've seen that there are a tremendous number of gender differences that should be taken into account as you're developing your marketing efforts. The value of the *Star* is that it organizes and consolidates these differences into a manageable framework. The four star points of female gender culture are defined as *Social Values, Life/Time Factors, Focus Strategies,* and *Communication Keys* (see Figure 3.2).

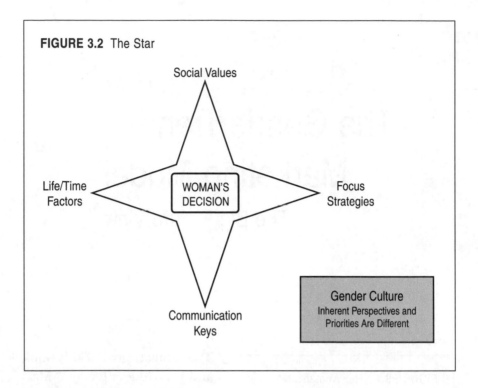

FIGURE 3.2 The Star

Social Values

Life/Time
Factors

WOMAN'S
DECISION

Focus
Strategies

Communication
Keys

Gender Culture
Inherent Perspectives and
Priorities Are Different

The core premise of this book is that each of these star points exerts a considerable influence on how a woman makes her purchase decision. We'll go into each of these in detail in Chapter 4. For now, as long as you follow the basic framework, we're ready to move on to the next component of the model.

The Circle

Whereas the Star captures what the woman brings to the equation, the *Circle* represents what the *company* brings (see Figure 3.3). Here, the keystones surrounding the Circle represent the 12 elements of the marketing mix: advertising, promotion, public relations, and so on.

Some marketers may not use all the marketing elements—for instance, some may not include event marketing in their plans. However, regardless of which elements you use, the Circle illustrates that *women respond differently than men do to every one of these elements*. Combined with the Star, the Circle provides a structure for organizing your thinking about these differing reactions, as well as a tool to help you plan your marketing approach.

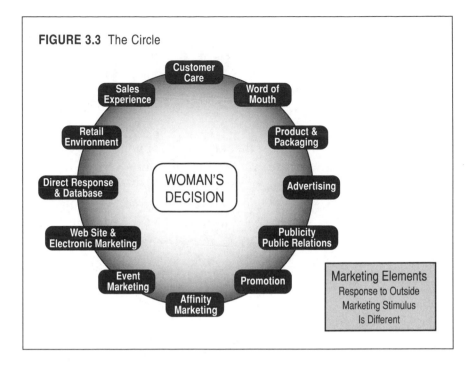

FIGURE 3.3 The Circle

Customer Care

Sales Experience

Word of Mouth

Retail Environment

Product & Packaging

Direct Response & Database

WOMAN'S DECISION

Advertising

Web Site & Electronic Marketing

Publicity Public Relations

Event Marketing

Promotion

Affinity Marketing

Marketing Elements
Response to Outside
Marketing Stimulus
Is Different

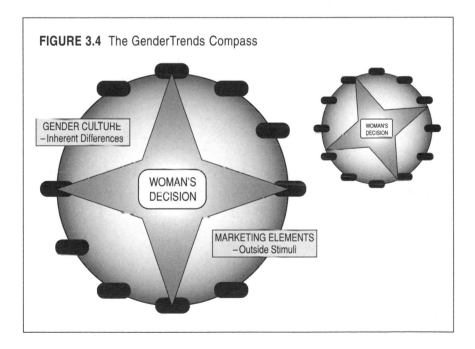

FIGURE 3.4 The GenderTrends Compass

GENDER CULTURE
–Inherent Differences

WOMAN'S DECISION

MARKETING ELEMENTS
–Outside Stimuli

WOMAN'S DECISION

The Compass

The GenderTrends *Compass* (see Figure 3.4) helps you visualize the concept that each of the four star points of female gender culture has a potential impact on each of the 12 marketing elements in the marketing mix. For example, star point one, women's differing Social Values, can and should change the way you develop your advertising, Web site, affinity marketing, and other elements that you build into your marketing plan. Alternatively, as you are developing your advertising, for example, you should be looking at it relative to all four star points: women's Social Values, Life/Time Factors, Focus Strategies, and Communication Keys. As you spin the Star inside the Circle and align each star point against the applicable marketing element, you'll create a systematic way to apply your gender learnings to the realities of the consumer marketplace.

The Spiral Path

The third component of the GenderTrends™ Marketing Model, the *Spiral Path* (see Figure 3.5), represents the consumer's decision process. Any consumer's purchase decision process can be simplified into five stages: *Activation, Nomination, Investigation and Decision, Retention,* and *Recommendation.* Chapter 6 will define these stages and talk about the gender factors that make a woman's purchase path different from a man's. For now, you need to note just two things:

1. While men's purchase path is depicted as a linear process, women's is shown as a spiral path.
2. The GenderTrends Compass moves with the consumer through all stages of her purchase path. This means that the insights on how gender culture interacts with your core marketing elements can be applied at each and every stage of the path.

The key to the GenderTrends model is that it brings together both gender expertise and marketing experience (see Figure 3.6). To create an effective program, you need both.

Without gender expertise, you can't have the in-depth understanding of your consumer that you need to create communications that motivate. Your programs will end up looking just like everything you've

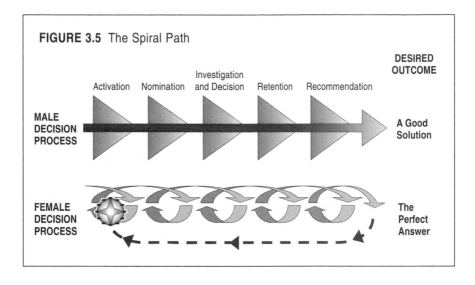

FIGURE 3.5 The Spiral Path

DESIRED OUTCOME

Activation   Nomination   Investigation and Decision   Retention   Recommendation

MALE DECISION PROCESS

A Good Solution

FEMALE DECISION PROCESS

The Perfect Answer

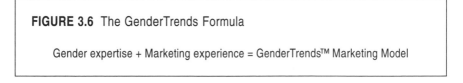

FIGURE 3.6 The GenderTrends Formula

Gender expertise + Marketing experience = GenderTrends™ Marketing Model

done before, just like everyone else's—and you won't be any farther ahead in capturing your share of the large, growing, and profitable women's market. *Without marketing experience,* you won't have the practical knowledge necessary to develop programs that are not only motivating to women consumers but also executable in the marketplace.

The value of the model is that it simplifies some very complex concepts and helps you structure your thinking about how they interact. It codifies the myriad manifestations of female gender culture and shows you how that culture affects each element of your marketing mix at each stage of the woman consumer's purchase path. It helps you to understand your consumer, focus on what motivates her, choose and use tactics effectively, and create communications that persuade.

So, what do you say? Are you ready to get started?

CHAPTER 4

The Star
Gender Culture

Chapter 2 provided an overview of the biologically based differences between women and men, and summarized some of the related variances in abilities and preferences. Now we need to go to the next step and look at gender differences in the context of *daily behavior and decision making*—the gender differences most germane to marketing. To structure the insights, we'll use the four-pointed GenderTrends Star, a useful tool with a surprising amount of power to guide your marketing.

Each of the four Star Points could potentially provide material for a whole separate book, but the encyclopedic approach makes for a fairly clumsy tool. The goal of this chapter is to give you the big picture: a concise yet complete overview of the key points. To add depth and additional understanding, I hope you will continue your reading with some of the excellent books and Web sites listed in Appendix B, "The Best Resources in the Business," at the back of the book.

If all you were trying to do with a marketing program was deliver straight information, like a journalist, gender culture might not matter too much. But as a marketer, you're trying to do a good deal more than deliver information: you want to persuade and motivate a consumer to take action. Not only that, but there are at least a half-dozen competitors trying to do the same thing you are—and you need to find a way to do it *better.*

The key to creating marketing programs that will win women's business is to understand what women value. Often, what they value—which may mean what they *cherish,* what they *enjoy,* what they *take pride in,* or what *matters* to them—is different from what men value. We'll also spend a little time on what they *don't* care about—things that men find fascinating or important that just don't ring women's chimes at all. You may be surprised to find that many marketing and advertising truisms we have all accepted as self-evident are actually rooted in male gender culture. It's just that no one has really put two and two together—gender thinking and marketing experience—so no one has ever really challenged them before.

A study conducted by Greenfield Online for Arnold's Women's Insight Team surveyed 1,000 men and women on how the two genders think they are portrayed in advertising.[1] A full 91 percent of women—*almost all of them*—said they think advertisers don't understand them. Even worse, the majority of women are downright annoyed by how advertisers portray their gender—far more women than men (58 percent versus 42 percent). This indicates there is an *enormous chasm* between the woman consumer and the marketer's understanding of her. It also means there is an *enormous opportunity* for the marketer who crosses that chasm.

Let the GenderTrends™ Marketing Model serve as your bridge. Once you become gender savvy about what the woman consumer is looking for and gain a real appreciation of what she does and doesn't value, there's no reason why every single one of your marketing elements shouldn't have greater impact and be more compelling than anything your competitors have in the marketplace.

The GenderTrends Star

The four points of the GenderTrends Star—Social Values, Life/Time Factors, Focus Strategies, and Communication Keys—signify four dimensions in which women's gender culture differs materially and relevantly from men's (see Figure 4.1).

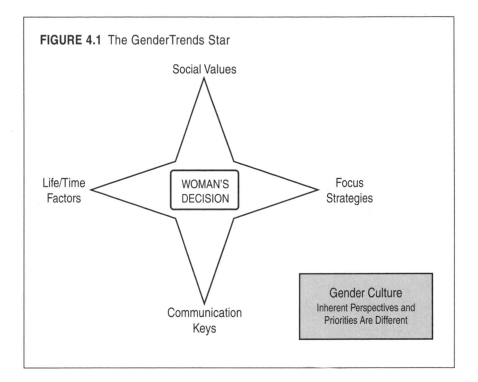

FIGURE 4.1 The GenderTrends Star

Social Values

Life/Time Factors

WOMAN'S DECISION

Focus Strategies

Communication Keys

Gender Culture
Inherent Perspectives and
Priorities Are Different

We'll spend some time with each of these Star Points and then wrap up the chapter by extracting a list of the key female values you'll want to think about as you're creating your marketing programs.

The Four Points of the GenderTrends Star

Social Values. Different beliefs and attitudes about *how people should relate to each other*

Life/Time Factors. Implications of the ways in which *women's roles differ from men's*

Focus Strategies. Consistent differences in how women perceive and process

Communication Keys. Different patterns and rituals of *expression*

Star Point One: Social Values

People First, Last, and Always

Personally, if I read one more article that says, "Women are all about relationships," I think I'll choke. *Relationships* is such a mushy word, don't you think? On one level, it's mushy-gooey—it sounds as if women go around desperately looking for someone to be nice to them. On another level, it's mushy-ambiguous: one poor, hardworking word has to cover our connection to our spouse or best friend, a work acquaintance, or a sales clerk in the department store.

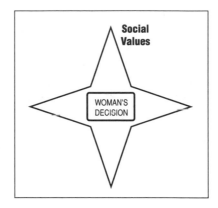

While I don't want to get mired in the relationship swamp, I do think it's fair to say that women are more likely than men to think that *people* are the most important and interesting element in life. To them, it's self-evident that when you come right down to it, it's all about people. As we saw in Chapter 2, you can almost say it's wired into women's evolutionary programming. Men, on the other hand, are more likely to hold the view that people are important, but no more important or interesting than current events or new ideas in computer animation or something more material like cars or cameras.

When comedian Jeff Foxworthy performs his song *Totally Committed*, he includes some great side comments, including "I do think men would take advice on relationships, but we're not gonna sit down and read magazines about it." And he's right. You only have to look at what sells magazines to see the difference: Women's magazines are full of articles about celebrities, the dynamics of blended families, advice columns about personal problems, self-help topics on how to enjoy life more, motivational stories about cancer survivors, and, yes, advice on how to make *him* happy. Men like to read magazines devoted to news, sports, business, computers, fitness, hunting, fishing, or other activities. But when it comes to reading about people and their internal workings, men tend to have one response: *borrring*.

In the pages that follow I'm going to expand on this different outlook toward people by addressing three separate but closely interwoven topics on which men and women differ:

1. Whereas men are soloists, women are ensemble players.
2. Whereas men aspire to be "winners," women prefer to be "warmer."
3. Whereas men occupy a pyramid, women occupy a peer group.

Each of these topics is rich with revelation on how women's values vary from men's, and each offers a wealth of marketing implications.

Men Are Soloists, Women Are Ensemble Players

Men are soloists. Each sees himself as the star of his life show and thinks everybody else, male or female, sees himself or herself the same way. Women see themselves—and everybody, really—as part of an ensemble company; it's the interaction and the chemistry that creates the electricity more than any individual's outstanding performance.

The way men see it. Men look at the world from the perspective of the *individual.* Their core unit is "me"; and it's important that the other "me's" recognize that this "me" is different, special. They take pride in self-reliance and self-determination. The way the world works (and should work) is like this: *I earn my own way, I deserve the rewards. I can do it myself, I don't expect help, don't want advice, I mind my own business—and so should the other guy.* As the saying goes, "It's every man for himself." When a Yankelovich survey asked who agreed with the statement "I feel I have to take what I can because no one is going to give it to me," the majority of men agreed (57 percent), but less than half of the women did (45 percent).[2]

The most desirable outcome by definition is for "me" to get what "I" want—what else? Is this a trick question? Freedom—autonomy, independence—is one of men's highest values, causing an almost reflexive resistance to being influenced by others, especially women, because that feels too much like mom telling him what to do. At the end of the day, what men want to see on their tombstone is this: *I left my mark on the world.*

The way women see it. Women look at the world from the perspective of the *group*. Their core unit is "we" (even if it's only two), and the best feeling in the world is being with people with whom you have a lot in common. They take pride in their caring, consideration, and loyalty, and one way they demonstrate that is by looking out for the others in their informal tribe—family, neighbors, friends, and coworkers. They offer frequent suggestions and help, and maintain a kind of "peripheral awareness," always conscious of things that might be relevant to someone they know and care about. Whether the issue is her husband's health, a colleague's upcoming trip, or a friend's son's college choice, a woman is constantly in "scan" mode; her clan is always with her, like voices in her head. Many women go so far as to build other people's happiness into their definition of success: "I'm happiest when I can succeed at something that will also make other people happy" garnered agreement from only 15 percent of men but 50 percent of women.[3]

One of women's highest values is a feeling of closeness and connection with another person. As far as women are concerned, when two people are really close, they want to know *everything* about each other. They want to know the other's dreams, doubts, and disappointments; their favorite food, shoe store, and vacation spot; their medications, worrisome moles, manicurist, and macaroni recipes. They even want to know about yesterday's tantrum and tomorrow's meeting with the contractor—*nothing* is too mundane or too personal. (I can feel the men recoiling, holding the book a little farther away in case it's contagious!) For women, though, that's the point, you see: getting personal. To women, that's a *good* thing.

Women believe that other people are just as important as oneself and that "we" all deserve equal consideration. That means each of us has a responsibility to other people as well as to ourselves, and the best outcome is the greatest good for the greatest number. The way the world works (and should work) is through cooperation and mutual support: "All for one, and one for all." Other people are a source of strength, a shoulder to lean on; everyone needs a hand now and then, and that's OK, because, as the song says, "People who need people are the luckiest people in the world."

FIGURE 4.2 The "We Not Me" Principle

Reprinted courtesy of GlaxoSmithKline.

The print ad in Figure 4.2 is a great example of the "We Not Me" principle. This ad from Tums uses just the right incentive to get moms to take Tums: "Think of him, think of her, think of THEM!"

Guardians of civilization. Somewhere along the way, women were handed the "guardian of civilization" cloak. It's generally agreed that when it comes to the altruistic stuff, women are in charge of everything: the earth, the arts, and the unfortunate; morality, spirituality, culture, and civilization—you name it, women are on the committee.

Women are more philanthropic, giving more time and proportionately more money than men. Whereas men are twice as likely to think the nation's most pressing issues are budget and cutting spending, women—across age, income, race, and social class—are more inclined to favor social programs and issues, such as education, health care, child care, poverty, joblessness, environment, world hunger, and the United Nations.[4] And both men and women say "emphatically" (according to the study) that women are the morally superior sex: they lie less, are more responsible, are more honest at work, and can be trusted more.[5] Recent headlines support these findings. Remember who the *Time* Persons of the Year were in 2002? Sherron Watkins of Enron, Cynthia Cooper of WorldCom, and Coleen Rowley of the FBI. All risked everything to make the world, and their work environments, better places.

Women care, and they vote with their wallets. The 2003 Cone Holiday Trend Tracker found that "women are overwhelmingly more supportive than men of cause-related shopping during the holiday season. Seventy-seven percent of women were likely to consider a company's reputation for supporting causes when purchasing gifts (compared to 64 percent of men). Sixty-five percent of female shoppers said they planned to purchase a product in which a percentage of the price is donated to a cause (compared to 54 percent of male consumers). Women were also more likely to buy holiday gifts from retailers that supported social issues (60 percent vs. 49 percent).

I coined the term *corporate halo* as the marketing implication that stems from this principle. Corporate halo is a bigger idea than *cause marketing.* Cause marketing is a marketing partnership between a business and nonprofit entity for mutual benefit. But corporate halo is more than just a business partnership—it is the sum of a company's acts of social responsibility and community citizenship for the benefit of the whole community.

The wonderfully insightful Grey Advertising study cited earlier puts women's commitment to altruistic aims in dramatic perspective. Their number one "fantasy," to use the report's language, is to make the world a better place; seeing their kids become really successful comes in second. Compare "I helped make the world a better place" to "I made my mark on the world." From a distance, they may seem to be saying almost the same thing; but up close, they capture a world of difference in men's and women's outlooks on life.

While we're here, let's take a minute to look at some of the other things on women's wish lists (see Figure 4.3). There's a 20- to 30-point drop between the top two dreams and either wealth, attractiveness, or career success. And wanting to be younger, famous, or live like a movie star almost doesn't make it onto the radar screen. Now, look at this list carefully and think about whether the majority of women-targeted ads you see actually reflect women's true values. Most advertising targeted to women keys in on getting ahead, fun and excitement, looking smashing (which, of course, means looking younger, right?), and tak-

---

FIGURE 4.3 Women's Aspirations

Make the world a better place	85%
See kids become really successful	83%
Have enough time to do what I want	82%
Travel more	72%
Accumulate wealth	62%
Be more attractive	53%
Be really successful in my career	48%
Nonaspirations	
Be younger	27%
Be famous	7%
Live like a movie star	5%

Source: *Women on the Verge of the 21st Century,* published in *Grey Matter Alert,* a white paper from Grey Advertising, Fall 1995.

---

ing care of household duties. This isn't to say that such advertising isn't at all relevant; only that it's missing the really meaningful messages. This goes a long way toward explaining the survey results we saw earlier: Most women feel that advertisers don't understand them and, worse, that advertising portrays their gender in a way that's actually annoying rather than appealing.

Men Aspire to Be "Winners," Women Prefer to Be "Warmer"

As we saw in Chapter 2, if women are evolutionarily programmed to be people oriented and nurturing, men are evolutionarily programmed to be competitive. It comes with the hormones.

The way men see it. Men think competition is *fun.* It's built into how they work, how they play, and how they communicate. From the time they're little boys, they self-organize into opposing teams, with someone who's the leader and gets to give the orders and usually a couple of lieutenants with some command power as well. The objective isn't conflict per se; there's a goal or prize, and whoever gets it is the winner, whoever doesn't is the loser. There are lots of rules, energetically disputed, resolved, and accepted, and a good deal of boasting, bragging, and swaggering on the part of the winners. The losers don't usually take it too hard—"you win some, you lose some"—and regardless of the outcome, the whole experience reinforces a sense of camaraderie and good fun.

Men also think competition is *good*. It brings out the best in people and helps unearth the best solutions. Challenging and testing one option against the other is how to strengthen what's good and weed out the weaknesses.

When it comes to personal interactions, experts agree that for a man, every encounter in his professional and personal life is a contest; and every contest a zero-sum game. As he sees it, either he wins or he loses: "For me to get what I want, you can't get what *you* want." "May the best man win."

Not surprisingly, this has implications for the types of personal relationships men form. Because even their friendships are grounded in competition, and their interactions take place in the language of challenge and aggressiveness, they have to be on guard against these same qualities in others.[6] Any imperfection could be construed as a sign of weakness, so it's better to keep as much as you can to yourself. If you're wrong or don't know something, don't let the others find out. Men's mentality is rooted *in concealing,* whereas as we saw earlier, women's is rooted *in revealing.* It's better to trust no one too far; it's safer to maintain a certain suspicion or at least distance.

Rules are very important in male gender culture for a couple of reasons. First, rules give boundaries to the competitive behavior, offering a structure within which varying levels of aggression can take place without resulting in the destruction of the individuals or organizations involved. They accommodate confrontation but make sure it doesn't get out of hand. Second, rules tell you when the game is over and, most important, who has won. Men need clarity on this so that they can get back to business and move on.[7] This role of rules in male society probably accounts directly for psychologists' observation that men are often more concerned with "matters of principle" and tend to be more inflexible when applying them, whereas women tend to feel "it depends" and adjust for the context and people involved.

The way women see it. Women make a distinction between the two core elements of competition: *interaction* is fun, conflict is not. Playing is fun, but losing isn't—somebody's feelings are going to get hurt. Whereas a man might say, "I like the game—I play to win—what's the score?" a woman would probably say, "I like the players—I play to play— whose turn is it?"

My next-door neighbor saw an example of this in action recently, while she was watching an informal soccer game played by her eight-year-old daughter and some of her friends. After about 20 minutes of active play, one of the fathers arrived. He immediately asked, "What's the score?" Not one of the girls had the slightest idea—and not one of them cared! He was flabbergasted: *What on earth is the point of playing if you don't even keep score?*

Girls play in small groups or pairs, are careful to see that everyone gets a turn, and for many activities, like playing house, don't even have winners or losers (shocking!). There's not much boasting and little obvious jockeying for status. In fact, a girl who flaunts her accomplishments is likely to experience a lot of peer pressure to stop: "She's so conceited! Nobody likes a show-off!"

As for competition bringing out the best in people and the best results, women don't see it like that. Researchers distinguish between *internal* competitiveness, which is a drive for personal excellence, and *external* competitiveness, described by the researcher as "the desire to beat somebody into the ground."[8] Compared to men, women test equally high on internal competitiveness or the drive to achieve her personal best, but the drive to conquer someone else is not nearly as strong.

When external competitiveness occurs among people within the same group, women find it at best pointless and, at worst, downright counterproductive. In a business environment, for example, they see many of the manifestations of peer-to-peer competition as unpleasant, unnecessary conflict, a tiresome waste of time and energy "full of sound and fury, signifying nothing."

Instead, the female focus is on teamwork. In women's view, true excellence comes from the merging of many talents with each person contributing his or her personal best. Every encounter—a sales negotiation, for instance—is an opportunity for mutual gain, every person is a potential ally, and negotiation is the way to find the win-win outcome for everyone. "I get what I want," says a woman, "and you get what you want, too."

Men Occupy a Pyramid, Women Occupy a Peer Group

Men think it's obvious that the natural social order is hierarchical. Women recognize that hierarchy and status differences are facts of life and may even make sense from a "law and order" perspective. However, in a social context, especially among themselves, women prefer to minimize hierarchical distinctions and expressions of rank, seeing them as uncomfortable, undesirable, and something to be downplayed rather than emphasized.

In a man's worldview, his relation to other people is organized in comparative terms: higher/lower, faster/slower, first/second, bigger/smaller, more/less, and so on. A woman's outlook is relational *without being comparative:* similar to/different from, know her/don't know her, far/near, and so on. You could say that men stack people vertically, and women arrange them next to each other.

The way men see it. Men are always conscious of where they stand in comparison to others, measuring and evaluating everything: their territory, their house size, their company prestige, and their success relative to other men.[9] Their goal is to be looked up to or admired as superior, a member of the elite at the top of the pyramid, one of "the few, the proud . . ." It's a given that when you say "get ahead," you mean "get ahead of the others." There wouldn't be much point in getting ahead of yourself, now would there?

Assuming you can attain alpha status, there are a number of advantages to life in a pyramid. The most obvious one is that you get more autonomy—the ultimate prize. The higher you get, the fewer people you have to listen to. Second, because of the rules, a clear delineation of rank brings order and reduces conflict. In a smoothly functioning hierarchy, lower-ranking people do what they're told instead of starting a discussion about it. Because of that, a system of command and control can keep things moving pretty fast. Finally, the top dog gets more goodies—and he doesn't have to share. As we've learned from many a bumper sticker: He who dies with the most toys wins.

The way women see it. Women believe that all people are created equal (to update the wording from the Declaration of Independence). Combined with the perspective that people are the most important and interesting element in life, that caring and consideration are high-priority values, that interacting with others in a win-win way ought to be anyone's idea of a good time, a place at the top of a pyramid is going to look pretty unappealing. It's lonely at the top. Women prefer to think in terms of *everyone* getting ahead—not *ahead of anybody else,* mind you, just moving forward together. Their motto is "the more, the merrier."

Women don't particularly want to be looked up to, any more than they want to be looked down on. In the world of women, the ideal position is side by side. A principle you will see repeated throughout this book is this: For women, the operative emotion is *not envy, but empathy.*

In advertising, it has been taken as a given for years that aspiration—the drive to be like someone higher up the ladder—was a fundamental motivating factor for everyone. It worked for men, right? How many ads have you seen founded on the premise, "When I get this product, everyone else is going to be *sooo* jealous!" Guys can really relate—it's just what you want when you're evolutionarily programmed to seek alpha status. But women think making other people jealous is sort of petty and small minded. They're more likely to relate to the premise, "Yep—that looks like *my* life. If that product works for her, it'll probably work for me as well."

One of my favorite print ads that exemplifies the "empathy" principle is this one from State Farm (Figure 4.4). The whole premise of the campaign, "We live where you live," is that State Farm agents (people, not a corporate office) live side by side with their customers. The implied message is "Of course we understand our customers because we have so much in common with them."

The benefits of the side-by-side arrangement are just as self-evident to women as pyramid power is to men. You'll always have someone to talk to, to bounce ideas off of, or to share experiences with. Your group will benefit from everyone pooling their talents and resources; and because you'll get input from everyone as you decide on direction, everyone will have a stake in seeing the group succeed.

Of course, the downside of this is the time it takes to negotiate and the reluctance of anyone to make the call for the others. Women often find themselves in a sort of "circle of deference." They'll say, "Well, I like Italian, but if you like Greek let's go to the Greek place." "No, no, we'll have Italian, Italian is great, let's do it your way." "No, no, really—*your* way!" It should come as no surprise that *this* is what men think is

---

FIGURE 4.4 Empathy

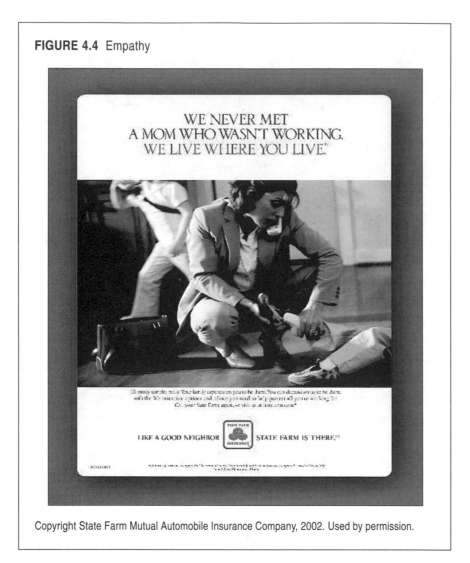

Copyright State Farm Mutual Automobile Insurance Company, 2002. Used by permission.

---

fruitless and counterproductive—and you've got to admit, they've got a point!

The bottom line is, when you're part of a peer group, the ideal world is just one big, supportive group hug—no one will ever be abandoned or lonely; you'll have people happy to help you and happy to have your help.

As a matter of fact, one of the more important manifestations of these different mindsets, in terms of implications for marketing and sales, is how men and women feel about asking for or accepting help.

Men don't like it—they feel it frames them as "one down" versus the other guy, and, worse, he's going to try to tell you what to do. Why would you do that to yourself? (Psychologists say that's why men hate to ask for directions!) Men prefer to see themselves as masters of a situation, whereas women are more likely to see themselves as students. With no barriers to admitting they don't know something, women are more likely to seek and welcome assistance from other people, and to relate to communications that characterize their view of themselves as "lifetime learners."

Degrees of Difference

From the descriptions above, it should be evident we're talking about some pretty significant differences of opinion here. Sure, to a certain extent *everybody* believes in being individualistic, and *everybody* believes in being communal, but to surprisingly different degrees— and the degree correlates to gender. A cross-cultural survey of six modern societies asked men and women to describe their ideal self— "the kind of person I would like to be." According to two reports on this survey, men in all these cultures overwhelmingly described themselves as bold, competitive, capable, dominant, assertive, admired, critical, and self-controlled. Women overwhelmingly chose a very different set of descriptors: warm, loving, impulsive, generous, sympathetic, and affectionate.[10]

The thing to keep in mind is that not only does each gender identify itself with a given set of characteristics, but depending on the context, each may be indifferent to, or sometimes even repelled by, the other gender's traits. Women may see what men call self-sufficiency as just a nicer name for selfishness and wonder how men can be proud of an outlook that seems sort of aloof and thoughtless. Men may see women's attention to others as foolish, wondering why anyone would *want* to spend so much time meddling and interfering in things that don't concern them—let alone why others would allow themselves to be interfered with in this way. Men are often horrified by the way women inquire about intimate personal details, seeing it as intrusive and none of their business; whereas women are appalled when men *don't* inquire, because in female gender culture, that's a silent snub that clearly says "I don't care."

FIGURE 4.5 Star Point One at a Glance

His	Hers
People + Things + Theorems	**People First, Last, and Always**
Soloist	**Ensemble Player**
"Every man for himself"	"All for one and one for all"
	Guardians of civilization
Winner	**Warmer**
"May the best man win"	"The more, the merrier"
Pyramid	**Peer Group**
"The few, the proud . . ."	"All people are created equal"
Envy	Empathy

Of course, neither is right—and both are right. As far as marketers are concerned, the important thing is to understand that we're talking about core beliefs and values here—the building blocks of motivation. Sometimes a word choice or the wrong visual is all it takes to transform a difference into a deficit. What male advertisers see as an image of autonomy and freedom (e.g., an investment company ad visualizing financial independence as a woman paddling a canoe in the wilderness, free to go wherever she wants) may have overtones of isolation and loneliness to women consumers: *a woman all alone in the middle of nowhere.* What men see as copy conveying healthy ambition and the natural drive to be in charge may strike women as self-aggrandizing baloney (GMC Yukon: "Victorious. That's how you feel behind the wheel.").

Understanding the underlying principles of gender culture will help you flag what's likely to work, what's not, and what sensitive areas need a little direct consumer feedback. In Figure 4.5, some of these underlying principles are summarized to give you an at-a-glance view of the very significant ways men and women differ when it comes to Social Values.

Star Point Two: Life/Time Factors

Women allocate their time differently than men do—partly because they have different roles in daily life, partly because they have a different style of getting things done, and partly because, thanks to their longer life spans, they simply *have* more time in their mature years. Each of these aspects holds important opportunities for marketers who recognize the underlying motivations and resulting needs that affect women in their purchase decisions.

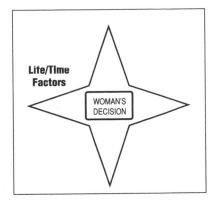

Daily Life: Women and the Double Day

Few would dispute that women's roles have changed substantially in the last 30 years—not only in the societies grounded in Western European culture, but throughout much of the rest of the world as well. Marketer Rena Bartos, in her 1981 book *Marketing to Women Around the World*, found that in most countries, the majority of women work outside the home—and the majority of work *inside* the home is still done by women.

Women in the workforce. These days, working women are more the norm than an anomaly. In fact, their labor force participation rate is fast approaching men's (see Figure 4.6). And whether or not women originally entered the workplace for economic reasons, now they're staying because *they like it there.* Grey Advertising's study reported that 78 percent of women say having a job makes them feel good about themselves; and 76 percent want successful careers. *Real Simple*'s "Values and Behavior Outlook" reported that 81 percent of working women say they would still want to work even if they didn't have to.[11]

By the end of their childbearing years (ages 40–44), the large majority of women have had kids: 81 percent, including 64 percent who have two or more children.[12] After their maternity leave, most mothers return to work (see Figure 4.7), and whereas ten years ago most of them said they felt guilty about it, today only 26 percent say they do.[13]

FIGURE 4.6 Labor Force Participation Rates

	Women	Men
1980	52%	77%
1990	58%	76%
2000	60%	75%
2003	60%	74%
2012 (Est.)	62%	73%

Source: Statistical Abstract of the U.S., 2004–2005.

For marketers seeking the higher-income market, it's worth noting that the higher a mom's education level, the more likely she is to keep working.

Consider this frequently published statistic: On average, women earn $.78 for each dollar earned by men. What is less well known is that single women earn 102 percent as much as single men—2 percent *more*—across the full spectrum of occupations, education levels, and age. When the Employment Policy Foundation looked at the earnings of full-time working women *without kids*, they found that in 2001 they earned 96 percent as much as men without kids. That's pretty darn close.[14] What pulls the average down to $.78 on the dollar is that post-kids, far more women than men shift from full-time to part-time work.

Women at home. Things may have changed a good deal in the office, but on the home front, not so much. In the average household, women devote considerably more time to household chores each week than men do: 14.2 hours compared to 7 hours for men.[15] Moreover, women's domestic responsibilities don't end with an empty nest. No sooner do the kids leave home then the family elders need help, and women take on the role of caregiver to older parents, in-laws, and other family members—not only on her side of the family but often on her husband's as well. Whereas sons give money, daughters give time. Most women will spend at least 17 years caring for their children and 18 more caring for elderly parents.[16]

The typical woman serves as the CPO—the Chief Purchasing Officer—in her home, doing most of the buying for the entire household. At the same time, she's got cabinet-level authority in a majority of the

FIGURE 4.7 Mothers in the Workforce

Mothers with . . .

Kids under 6	63%
Kids 6–17	79%

Mothers with . . .

Some high school	38%
High school graduate	58%
At least 1 year of college	68%

Calculations based on data from Statistical Abstract of the U.S., 2004–05.

other primary areas of family life. She's the Secretary of Health, Education, and Welfare, for instance, typically taking on primary responsibility for health care, school issues, and budgeting/financial management. She's the Secretary of the Interior, making sure that everyone's emotionally stable and getting along, and the Secretary of the Environment, dealing with everything from clearing a path through the socks on the floor to putting up wallpaper to making sure the Christmas tree is decorated or the menorah lit. She runs the Office on Aging if her parents—*or* her husband's parents—are elderly and ailing, and she even moonlights as Julie, the cruise director, planning family vacations and other activities. It's a tough job, but somebody's got to do it—all of it, *all of the time.*

In the 1990s, many advertisers sought to show sympathy for women's situation by portraying their life as harried and almost overwhelming. However, a recent study found that women see their life as very full and busy but not disjointed or unmanageable. According to the *Real Simple* "Values and Behavior Outlook" report, 90 percent of women say they feel their career and personal life are well balanced right now.[17] They move easily among their roles and integrate their activities into an organic whole. The reality is that most women these days *don't* feel exceptionally stressed out—no worse than men—and are pleased with how well they cope with everything they have to do (see Figure 4.8).

FIGURE 4.8 *Self-Defined for the New Millennium* (Yankelovich study conducted in 2000 for *Self* magazine)

I have found ways to successfully manage stress in my life.	73%
When I have too much to do, I find that I get more done than expected.	63%

One thing all women agree on is that there just isn't enough time in the day to get everything done. Women are not just busy, they are time starved. In fact, time is the single most important resource that people have nowadays, according to DYG Inc., one of the nation's leading research organizations. When DYG asked women to choose between gaining additional moderate amounts of time or money, they picked more time by nearly two to one.[18] We used to say "Time is Money." Well, not any more. *Time means more than money.* Time is the ultimate luxury for women. One way women deal with the time crunch is by multitasking.

Multitasking

One of the findings from Chapter 2 was that men tend to *be single-minded and focused,* whereas women tend to be *multiminded and integrated.* In addition to the "people first" orientation, this is one of the most consistent and systemic differences between the genders. It manifests itself not only in brain structure, perceptual abilities, and processing preferences (more about that in a moment) but also very pragmatically in terms of how men and women run their life.

Men like to structure their life linearly: first things first, finish one thing before going on to the next, get the most important things done before tackling anything lower on the list. Women pursue several tasks simultaneously. Each task spans a longer period of time, and outcomes can't always be timed as precisely, because the attention allocated to each is adjusted continually based on what comes up—what else needs to be integrated into the time stream.

To women, this is the most efficient way to work within their "many hats" lifestyle. As they move across their roles at work, at home, and at leisure, it allows them to accomplish more—just less predictably. In fact, if women *aren't* doing more than one thing at a time, most feel a vague sense of unease and start looking around for something to add into the mix. Just cooking dinner isn't enough, but if she can return a phone call, get the mail opened, and sort the laundry at the same time, now that's getting something done!

Multitasking makes men nervous. To them, it looks a little like herding cats: disorganized, unstructured, and out of control. They're sure things aren't progressing as they should be—"How can you get it right if you don't give it your full attention?" They shake their heads at how those ditzy women are easily distracted, can't focus, and are lousy at prioritizing. For their part, women feel a little sorry for men. The poor dears seem to be able to handle only one thing at a time, kind of sad, really.

Let me give you a brief example: Suppose a man tells his wife that he is going to run out to the drugstore. As far as most women are concerned, "I'm going to the drugstore" is an incomplete sentence. Any woman knows that the sentence should end with "and do you need anything while I'm there?" It's just a female reflex to scan for anything the tribe might need. Most women are accustomed to this difference in how men and women think, however, and nudge men by completing the sentence for them.

"Great!" a woman will respond. "Can you take the videotapes back to the Blockbuster next door?"

"I'm not *going* to Blockbuster; I'm going to the drugstore!" he's likely to grumble.

"But Blockbuster is next door to CVS!" she'll answer, astonished. "It's on the way."

Understand: All he wanted to do was to get in and out of the drugstore without a bunch of additional tasks being piled on. To the typical male, a request to add on tasks like this is *in* the way, not *on* the way.

The flip side, of course, is that men are typically very sparing about asking women to do similar errands for them—though women generally don't mind when men make these requests. Women *look* for additional tasks to group together. When a man asks a woman to drop off something at the post office while she's out, she thinks, *Great! Combined with the dry cleaning I've got to drop off and the grocery shopping I need to do, I've almost got the critical mass I need to make it worth my while to get in the car and drive to town.*

To women, it simply doesn't make sense to get in the car for just one errand. Until critical mass is attained, the dry cleaning and grocery shopping will just have to wait.

These two different approaches aren't right or wrong: they are just two alternate strategies for getting the most out of the limited time we all have. Conceptually, let's say you give a man and a woman the same to-do list of five prioritized items. At the end of the day, the man will come back with the top two items crossed off the list. The woman may return with the first priority undone—but the other *four* items are all crossed off. The man prioritizes; the woman *maximizes*. In her life, just because it isn't "most important" doesn't mean it doesn't have to get done eventually—might as well be now.

A UN study of men and women in 130 societies concluded that in all cultures, women multitask and "demonstrate a facility for juggling many activities at once."[19] All over the world, we do it the same way. Retail designers, event marketers, salespeople, and customer service reps can all leverage this insight to their advantage (wait until we get to Chapter 8—you'll see!).

Milestone Marketing

Anyone who has been through a few of the big "life transitions"—marriage, moving, new baby, new business—knows how demanding they can be. Each life event launches a host of additional needs and generates a flood of errands and activity. Because of women's roles in daily life, *family milestones affect women substantially more than they do men.* For one thing, she's usually the one to handle all the logistics. From calling the caterer to plotting the plantings, she's the one who plans and manages the event. For another, each time the household adds a person, the woman's workload shoots upward for the long term. The household needs new products and services, and as household CPO, it's the woman's job to get them.

Many articles have pointed out the advantages of organizing marketing thinking by life stage rather than by age. With the advent of cohabitation, postponed childbearing, divorce, and second marriages, current lifestyles are far too varied to peg a particular life event to a specific age range.

"Milestone marketing" takes the concept a step further by focusing on the people actually going through the event right now—not the people who have been through it at some time in the past. Married women have a chronic condition (if you'll excuse the analogy); women getting married have an acute emergency—they need help *now*. Marketers who tune in to women's immediate concerns and find a way to lend a helping hand in a relevant way will earn women's eternal gratitude.

"Live Long and Prosper"

With advances in health care, healthier diets, different lifestyles, and other choices now available to us, we're all living longer. In her book *New Passages,* Gail Sheehy pointed out that although we think of longer life expectancy as adding more time to the end of life, in reality it's more like adding an extra decade to the middle, somewhere between 50 and 60. These days, 55 is very alive; it's Prime Time, not the darkest hour before dawn. As the baby boomer population moves into prime time—and becomes progressively more female—we're going to see some major shifts in both popular culture and marketing opportunities.

Between the years 2000 and 2010, the 55–64 population will grow an astounding 48 percent; by contrast, the 25–54 age segment will grow a mere 2 percent.[20] And because women live longer, as any population ages it becomes more female: in 2001, among Americans aged 65+, 14.6 million were men and 20.5 million were women.[21]

Most older women will be healthy and can look forward to many years of an active lifestyle. According to Diane Holman of Woman-Trends, if a woman reaches her 50th birthday without cancer or heart disease, she can expect to see 92.

Whereas baby boomers' grandmothers may have sat in a rocker sipping tea while reading a book, today's boomer grandma is more likely to be sitting at her computer sipping Evian, having just come from a tennis match. These will not be women pining for the good old days of their lost youth. As a matter of fact, the Grey Advertising study found that the great majority of women, eight out of ten, feel *stronger and more confident* in themselves as they grow older. In fact, women of all ages seem to feel that "the best is yet to come." When they were asked to identify the peak age for success in a woman's life, women

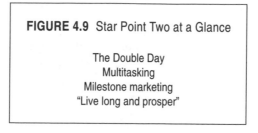

FIGURE 4.9 Star Point Two at a Glance

The Double Day
Multitasking
Milestone marketing
"Live long and prosper"

aged 25–34 said 41 years old. Women ages 35–49 said 50 years old. And women over 50 said 58 years old.[22]

I'm going to be discussing PrimeTime Women™ in more detail in Chapter 11, but suffice it to say that yesterday's "little old lady" will be tomorrow's financial powerhouse. Marketers unable to let go of outdated notions about men carrying the cash and consumers shutting down spending at age 55 will find themselves outflanked and outrun by savvy companies eager to serve America's target market bull's-eye— PrimeTime Women™.

From a woman's roles in daily life to her propensity to multitask, the dramatic impact of life transition milestones and her longer life span, women's attitudes toward, and uses of, time are very different from those of men's (see Figure 4.9).

Star Point Three: Focus Strategies

A little while ago, I mentioned that one of the most pervasive differences between women and men is this: Men are single minded and focused, while women are multi-minded and integrated. Relative to men, women see more details, care more about them, and via those bilateral brains and multizone processing, prefer to integrate them into a comprehensive whole rather than strip them away as extraneous.
As I said in Chapter 2, men analyze (take apart) and women synthesize (put together).

Details, Details

She notices more. Women pick up on things that men don't even register—either because they physically can't, or because they can't be bothered. This is partly because of women's "extrasensory sensitivity"; their radar screens seem to be set on a higher resolution. And women's "bandwidth" for screening distinctions is made of a finer-gauge mesh. If you can touch it, taste it, hear it, see it, or smell it, she's probably noticing it at some level, and it's figuring into her assessment of your product, service, and communications.

Even beyond the five senses, women possess a more *hidden* sensory ability. They can read subtle variances in tone of voice, facial expression, gestures, and body language, which gives them a sort of "emotional X-ray vision." If you're face-to-face with a female customer, any insincerity—or any of the unfortunate gender judgments we've been talking about—is likely to be much more apparent to her than you may realize.

She cares more. Although it's true that men care only about "the important stuff," the corollary is *not* that women care only about the details. Researchers and salespeople get confused when they hear women talking about criteria that seem minor in the grand scheme of things (storage pockets and a security purse holder in the minivan, for example) and sometimes conclude that women have different needs than men. The way it really works is that women want all the same things as men—*and then some*. They have a longer list.

In the film *When Harry Met Sally*, the two friends are in a diner ordering dinner. Harry places his order, quickly requesting an item on the menu. Sally names her item—and then launches into the specifics: "I'd like the pie heated, and I don't want the ice cream on top, I want it on the side. And I'd like strawberry instead of vanilla, if you have it. If not, then no ice cream, just whipped cream, but only if it's real. If it's out of a can, then nothing." Harry thinks she's crazy, obsessed, demented, but as Sally says, "I just want it the way I want it."

That's what your women customers want, too. Details matter.

Integrate versus Extricate

When it comes to absorbing a problem, sizing up a situation, or making a big-ticket purchase decision, men and women couldn't be more different. Both believe in getting "the big picture," but they approach it from opposite points of view.

The way men see it. Men believe in peeling away the "extraneous detail." If it's not one of the top three to five factors, forget about it. To stay focused on what's important, remove the topic from its context and reduce it to its basic elements. Analytical and minimalist, this approach is grounded in the benefit of extricating the bare essentials from the morass of smothering detail. Clarity comes from simplification, stripping away the small distinctions, discarding the data that clutter up the main points.

Apparently, men operate this way even at the molecular level. In the November 1999 issue of *Science*, the Whitehead Institute in Massachusetts tackled the case of the diminishing Y (male) chromosome. *The modern X chromosome has about ten times more genes than a modern Y chromosome, which has been casting off genes that are not useful to the male for the last 320 million years.*[23]

In addressing a high-involvement purchase decision, then, men prefer to focus in on the *important* things—namely, the top few items on their list of criteria. Once they find something that meets all the key criteria, they're ready to move ahead on a decision.

In absorbing advertising, they like simplicity, broad strokes—a message and creative approach that allows you to get in, get out, get on with it. In his book *Male and Female Realities,* Joe Tanenbaum, one of the few male authors to write on gender differences, says: "Men are very simple. They're not very complicated. They're not very sophisticated in the way they approach things."[24] In female vernacular, this statement is not particularly flattering. To be candid, it borders on being a put-down. I hesitated to include it without checking it with some male feedback first. To a man, they said, "That's right—simple and proud of it." I always get laughs and many nods of agreement when I present Figure 4.10, which is the visual representation of this idea.

FIGURE 4.10 Men Are Simple, Women Are Not

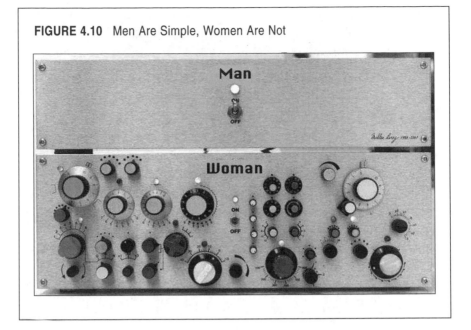

The way women see it. With women, it's an entirely different story. In their view, details not only add richness and depth but are *necessary* to an understanding of the situation. How can you possibly grasp the big picture without a detailed knowledge of the specifics? How can you appreciate the real issues without a thorough familiarity with the context? Women look to *add* information, not cut it away. While men see this as complicating the situation, women see it as integrating all the material necessary for a comprehensive perspective. Anything less would be superficial and meaningless.

It is an accepted philosophy in advertising that to be effective, ads must be single minded and focused: one and only one central premise, with a single—or at most two—support points. Take a Nissan print ad I saw recently: The visual is clean and simple—a gleaming car dashing through a spray of water. And the copy is straightforward as well— *Horsepower increased: 17 percent. Torque increased: 6 percent. Bragging rights increased: 100 percent.* Aside from the fact that the copy is *perfectly* aligned with male gender culture, the execution is well designed for the way men absorb information: a two-second scan and they register all they need to know. It's not great for women, though: a two-second scan and they forget about it two seconds later.

Even if most women cared about torque (and I'll wager that most women don't have any idea what torque is, let alone why anyone would want it), there's not much to engage with. The ad leaves women either cold or hungry for more to work with. In either case, they turn the page no more persuaded or motivated to check out the car than when they first picked up the magazine.

The Perfect Answer

The "longer-list" factor (wanting all the same things as men and then some) and the drive for a complete, integrated solution combine to create what I call the "Perfect Answer" syndrome. The Perfect Answer syndrome is a fundamental premise of the GenderTrends™ Marketing Model and an important key to understanding how women buy. Basically, women set the bar higher than men do; and if that means it takes longer to get over the bar, so be it. Women don't settle for "good enough."

Let me give you an example. A close colleague of mine was in the market for a cell phone, and she described several criteria she had in mind. Like many women, she doesn't like shopping for technology products, probably because they're not marketed in a way that makes any sense to her or to most other women. Who cares about the technical differences between digital and analog? What the heck is a gigahertz? Never mind—don't answer that. Who cares?

After she got the phone, she described how the selection and purchase had occurred, knowing I'd get a kick out of how gender differences showed up in the whole process (and she was right, I did). It seems that her husband, who loves gadgets, offered to do the research for her. The most important things to her, as she travels frequently, were that the phone work well just about anywhere ("Can you hear me now?") and that it not rack up ridiculously high roaming fees. She also wanted it to be lightweight, with no stubby antenna that would stick out and catch on things in her bag, and, all else being equal, she wanted it to be a cute phone, like the Motorola StarTac. My colleague's husband spent a day or two on the research and concluded that she needed AT&T's Digital One-Rate Service.

"Fine," she responded. "And what kind of phone do I get?"

"What does it matter?" he asked. "You get whatever phone comes with that service."

"Uh-*huh*," she said. "Well, it's very *manly* of you to listen only to the first thing I said, but, actually, I care about the other considerations I listed too."

So, she looked into what phone models AT&T offered with the service plan her husband had recommended, and it turned out that Nokia was one of the phone options. Nokia was the first company to offer cell phones in any color other than black matte plastic. Its early phones came in three colors, and one was a dark metallic navy called Ocean Blue. It was flying out of the stores, apparently, and was extremely hard to find—except in women's purses and briefcases, probably. She had found *her* phone, though, and so she proceeded to call all over the greater Philadelphia area until she finally located an Ocean Blue Nokia. It was at a retail store almost an hour away.

When she returned from her expedition, she showed her phone to her puzzled husband. "You drove *two hours* back and forth to get that?" he asked, astonished. "I had no idea the color of the phone was the most important thing to you."

I completely understood what my colleague said next: The color *wasn't* the most important thing; in fact, it was the *least* important thing. But like Sally with her pie and ice cream, my colleague wanted what she wanted. If she was going to go to all the trouble to get something she was going to have for a long time, she wasn't going to settle for something that was only 90 percent of what she wanted. She was willing to put in a little extra effort to get *100* percent. "Every time I use my elegant little Ocean Blue phone," she concluded, "I'm glad I did!"

Now here's the big "Aha!" for marketers: the color of the phone was not the most important factor. But it was *the deciding factor.* It was the reason my colleague chose Nokia over Ericcson. This insight represents an enormous opportunity to add incremental business and capture share from competitors. Companies today generally focus their research and their marketing messages on whatever has been identified as the "most important" factor(s). That works for a male buyer. The first option he encounters that checks off all the "Top Box" criteria—problem solved. Buy it. Proceed to the next priority.

The problem is, in most categories all the main competitors offer all the same "most important" features. So which brand a man buys is based almost as much on proximity as anything else—whichever qualified option he encounters first. But a woman has a longer list, and her decision is based on the whole package including the "nonessential but nice to have." That's great for the share-seeking marketer because she actually cares about the things that make you different from your competitors.

To coin a phrase . . . *the diva's in the details.* Women are constantly scanning, integrating, and *acting* on the details. And these are often details that guys don't say anything about. Does that make women "demanding" customers? You bet. But it also makes them more *discerning* customers, and you can apply that to your advantage.

Several companies have found that paying attention to what women want has helped them increase customer satisfaction among their male customers, too. For example, Wyndham Hotels installed magnifying mirrors in their bathrooms, based on suggestions from women travelers who found it difficult to apply makeup leaning way over the sink. (You can't wear your glasses when you apply eye makeup, you know.) Men didn't request the mirrors, and it's likely they never would have, but once the mirrors appeared, men noticed they made shaving a lot easier, and they appreciated having them.

Kimpton Hotels, which operates the Hotels Monaco, Hotel George, and Summit Lodge, to name a few, has taken this "diva is in the details" principle even further.

Kimpton Hotels

Opportunity:

Women constitute 40 percent[25] of all business travelers today and are estimated to constitute 50 percent[26] of frequent fliers. They spend $175 billion on 14 million trips annually[27] and influence 80 percent of all luxury and family travel.[28] We've come *and* gone a long way, baby—just 30 years ago, female executives constituted only 1 percent[29] of business travelers. A glance around any airport or train station confirms that things have changed dramatically. But as an industry, travel is very operations-intensive with a lot of moving parts, making it difficult to change and slow to recognize and act on these demographic trends.[30] This is a wake-up call!

FIGURE 4.11 Kimpton Hotels: Om Away From Home

Kimpton Hotels offer everything you need to take your yoga practice on the road. The following pages offer restorative poses to relieve travel fatigue.

Start with a yoga basket delivered to your room at no charge, that includes a yoga mat, strap and block from Gaiam and an issue of *Yoga Journal* Magazine.

Free instruction is available on your television. Please dial the operator at '0' to request a yoga basket.

We invite you to take your yoga basket with you or have it sent to a destination of your choosing. A nominal fee will be charged to your room upon request. NAMASTE.

OM
away from home

Kimpton Hotel & Restaurant Group, LLC

Strategies:

Kimpton is known for its collection of stylish boutique hotels that are coupled with bustling chef-driven restaurants. The company is also known for its social responsibility and diversity initiatives, internal and external. And now Kimpton is becoming known for its Women In Touch program, designed to serve the unique wishes and needs of women guests:

- Stylish surroundings—From whimsical elegance created by world-class designers to honoring architectural history, Kimpton sites reflect style in spades.
- Fun—Kimpton believes that travel should always be a delightful journey, so they provide a friendly and welcoming atmosphere with wine

hours, complimentary neck and shoulder massages, tarot card read-
ings, and more.

- A sense of personal hospitality—Kimpton employees pride themselves on creating a "home away from home" atmosphere and demonstrate a personal and genuine sense of caring for all guests.

- Locally loved restaurants adjacent to the hotel—Kimpton has found
that women really appreciate never having to leave the hotel to have
an exceptional dining experience.

- Safety and security—Kimpton provides that with small hotels that typically have around 200 rooms.

Insights that Kimpton tapped into:

- **Details matter**

  The "diva" is in the details. Women want the same things as men, *and
  then some.* Kimpton's "Forgot it, We've Got It" program saves the day
  when guests have forgotten to pack an essential item. No more frantic
  trips to a drugstore; guests can get the following complimentary items
  during their stay: Static Guard, spray wrinkle remover, hand-held
  steamer, make-up mirror, umbrella, tweezers, sunscreen, nail care items,
  lint brushes, and more. And for a small extra charge, you can even get
  flattening gel, phone chargers, and hair spray! Talk about stress relief!

- **Multitasking**

  When women are on business trips, they want to do more than just
  business. Kimpton's "Om Away From Home" Yoga Program is the first
  ever in-room yoga program and a great way for women to take care of
  their health and well-being while taking care of business. (See Figure
  4.11.) Yoga instruction is made easy and accessible through the Yoga
  Channel offered on in-room televisions and via a complimentary copy
  of *Yoga Journal* and a little travel yoga booklet. Complimentary yoga
  baskets complete with a mat, block, and strap are available for guests
  to use during their stay and take home; instructional yoga CDs are
  available for purchase in the honor bar. In-room meditation, pilates,
  and spa services are coming soon.

- **Corporate halo**

  Altruistic elements play a major role in women's purchase contemplations. Kimpton Hotels has leveraged this principle and recently
  launched its partnership with Dress for Success as the exclusive

hospitality sponsor in March 2005—Women's History Month. Guests booking a room during the month of March could designate a portion of their room rate as a donation to the organization, which is an international not-for-profit organization that assists economically challenged women transitioning from unemployment to self-sufficiency. (See Figure 4.12.) Dress for Success supplies its clients with an interview suit as well as ongoing support and career development. Events, such as fashion shows, volunteer recognition receptions, and "mistake shoe" drives, were held across the country at various Kimpton locations to help raise funds and collect donations.

- **We not me/peer group**
Women look at the world from the perspective of the group. Their core unit is "we" not "me" and their mottos are "all for one, and one for all," and "the more, the merrier." Kimpton recognizes the value of "girl-friends" and shared experiences and has introduced several "Girl-friend Getaway" packages including "Downtown Divas," where guests receive chocolate-covered strawberries and Veuve Cliquot champagne, town car service to and from the hotel to Nordstrom, a Nordstrom personal shopper, a pint of Haagen–Dazs ice cream at turndown, and more. Sometimes a girl's best friend is a pet. Kimpton offers another special package that includes canine welcome amenities and even pet psychics. Can't travel with your pet? Several properties offer goldfish to keep you company!

Results:

Niki Leondakis, CEO of Kimpton Hotels & Restaurants, spearheaded the Women In Touch loyalty program and has seen the results. "We knew that we were attracting a higher percentage of women travelers. But our programs have also made our hotel experience better for male travelers as well. For example, the 'Forgot It, We've Got It' program is not labeled for the 'harried, haggard female business traveler.' We've done transparent marketing, and this is when you win—when the men also appreciate the things you've done to market to women."

Kimpton's marketing savvy has turned into sales success; it has gained three percent market share over its competitors, indicating that the company is serving the needs of guests better than anyone else in this rough travel economy. Within a six-month period in 2004, more than 200 women's packages

FIGURE 4.12 Kimpton Hotels: Dress for Success

Kimpton Hotel & Restaurant Group, LLC

were booked, which represents a 50 percent increase. And new members to the Kimpton In Touch program are equally split between men and women, demonstrating that meeting the expectations of women generally translates into more business from men as well. It's a win-win situation for everyone. I know where I am going to stay on my next business trip. I bet you do too!

FIGURE 4.13 Star Point Three at a Glance

Details, details
Integrate versus extricate
The Perfect Answer

Figure 4.13, Star Point Three at a Glance, summarizes the distinctly different orientations women and men have toward details. They not only scan their environments in different ways, but they also take in, remember, and respond differently to the details of life. This has significant marketing implications, as I'll discuss in greater depth as we continue. For now, let's look at Star Point Four, which illustrates the communication differences between men and women.

Star Point Four: Communication Keys

The Communication Keys of male and female gender culture evolve, not surprisingly, from the values and principles of the other three Star Points. However, because we're all in the communications business here, I thought they were worth pulling out for separate consideration. The five keys are such a core part of male-female gender difference that a dedicated section will help you by serving as a quick reference when you're checking your executional approaches.

Headline versus Body Copy

Consistent with men's inclination to simplify and strip away extraneous detail, they believe in starting with the main point and supplying specific detail only if the listener asks for it. Conversely, women will often start with a lengthy background and build up to the summary conclusion—an approach consistent with their belief in context and richness of detail. To women, the details are the *good* part: what he said, why she answered as she did, and what the significance of that event was. The guys are patient up to a point, but then they start rolling their eyes and looking at their watch.

But a woman wants the full story—and "making a long story short" is not usually the best way to get and keep her attention. To engage her with your message in the first place, she needs some specifics to work with. And to serve her in her search for the Perfect Answer, she'll require a lot of product and service information to compare against her longer list.

"Report Talk" versus "Rapport Talk"

Sociolinguist Dr. Deborah Tannen characterizes men's conversation as "report talk," whose role is to transmit information, solve problems—and *establish or defend individual status.* When every encounter is a contest, the contestants have to be ready to fend off others' attempts to win the point. She calls women's conversation "rapport talk," whose purpose is to transmit information, solve problems—and *create connections among individuals.*

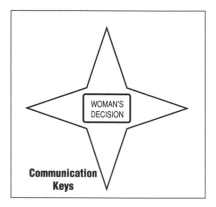

According to a *People* magazine study, conversation serves many purposes in women's life. It helps them recharge—71 percent of women (and only 49 percent of men) agree that "having a good conversation with a friend helps me recharge my battery." It helps them learn—41 percent of women agree (and only 34 percent of men) that "I learn a lot from hearing stories about what's going on in other people's lives." It helps them connect with others *and* themselves. As Pulitzer Prize-winning journalist Anna Quindlen says, "I only really understand myself, what I'm really thinking and feeling, when I've talked it over with my circle of friends. When days go by without that connection, I feel like a radio playing in an empty room."[31]

When male and female students in a communications class were asked to bring in an audiotape of a "really good conversation," one young man brought in a lunch conversation with a fellow classmate that included lots of animated discussion of a project they were working on together. The women students were puzzled, because there wasn't a personal word on the whole tape. *You call that a conversation?*

This is not an extreme example; it's how women *define* "good inter-action." If you want to have a good conversation with a woman cus-tomer, either face-to-face or via your marketing materials, you need to build in some rapport. And as we'll see in Chapter 9, if you don't lose the "establishing status" element during a sales interaction, you're likely to lose her as a customer.

Making the Connection

I've come to think of the ways men and women connect within gen-der as games—games as different as football and figure skating. Men have three games: One-up, One-down, and Put-down. Women have three games, too: Same-same, Scoop, and Gift Exchange. And each gender has its own "social currency": for men, it's facts and features; for women, it's stories and personal details.

Connecting through competition—establishing rank. Men actually con-nect through competition. They see verbal jousting and challenging banter as a friendly way to size each other up—the first step on a road to becoming buddies. And the better friends they are, the worse they treat each other. When girlfriends Debra, Lisa, and Ellen are having lunch, they call each other Debra, Lisa, and Ellen. But buddies Dave, Mike, and Brad call each other Monkey-butt, Loser, and Dogbreath—and that's how you know they've been friends forever.

"One-up." Men who don't know each other usually play One-up. You know how this goes. The goal is to establish who's "higher"—any crite-rion will do. The topic can be money, sports, music, or fitness, and "higher" can mean knows more, owns more, is better connected, or has gone where no man has gone before—you name it.

One guy will open with a remark that sets the topic: "Have you seen the new PDAs they're coming out with?" Second guy ups the ante: "Yeah, sure. Matter of fact, I just bought the latest model. It's incredi-ble. You can get stock market reports from anywhere anytime, down-load tunes, take pictures, send them to the subsidiary in Germany, you name it." Third guy says: "You know, when I was beta-testing that model last year, I told them they should change the way the controls

worked, because most people were going to find them too complicated. What do you fellows think?" The other guys know they can't
beat that one—they fold.

"One-down." The game of One-down works much the same way, but
it's for guys who know each other a little better, so the competition is
a little more overt. One-down is the "ongoing game show" mind game
consisting of test questions that pop up at every opportunity. Say two
guys are disputing a point in baseball. Sooner or later, Jim's going to
say to Joe, "You don't know what you're talking about!" "Oh yeah?"
says Joe. "Who hit the winning home run in the 2001 World Series?"
If Jim gets the answer, he gets a point. If not, he is now *one-down* and
has already started thinking about how to get back at Joe and stump
him with his next question.

Social currency: facts and features. Both of these games rely on a
special kind of social currency: facts and features. It's what men exchange during small talk. So if you're like me and have been wondering why so many men walk around with huge inventories of apparently
useless factoids, now you know. The bigger picture, though, is that this
is one more case where male preferences skew away from the personal
and as we'll see in a moment, women's don't.

"Put-down." The endgame in male bonding is the Put-down, and it's
reserved for family and longtime friends as a sign of affection—and for
all coworkers, as a good-natured bid for dominance. The basic premise
is to see who can deliver the better insult. So a couple of guys who haven't seen each other in a year might have this exchange: "Looks like
you've put on a little weight, buddy. Is that where you carry your spare
tire nowadays?" "Look who's talking. With that pot you've got, I bet
you haven't seen your feet in five years!" It's not malicious, it's not
mean, it's all in good fun—but if one of my girlfriends ever talked to
me like that, I'd go to my room and cry.

Men actually use this routine to show affection and good faith. In
fact, one of the highest accolades in the male kingdom is to be the
honoree at a roast: an event where a series of speakers gets up to deliver a tirade of insults all meant to show respect and affection for the
guest of honor. To women, this style of humor is as foreign as camel's

milk. *You call that funny?* As for the marketing implications, wait until we get to our discussion of women's humor in Chapter 9.

Connecting through affinity—establishing links. Guess what? Women's games are about as opposite from the men's as they could be. Surprised? I hope not. The insight here is that instead of connecting through competition, women connect through affinity; instead of seeking to establish rank, they strive to establish links. The key word is *empathy*—and the force is strong.

"Same-same." One of the settings of women's scan mode is "things in common with someone else." Almost without thinking about it, a woman will seize the opportunity to reinforce virtually any similarity between herself and the speaker. "I know what you mean—my boss does the same thing!" or "You're kidding! That's my favorite shoe store, too!" One ad that exemplifies this principle is for McCormick spices. It shows a smiling but clearly tired woman at the end of a tough day, and the headline reads "If you're a vegetable by the end of the day, just add chicken." It goes on to give an easy stir fry chicken recipe. Instead of prodding women to aspire to pert and perfect mommyhood, McCormick says "We get it. We understand what your life is like. This woman is just like you, and if our solution works for her, it will work for you too."

"Scoop." This game is the opposite of put-down. It's women's instinctive show of support when someone else might be feeling bad about something. The minute she senses someone is embarrassed or at a loss, a woman will step in to scoop up the poor soul and rescue the situation. Imagine this scenario: A conference participant briskly rounds a corner in an unfamiliar hotel, only to find himself face-to-face with an oddly placed brick wall. You can tell it makes him feel a bit foolish, as he stops abruptly and looks around to find his way. A few of his fellow conference-goers, friends of his, are standing nearby and call out a comment or two. For his male friends, it's the perfect opportunity for a slam-dunk put-down: "Walking into walls again, Jim?" or "Can't find your way around the corner, good buddy?"

But the women in the group take a different tack, instantly scooping him into their care and protection. "You know, everyone's been doing that," one woman says right away. "I don't know why they designed this corridor like that." Another says, "I almost did that myself a minute ago! Are you looking for the phones? Because if you are, they're over there."

Gift exchange. This is the big game for women. Women exchange compliments, and although to men it might look like a random little ritual, it's actually rooted in two ways of establishing links. First, it's a way of showing affinity. When a woman tells a friend or a new acquaintance she likes her bracelet or her shoes or her dress, it's an indirect way of saying she likes her. Second, it opens the door to the way women exchange social currency, which is through stories, personal details, and confidences.

Social currency: stories and personal details. When Jill tells Janet she likes her bracelet, Janet is unlikely to reply with a simple thank-you and move on. Instead, chances are she will launch into a story. *You know where I got this bracelet? I was on Cape Cod to spend Christmas with my folks last year. My sister and I went into town to do some shopping, and I saw this bracelet in the window. I was dying to buy it, but I had just splurged on a new handbag two stores down, and I really didn't think I should. So guess what? My sister gave it to me for my birthday last April!*

At this point, every guy's eyes in the room are glazed over—this is *way* more personal information than they are interested in. But, the other women in the conversation have just been given a pile of gifts, all kinds of leads to find something in common and build up the relationship. There's so much to work with: Cape Cod, Christmas, parents, sisters, April birthdays. Something in there is bound to strike a chord. A woman can tell you a story about almost every piece of jewelry she owns, every scarf, every pair of shoes! So gentlemen, if you've been wondering why a woman launches into the detailed personal "story of her life" at the drop of a hat, now you know. What are the marketing implications? Again, you'll see all kinds of applications in Chapter 9.

There are scholars who spend their entire careers examining, documenting, and explaining the implications of the differences in how men and women communicate. We've barely scratched the surface of the subject. With Star Point Four, there's room to provide only the

---

FIGURE 4.14 Star Point Four at a Glance

Men	Women
Key Points	**Full Context**
"Headlines"	"Complete article"
"Report talk"	**"Rapport talk"**
Establish status	Build connections
Connect through Competition—Rank	**Connect through Affinity—Link**
One-up	Same-same
One-down	Scoop
Put-down	Gift exchange
Facts and Features	**Stories and Personal Details**

---

bare bones framework essential to understanding a great number of the marketing applications we'll cover. My guess is many of the men reading this will think that's just fine. *Come on. Let's get to the action steps!* For anyone serious about building his or her business with this huge and lucrative market, I urge you to continue your studies with the books listed as essential reading in Appendix B.

In Figure 4.14, you'll see a summary of the major variances we've just discussed regarding men's and women's communication styles and patterns. As with the topics covered by the other Star Points, this summary can provide a quick detailing of the main areas in which gender differences can influence marketing outcomes, a topic we'll address in greater depth in the chapters ahead.

Women's Values

How does gender culture connect to your product? It may be true that women value warm relationships more than men do or value independence less—but what does that have to do with the price of tea in China or with selling more stereos or insurance policies? The answer is simple: To motivate and persuade people, you have to talk to them about things they care about, in terms that matter to them—what they cherish, what they're proud of, what they enjoy, what they're hoping to accomplish in life, and so on.

The four Star Points of gender culture allow us to pull apart and clarify four discrete points of differences between male and female culture—and wouldn't it be convenient if human behavior would just align itself as neatly? But in real life, in real situations, people don't operate on abstract principles. So as marketers, it's our job to go to the next step: translate the concepts of gender culture into an understanding of women's lives and values.

I'm closing this chapter with a summary of some of the key *values* women bring to their decision making, with emphasis on the ones that most differentiate them from men. It's a broad topic, so we can't go too deeply into any individual point and give it the thorough attention it deserves. Some of the values are what you would expect, some are unexpected, and some have simply been overlooked. But the list will be a useful tool for you to use in jump-starting your strategic and tactical thinking on innovative marketing approaches for the women's market.

What Women Cherish

Warm, close relationships. The closer, the better. To women, personal ties are a good thing—in fact the best thing. Freedom is not nearly as important as friendship. Who cares if you can do anything you want; if nobody likes you, what's the point?

Girlfriends. Women's relationships with their close women friends are some of the most cherished elements in their life. Yet most marketers have barely begun to explore the possibilities to tap this insight for advertising and other marketing elements. Women are portrayed as individuals, which they are, of course, and as wives, mothers, and coworkers—all perfectly valid and rich with opportunity. But women in small groups, animated by lively conversation and laughter or warmed by caring concern, are a brave new world beckoning.

According to an article in the *Chicago Tribune* (May 18, 2005), for women, friendship not only rules, it protects. It buffers the hardships of life's transitions, it lowers blood pressure, boosts immunity, and promotes healing. It may help explain one of medical science's most enduring mysteries: why women, on average, have lower rates of heart disease and longer life expectancies than men.

FIGURE 4.15 What Women Cherish

Ad by Brainsaw. www.brainsaw.com

I found this great "girlfriends" ad example in the most surprising category—golf (Figure 4.15). To women, golf would never be played alone (why bother?). Cleveland Golf equipment is tapping into this nontraditional golfers' market in a relevant and appealing way.

One of the best examples of girlfriends in action is a story I read about six 40-year-old women getting together for a mammogram party in Dallas. No one wanted to go alone, so these creative ladies decided to have a Girls' Day Out at the doctor and go as a group. Now their mammogram appointments are annual "Girlfriends" parties, and the typical fear and dread is turned into shared hope and optimism. "You're taking instant support with you," said one woman. It's time for marketers to create these opportunities, so women don't have to do it for themselves.

Men who are thoughtful, caring, and considerate. No, not men who are women; rather men who are men and then some. (You remember women's longer list, right?) Women long for a man who understands and empathizes with them, is proud of them for the things they take pride in, and "gets" the metamessages. You don't usually get a whole man like this, but occasionally you get moments—so women cherish the moments. The long-running "A Diamond Is Forever" campaign, with its unmistakable music and distinctive silhouette, does an excellent job portraying the kind of romantic moment that makes women swoon.

Children's accomplishments. This is under the "cherish" heading instead of "takes pride in," because the emotion women experience goes far beyond parental pride. As one of women's highest values, helping their children succeed and be happy engenders a feeling of love powerful enough to warm a village.

What Women Take Pride In

A warm, comfortable, and orderly home. Yes, women take pride in this. The key is to keep in mind that it's not the *only* thing they take pride in, romanticized home care advertising notwithstanding. (I'm afraid I actually laughed out loud in disbelief when I read a recent quote from a Fieldcrest Cannon executive commenting on a new ad campaign: "The ads recall a better era, when Mom had time to do the laundry and hang it on the line, days when we had time to enjoy ourselves." Ah yes, the good old days before we had labor-saving appliances.[32])

Appearance: figure, clothes, jewelry, hairstyles, grooming, and the like. As we saw early in this chapter, for most women (except for teenagers and 20-somethings), appearance is on the list but not as the all-consuming obsession marketers seem to think it is. The other radical revelation, which I've seen reflected in only one or two advertising campaigns, is that looking good is not just about *luring men*. For younger women, maybe. But as many women have discovered to their chagrin, most men simply don't notice elements like hair, clothes, jewelry, and shoes. Not to worry—at least other women can appreciate good taste. And besides, accessories make such good compliment prompts!

Their own efforts to be caring, considerate, thoughtful, generous, and loyal. That cross-cultural survey we saw in the beginning of the chapter highlighted women's identification of these traits with their "ideal self."

Multitasking. As we said, men see no sense in multitasking as a way of getting things done. Because it doesn't focus on "first things first," men see it as an inefficient way to run their life. But women feel they get a heck of a lot more done than men who tackle only one thing at a time, and they're proud of being able to juggle a lot of balls at once—especially when they can manage to make it look easy.

Being needed. As opposed to men who feel a sense of power when they attain the autonomy to do whatever they want *unfettered by others*, women feel powerful when *others come to them for help.*

Making the world a better place. This is related to the previous motivation but on a macro scale. As we saw in the survey earlier, this is women's number one dream for themselves.

Corporate halo. Altruistic elements play a major role in women's purchase contemplations. Beyond any product quality or sales or service considerations, a company's corporate halo—its acts of social responsibility and community citizenship—mean a lot to women.

Recognition. Just because women don't boast and push themselves forward doesn't mean they don't like being recognized and admired— for the right reasons, in the right way. Marketing messages that acknowledge women's accomplishments are appreciated not only by the honoree but also by the female audience, which feels that very often deserving women get passed over for these kinds of recognition.

What Women Enjoy or Care about More Than Men Do

Before we get started, in selecting the traits listed below, I based my choices on traits that distinguish women from men. Women also enjoy good food, a day at the beach, or a great movie, but if there are no relevant gender-based differences, I don't discuss them here.

Being around other people. Women feel *good* about being in a group. Whereas men are often inclined to think of other people as a *drain* on their energy, women see others as a *source* of energy and go to other people whenever their reserves are low (the "tend and befriend" factor).

Collaborative interaction. Add to the pleasure of being around others the fun and satisfaction of collaborating on common goals for a project that is important to all of us, and you'll show women a day in the life they'd like to live.

She wants it the way she wants it. Just because *you* don't notice a given detail or don't think it's important, doesn't mean she doesn't. Just because you think it's obvious that people prefer minimalist communication doesn't mean that's for her.

Things Women Enjoy the Same as Men— but Are Sometimes Overlooked

Challenge and achievement. Women are as motivated as men by the challenge of achieving excellence. However, unlike men who care deeply about being a winner and defeating a loser, women frame their ambitions in terms of achieving their *personal best*. They take a great deal of pride in attaining excellence and surpassing their previous efforts; whether anyone else is surpassed is immaterial.

Working. Just like most men, the majority of women like their jobs. In fact, when asked, "If you were to get enough money to live as comfortably as you would like for the rest of your life, would you continue to work or would you stop working?" 68 percent of women said they would continue to work (as would 70 percent of men).[33]

Things Women Don't Want/Don't Do/Don't Care About

Isolation, loneliness. Nobody wants isolation and loneliness. The point of calling out these factors for women is twofold: First, many psychologists believe feelings of isolation and loneliness are at the *top* of women's aversion list; even if men don't like loneliness, women don't like it more. Second, for women, freedom almost always takes a back seat to friendship. Many marketers who think they're expressing independence and self-sufficiency need to check their communications explicitly to make sure they're not casting shadows of solitude and distance.

Getting ahead of the Joneses. Many ad executions are platformed on the assumption that everyone wants to get ahead of everyone else—code word: *aspirational.* However, female gender culture is grounded in the idea of empathy, not envy. Women would rather be hanging out with the Joneses than scrambling to get ahead of them.

Gloating. I've seen a couple of women-targeted ads lately with a "gloating" theme—some of them over pretty trivial product benefits. I wonder if those advertisers know that to women, gloating doesn't mean "rightful pride of the victor over the vanquished" but rather "mean, smug, and self-satisfied."

Boasting, bragging, and swaggering. Women may be resigned to men's self-reinforcing statements and carefulness to claim credit where credit is due, but they are quite uncomfortable with this behavior from themselves or from another woman. They may feel boastful inside, but strutting around shouting their virtues to the world is definitely not their style.

Facts and features. Women's people-first orientation causes them to see life problems and purchasing solutions in terms of how they impact people; facts and features are strictly secondary. They don't care nearly as much about your fund's one-, three-, and five-year performance or its Morningstar rating as they do about whether this investment is going to be enough to send Jack and Emily off to the colleges of their choice.

How the thing works. You can give women all the wonderful mechanical drawings and blueprints you want; just don't get your hopes up that they will ever look at them. And, frankly, you'd get a higher return putting the money into making sure the products are simplified and easier to work with in the first place. Let me clarify a bit . . . I think women may sometimes want information on how things work . . . because women often want lots and lots of information on everything, important and unimportant in order to get a comprehensive understanding of what they're buying. But I believe they hardly ever "care" about automotive drive trains and computer gigabytes and digital versus analog electronics features. Their interest is in what benefits the products deliver, not how they work.

What Women Expect or Are Open To That Men Don't Want

Help, advice, and others' opinions. Women don't share men's barriers to offers of assistance and instead see advice as valuable, both for its immediate content and for the learning it provides for future reference.

Emotions. Whereas men regard self-revelation as "indecent exposure," women look on positive emotional candor and expressiveness as natural and to be encouraged.

If there's one key takeaway from this chapter, it's this: Women and men are not the same, and using the same marketing strategies to reach them means at best a near miss. And a near miss is like *almost* making that sale: it doesn't line your pockets and doesn't send products flying off the shelves.

Because the concept of different male and female gender cultures is relatively new, as is the thinking about how to apply gender culture insights to marketing, men don't generally know women well enough to portray them the way women see themselves or the way they would like to be seen. As a default, women are portrayed as having the same drives and aspirations as men—to be perfect, slim and youthful, self-involved and self-sufficient, seeking status and excitement, in control at every minute. And that's *not* what women want—not most women, in any case.

Ironically, as we've seen, one of the things that women want most is a sense of belonging, a feeling of being understood. And that message is missing from most marketing communications. And as far as women are concerned, until now that intent has seemed to be missing from most marketers.

The purpose of the GenderTrends™ Marketing Model is to give you an understanding of female gender culture and show you how to translate your insights into intelligent action. This chapter has focused on developing the gender understanding. Chapters 5 and 6 offer the "translator tools" and show you how to apply your new gender savvy. The final part of the book outlines specific strategic and tactical implications for marketing, sales, and consumer communications.

Figure 4.16 brings together and illustrates the four Star Points we've discussed: Social Values, Life/Time Factors, Focus Strategies, and Communication Keys. In each of these four areas, women and men show significant differences. These differences influence the process and outcome of women's purchasing decisions—which is the ultimate goal of this book and its readers.

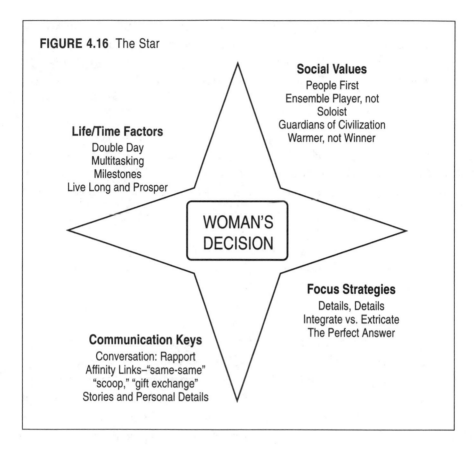

FIGURE 4.16 The Star

Social Values
People First
Ensemble Player, not Soloist
Guardians of Civilization
Warmer, not Winner

Life/Time Factors
Double Day
Multitasking
Milestones
Live Long and Prosper

WOMAN'S DECISION

Focus Strategies
Details, Details
Integrate vs. Extricate
The Perfect Answer

Communication Keys
Conversation: Rapport
Affinity Links–"same-same"
"scoop," "gift exchange"
Stories and Personal Details

CHAPTER 5

The Circle and the Compass

Response to Marketing Contacts

Bombarded by an arsenal of marketing contacts, women select, react, and respond differently to those contacts than men do. This chapter will identify the 12 marketing elements that companies use to communicate their offerings and persuade their consumers (*the Circle*), as well as demonstrate the basics of applying the gender culture insights of the last chapter to the marketing elements in your plan (*the Compass*). Actual recommendations and examples will be covered in Chapter 8, within the context of the consumer's purchase path.

As we previewed in Chapter 3, the core concept of the GenderTrends™ Marketing Model is that each Star Point of female gender culture holds implications and insights for almost every element in your marketing mix. To visualize the idea, think of the Star spinning within the Circle to align each Star Point in turn with each of the keystone elements. (See Figure 5.1.)

Even in its simplest form—4 Star Points multiplied by 12 marketing elements—a systematic application of this process would yield almost 50 discussion topics. In fact, because each Star Point is composed of *several* related insights, the model yields many more than 50 observations for you to consider as you design and execute your tactical plan. In my seminars and workshops, I can customize a workbook to the

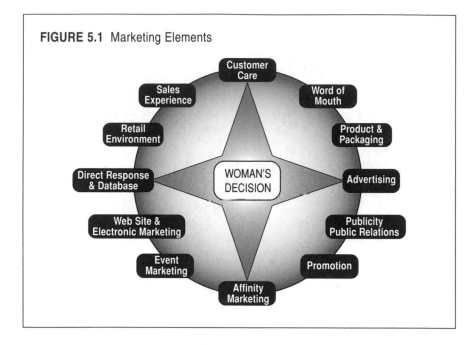

FIGURE 5.1 Marketing Elements

specific industry and/or functional area I'm working with, which helps to focus the discussion on the applications most relevant to the participants. However, because readers of this book are from many different industries and deal with many different functional areas, that's going to be a tad difficult.

To streamline the process, I'm going to select three areas—*advertising, product/packaging,* and *Web site/electronic marketing*—as sample applications to demonstrate how the Star Point insights interact with marketing elements. Given the space constraints, the notes must necessarily be abbreviated. But they will give you several concise examples of how to apply the model so that you can do this yourself in the context of your own brand, consumer, industry, department, and marketing objectives.

For companies *organized by function* (such as product development, advertising, Web site/electronic marketing, and so on), I suggest that each department head set up a brainstorming session with eight to ten people familiar with the GenderTrends principles in this book. Going through each Star Point as it applies to their department will result in a deep understanding of their consumer and appreciation for how to reach her effectively.

The limitation of this approach is that it's difficult to ensure that all of your company's diverse communications reach the consumer with "one look, one voice." With each department working separately, the insights will be deep but not broad. The "one look, one voice" philosophy across departments will strengthen your communications no matter how you define your target, but it's *especially* critical for women, who are so much more sensitive to context and specifics than are their male counterparts.

In companies that have an alternative *brand-based organizational structure,* managers charged with guarding the brand identity generally have control of most of the communications elements that deliver this identity to the consumer. These companies, therefore, have a somewhat better shot at delivering a consistent point of view across the board to the customer in the marketplace. The downside to this approach is that applying all of the learnings and insights of this model to all 12 of the marketing elements will be a comprehensive process, requiring an extensive time commitment.

Advertising

Advertising is probably the easiest element to work with, because there are so *many* ways to apply gender culture principles. It would be overkill to try to cover them all, so here are a representative few to get you started.

Social Values

People first. Step away from the conventional "product as hero" perspective and focus on people as the axis in your advertising. The people may be product users, as in Apple's iPod TV ads, or company representatives, such as Bill Ford for the Ford Motor Company or the late Dave Thomas for Wendy's.

"Warmer" instead of "winner." Avoid premises founded on command and control, going solo, status, defeating opponents, outranking others, making others jealous, being the top dog, and other qualities or values that don't connect for women. Fidelity Investments used to run a print ad showing a square-jawed, vigorous-looking older man on the

phone with the headline, "Fundsnetwork. To a mutual funds investor, it's command central"—perfect for men, less resonant for women. Saturn seemed to forget its "different kind of car company" heritage when it ran an ad promoting its latest line of cars as "faster, roomier, more luxurious and yes, more expensive." Hits the mark (even though it doesn't differentiate) with men, not with women. Merrill Lynch ran an ad for its financial planning services showing a perfect couple in a perfect house with expensive art on the walls with the headline "Dan and Patricia are always searching for the best of everything." While I can see that they are clearly wealthy and successful, this high-society couple strikes me as shallow and vain. I don't want to be like them—in fact, I don't even want to know them!

Instead, seek positioning platforms that emphasize bringing people together; creating a sense of belonging and closeness; offering the opportunity to help other people; values like excellence through teamwork, consensus, and mentoring; and making the world a better place. Another print execution from Fidelity, you could almost say a "sister ad," takes an approach women are likely to find more relevant and appealing. It shows a pleasant-looking woman, also on the phone, next to the headline "New job? Call family, friends and Fidelity." Saturn also has a "sister" ad that is much more female friendly—it shows a woman and her children casually posed outside and says "There's a point where luxury becomes somewhat silly . . . overdone." I couldn't agree more. Merrill Lynch's "sister" ad is quite a contrast to the high achievers above—a normal, nice-looking family is shown smiling with the headline "Will and Elizabeth Burns have outgrown their old portfolio. Their kids have outgrown everything else." Now *that* I can relate to! I like to present these ads together in my seminars, because they are literally a side-by-side demonstration of the different approaches more likely to appeal to men and women.

Similarity instead of superiority. Feature people your target audience can identify with and relate to, attractive "normal" women rather than perfect "aspirational" women. Most women don't even want to be supermodels—honest! One brand that really knows women is Procter & Gamble's Olay. Its advertising typically portrays its users' natural beauty reflecting a sense of personal warmth, never the unattainable air-brushed perfection of most beauty care products.

Recognize that women are not driven by an operative emotion of envy. They don't think, *When I get that product, she's going to be so jealous of me!* Instead, they operate from empathy, thinking, *I have that same problem—maybe I'll look into doing what she's doing.*

Corporate halo. Let your consumer know about your good corporate citizenship, the good works done by your foundation, your donations to those in need, your support of the arts or environmental causes. Target prides itself on "giving over $2 million a week to the communities we serve" and has done an exceptional job of developing and advertising its Take Charge of Education school fundraising program, whereby a percentage of every qualified purchase goes directly to a designated school. The retailer actively reminds its "guests" of the company's good deeds via advertising as well as in sales flyers, store displays, on its Web site, and even via its salespeople. A recent ad campaign drew attention to its program by featuring celebrities such as Vanessa Williams talking about how important their favorite teachers had been in their life. Target is not seen as exploitative when it promotes its good citizenship—it is offering women everything they need "*and then some*" and is also offering a differentiator. Today, many products are viewed as interchangeable commodities—so if a brand can't be differentiated via quality, selection, and price, an impactful way to break away from the crowd is by using the "corporate halo."

Life/Time Factors

The double day. Acknowledge women's multiple roles in a positive way. Don't portray women as harried, frenzied, and at the end of their rope; instead, create advertising that shows them realistically as busy, yet handling the chaos with confidence and a sense of humor.

Milestones. Tap into her mindset at a time when you know what's uppermost on her mind. Use milestone-specific media—wedding Web sites to reach engaged women, for example. And tailor your creative strategies with an event-relevant hook. Epson recently ran an ad for its printers at back-to-school time showing an excited grade school student getting on the bus with the headline "He'll never forget his first day of school, and now neither will you." Milestones can be large or small, but women mark them all.

Focus Strategies

Details, details. Provide plenty of specific information in various long-format media. Although credit card companies like MasterCard and American Express focus their TV ads on a single benefit, they always back them up with detailed newspaper ads and fairly lengthy direct mail contacts.

Integrate versus extricate: the big picture. To make a decision, she'll want more than the bare bones that a man would call the big picture; she'll want a comprehensive grasp of the product, with options and contingencies, within the context of its intended usage.

Integrate versus extricate: immersion. Instead of assuming that super-clean, streamlined copy and visuals are by definition the best way to engage and motivate her, consider and test richer, more involving executions. In contrast with the car ad I described earlier with the three quick hits on horsepower, torque, and bragging rights, I often show a Ford ad focused on the company's environmental/recycling story. Those who espouse the "clean visuals" school of thought would say the ad's a mess: it's a two-page spread, and scattered across some sort of textured background are numerous little "vignettes," like a few soda bottle caps with a slip of paper saying, "The two-liter bottles we recycle each year would fill a 100-acre lake." On the right is a short, informal "from the desk of" memo from a woman named Audrey White outlining a few of Ford's environmental efforts. There's a little wallet photo of her too; she looks like a nice person, someone I can relate to.

There's more, but already you can see that the ad gives readers a lot to work with. There are plenty of little points of entry into the ad, and they pull you in and move you around the page without your even realizing how completely and agreeably you've been engaged in the process of educating yourself on the company's message. I think this "immersion" approach to advertising may well be more successful in reaching and persuading women than the conventional "clean hit" headline and single visual most of us have been taught to strive for.

Another good example is Phoenix Wealth Management, which has managed to create an ad with the women-friendly attributes of immersion, people power, and storytelling all in one. The ad features five professional-looking women of various ages and races, and beside each woman is a caption that states *her* power story, such as: "Gives her broker investment ideas," or "Is taking her company public," and "Earns more than her CEO husband." Now I want to get to know these women, find out more about them, and find out about the company that's helping them.

Integrate versus extricate: details as differentiators. She has a longer list, and the top benefits are a given: the price of entry. Make sure you dig out the differentiating factors and get them across. While ads for other cell phone companies were still duking it out with each other over who had the better technology and features, Nokia, taking its point-of-difference insight a step further, extended the line of colors for its faceplates and started running whimsical ads showing its phone as a fashion accessory. It worked!

Communication Keys

Personalize the communications. Use anecdotes and personal details to introduce a person or convey a situation or highlight a set of values your female audience can identify with. Use everyday language; stay away from corporate-speak and abstractions. Instead, use a lot of first-person and second-person language. One of my very favorite campaigns of recent years is for Citibank. Among its many wonderful print ads is one that shows a woman among a group of female friends (the girlfriend factor). The copy, laid out very much like a poem, says "Money can't love you back. Not to say you shouldn't make the most of it. You should. That's why we provide tools like online banking and free financial checkups. Just don't forget to amass a fortune—in friends. Save money. Hoard friends. Citibank—Live richly."

Focus on human benefits, not facts and features. Even the most high-tech, rational product translates into human situations with human benefits. Facts and features may be important to the final sale, but that won't be relevant to your brand unless you capture a woman's attention favorably first. Most consumer electronics ads concentrate exclusively on the "product as hero," with a close-up of the device and copy touting the highly technical features of it. However, a recent Best Buy ad is quite a departure from the norm—it features a close-up of a woman holding a digital camera. The copy reads "HEY, if I took pictures of the baby and e-mailed them to the in-laws, maybe they wouldn't visit as often. WAIT. What if that just made them want to visit more?"

Show some emotion. Showing that somebody cares one way or another is always going to be more powerful—and memorable—to women than a sterile, high-tech presentation. A Hertz flier I got recently in my Mileage Plus mailer had a wonderful, warm visual of a woman's delighted reaction to some news from her husband: "He just told her they're going to Paris. What will you do with your double miles?" Not a real breakthrough message—it's the visual that adds interest and excitement to the story.

One of my favorite "emotional" ads is from the South Carolina Tourism Board, and it features storytelling as well (see Figure 5.2). The visual is of a family playing golf on a lovely course, and the copy reads as follows: "This morning, my daughter made her first birdie. After her brothers were done carrying her around the green like some kind of princess, she came running over and gave me a big hug. And she said, 'Mom, I will never forget this day.'" I don't play golf, as it happens, so the visual alone would never have held my attention. But combined with the warmth of that little vignette—well, what mother wouldn't want a family vacation experience like that?

Web Site/Electronic Marketing

Web site and electronic marketing derive many of the same implications from gender culture as advertising—and then some. The medium warrants special consideration when marketing to women, because a number of its benefits are directly aligned with the tenets of female lifestyle and culture. In fact, the Internet is one of the key ways that increasing numbers of women are finding to connect with each other. Women say they value the Internet because it strengthens their bonds with others; 60 percent of women claim that the Internet has improved their connection to parents, siblings, and children.[1]

FIGURE 5.2 Show Some Emotion

The Bounce Agency

It's perhaps hard to remember that as recently as 1998, pundits were saying that the Internet was basically a man's medium; at the time, it was high tech and not particularly user friendly. True to form, women didn't jump in until the novelty had developed into something useful. Forrester and Jupitermedia seemed a little surprised when, by 2000, women constituted 51 percent of online users. Today, 52 percent of the online population is female—mirroring their percentage in the population at large. By 2008, though, there will be roughly 10 million more women online than men. And women's influence and power in online purchasing is growing as well. In fact, women are already in a position of buying dominance, as a 2003 Goldman Sachs/Harris Interactive/Nielsen/Net Ratings report showed they were responsible for 60 percent of total online spending.[2] Today 63 percent of women have access to the Internet, and almost every single one of them (62 percent) buy things online at least once a year.[3] I predict that women will evolve fairly rapidly into a 60 to 65 percent majority of online users, accounting for perhaps 70 to 75 percent of the online *spending*.

The "Five Cs" that make the Net a *woman's* medium are as follows:

The Five Cs Connecting Women and the Internet

1. **Communication**—E-mail makes it easier than letters or even the phone to keep those connections active.
2. **Content**—As voracious information seekers, women see the Net as a godsend. Count on them spending lots of time online researching questions on the myriad topics that matter to them—including seeking out product information.
3. **Commerce**—The most likely scenario is that women's share of online spending will rise fairly quickly to approximate their share of offline spending, currently 80 percent.
4. **Convenience**—Communication, content, and shopping are all available to her in her pajamas after the kids have gone to bed. What could be better?
5. **Community**—In some ways, chat groups are even better than an "old-fashioned" neighborhood: everyone in a chat room is fascinated with *exactly* the same thing you're passionate about. If you're into silk-screening gingko leaves on T-shirts, for example, you're not likely to find many fellow enthusiasts on your block, maybe not even in your state, but I bet they're out there in the e-world somewhere.

Women are crossing the threshold of cyberspace at a rapid pace, but, so far, once inside they're not wild about the décor. Many marketers do not yet realize this and are still leaving their Web design in the hands of young male programmers. These guys may eat megabytes and breathe gigahertz, but they're not well versed in how women shop the Net—which is the opposite of how they shop bricks and mortar, incidentally! If the online construction crews don't understand which site features women value and which ones just frustrate them, now would be a good time to get them up to speed on gender culture, because they are just about to experience a huge surge of increased female access and buying.

Life/Time Factors

Milestones. Sponsor the sites women go to for help at the time of a major milestone. Or get her permission to send her an e-mail. If you can relate your product to a solution she's looking for, she'll be happy to link directly to your site for more information.

Focus Strategies

Details, details. Women buy most of the stuff, and women notice details. Who could be better qualified to serve as your R&D advisory board? Deliver surveys on your site, on your partners' sites, or via e-mails asking women in your target audience for input on your product and/or service.

Context. For those who sell directly off the Net, leverage its interactive capabilities to suggest related products while she's shopping—cross-selling and up-selling via the "buy an outfit instead of an item" theory of shopping. Peapod, an online grocery delivery service, is a master at this: no sooner do you click on hot dogs than electronic coupons pop up suggesting buns, mustard, relish, and napkins.

The Perfect Answer. Another potential use of your Web site's interactive capabilities is to help shortcut her search for the Perfect Answer. By providing plenty of information and supporting it with links to third-party sources commenting favorably on your product (online magazine articles, etc.), you can help accelerate the due diligence phase and keep her within your brand's framework while she's doing it. (More on this in the next chapter.)

From the *advertising* and *Web site* examples above, it should start to become at least superficially evident how to use the model to tailor your plan for women. Since about half of the marketing elements are straight communications tools, many of the gender culture implications for one element will also have applications to the others. But *each* element, of course, also has its own unique characteristics, and many of these can be enhanced through gender-specific insights as well.

Communication Keys

Personalize the communications. How many Web sites have you gone to where there is just text all over the page, and you can't tell if it's a site for a bank or a retailer or a travel agent or just news? For women, the Internet is about connecting, and if there are no people on your Web site, then how are they going to connect to your brand? Show people on the home page (preferably women). Personalize your site with an "Ask the Expert" column using real people with real questions and answers. Shutterfly, an online digital photo source, does a great job of this with their "Ask Mike" column. Create peer reviews (Amazon has done so successfully) and feature customers' success stories about their brand experiences. (One of my favorite sites—be-jane.com—is doing this well.)

Product and Packaging

While "woman-specific" products are rarely necessary—and usually not even advisable—there are definite opportunities to enhance female-friendly features before your competition gets to them.

I chose product and packaging as my last "sample" category because, in addition to gender culture factors, there are a few other considerations you should look at that didn't make it onto the Star, because they affect only one or two of the marketing elements.

Social Values

People first. In this day and age, differentiating your product at the shelf is one of the most difficult tasks for any manufacturer. And at the shelf is where the vast majority of purchase decisions are made. One way to do this is by featuring people on the packaging, just as Kashi cereal has done so creatively. Both front and back panels feature close-ups on one, or sometimes two, friendly, "real" faces, and the package really stands out in the cluttered cereal aisle.

Displaying status. Status displays are not encouraged in female gender culture, where peer-to-peer linkings are preferred to pyramid rankings. So when you're tailoring your products for women—a cell phone, for example—think "tool," not "cool." Save money on the fancy features and put it into warranties, guarantees, and hotlines.

Corporate halo. Women are more likely than men to change brands based on environmental concerns. Make certain your product and your packaging are as environmentally friendly as you can make them—and be sure to communicate that on the package itself. One pet peeve I've heard several women talk about is software packaging. What you take home from the store is a glossy, heavy-duty cardboard box about 12 inches square and 2 inches deep. What you're left with when you retrieve the actual product is a slim CD-ROM—and about a pound of cardboard you have to cram into the recycling bin. As a marketer, I understand the manufacturer is going for shelf impact, but to women, it just seems wasteful. Music CDs don't need all that extra packaging, women say, so why does software?

One example of leveraging corporate halo on the package is Paul Newman's "Newman's Own" brand, which was founded as a vehicle for him to donate to worthy causes. Over $150 million has been given to thousands of charities since 1982, and each and every ad and package states just that.

Another example of corporate halo messaging on packaging is from Marshall Field's. It used the side panels of its famous green shopping bags to communicate support of Project Imagine, a community-based arts program. And M&Ms recently had a special breast cancer product and package, which featured pink and white candy, a pink ribbon, and a donation for each package sold to help fight breast cancer.

Life/Time Factors

A question for all busy women reading this: How many times have you gone through the day and just forgotten to have lunch? "Lunch? Who has time for lunch?" you say. Well, Campbell's developed a clever product and advertising campaign to solve this midday problem: Soup at Hand. Made in four yummy flavors in an insulated cup contoured to fit your hand and with a convenient "sippable" lid, Soup at Hand has been one of the Campbell Soup Company's most successful new product introductions ever.

Another savvy marketer has created a product that helps women multitask. It's the "Trim Trolley" (for Tesco supermarkets in the United Kingdom), which has attachments that would normally be found on a machine in the gym (Figure 5.3). It shows a shopper's heart rate through sensors on the bar used for pushing the trolley and how many calories are being burned while they shop. The trolley, designed by German company Wanzl, even allows shoppers to make their shopping workout harder by increasing the resistance on a large wheel between the two rear wheels on the trolley. Shoppers are thought to burn around 160 calories during a typical 40-minute visit to the supermarket pushing a standard trolley. But pushing the Trim Trolley for the same time, with the resistance level set at 7 out of a possible 10, the average person would burn around 280 calories, the equivalent of a 20-minute leisurely swim.

Milestones. These life event transitions are often momentous enough that consumers want to commemorate them in the products they choose. What about a financial services "wedding package" that includes joint checking and savings accounts and a CD that sets aside all the cash gifts from the happy day to grow in value and mature on the couple's 20th anniversary? Or perhaps a "celebrating our retirement" SUV outfitted for a combination of comfort (leather seats), exploration (global positioning maps), and reliability (run-flat tires) might catch a woman's eye while she's doing research on where she wants to retire?

FIGURE 5.3 Tesco's Trim Trolley

Focus Strategies

Integration. Seek opportunities to create "suites" or "collections" of related products that can be sold together: a collection of family room consumer electronics components designed by Michael Graves, for example; or a home office desk set of coordinated computer, peripherals, phone, and recharger stands for a PDA and cell phone.

The Perfect Answer. Whenever practical, present the answers to as many of the consumer's due diligence concerns as possible on the package: perhaps a comparison of your product and the category's two leading competitors—highlighting your product's advantages, of course.

Other Factors

In addition to the gender culture factors that make up the Star, the product and packaging element should take a number of additional points into consideration.

Physical size and strength. A woman may choose a Jeep Cherokee over the competitive brands because it was the only one whose hatch she can easily flip open. Here are some examples of companies who have designed their products with women's physical differences in mind.

- Finally acknowledging the weaknesses in paint can design, Dutch Boy introduced new packaging, the Twist and Pour paint containers. They work much like a liquid laundry detergent container and are easy to carry, the pour spout reduces the dripping and spillage, and it doesn't dent or rust.
- Barbara Kavovit, a single mother and former Wall Street trader, was fed up with tools that were too big and cumbersome for her size and frame, so she created Barbara K Tools, a compact box packed with lightweight tools with nonslip grips.

Sensory sensitivities. Women are going to be more put off than men by anything overly rough, sharp, smelly, or loud. They'll be more attracted, meanwhile, to pleasing styling, textures, sounds, smells, and so on. Seek opportunities for sensory enhancement of your product, even if it's only secondary to the product's prime function. Computer accessory manufacturers are making good use of this when they design packaging for their mouse pads and fabric-wrapped gel wrist rests. Have you noticed how more of them are starting to build "touch here" openings into their cardboard and plastic outer packaging? Retailers also put this principle to good use: Did you know that some cookie shops vent their ovens toward the front of the shop rather than the back (where most kitchen odors go), because they're counting on the aromas wafting out to bring passersby in?

Storage. As manager of the household, decisions and responsibility for product storage usually fall on the woman. Make sure you check your package dimensions and bulk for easy lifting and "fit." And another thing: Have home appliance manufacturers visited any homes with children lately? Do any of these engineers or executives have *teenagers* in the house? If these engineers and executives were the ones who did the grocery shopping, cooking, and dishes for the home crew, day in and day out, they would understand that larger appliance options—more refrigerator space, more freezer space, more room in the dishwasher—could reduce the number of shopping trips and load/unload cycles someone, usually Mom, has to do every day. Home building is a sophisticated industry these days. There's got to be a way manufacturers and contractors can figure out how to incorporate the woman's lifestyle and preference into their designs and plans.

Instruction sheets and manuals. As we saw in Chapter 2, women find the inner workings of various technical/mechanical products neither fascinating nor particularly understandable. As far as most women can tell, there's hardly a manufacturer on the planet who has put one moment's thought into reducing women's frustrations in this area, except maybe Xerox and one or two of the other office copier makers. Many of these now come with interactive control panels that walk you through the settings and steps you need to operate some of the machine's more advanced features. Lower-tech versions have pull-up, laminated troubleshooting booklets secured into a pocket on the front panel, so they won't go "walking off" under someone's stack of papers. Why couldn't VCR manufacturers apply a couple of ideas like that? Would women be willing to pay a little more? You bet they would. It sure beats not being able to operate the machine at all and having to beg your seven-year-old son for help!

Best Buy (Figure 5.4) is a best practices paradigm of how to apply GenderTrends principles to improve a retailer's product/service offerings.

Best Buy

Opportunity:

According to a 2004 study released by the Consumer Electronics Association, women buy 57 percent of consumer electronics. They represent over $55 billion worth of sales to the industry and influence as much as 90 percent of purchases in the category.[4] Best Buy took notice, especially when it realized that only 40 percent of its revenue came from female customers.[5]

Strategies:

In 2003, Best Buy realized it needed to become more customer focused in order to gain sales against new competitors in the category (e.g., Target, Wal-Mart). As part of its "customer centricity" growth strategy, Best Buy identified five customer segments with the most potential for profitability and growth, and one key segment is "Jill," the busy suburban mom who wants to enrich her family's life with technology and entertainment. In a select and growing set of stores, Best Buy has customized store designs, customer service, marketing, and product mix just for "Jill." Just step inside and see for yourself.

Insights that Best Buy tapped into:

- **Customer services**

  There is no such thing as customer service in the consumer electronics industry, at least according to women shoppers. Women report that they often feel invisible, ignored by sales associates who chase after the "real" purchasers of technology gadgets, men! Best Buy is addressing this poor service expectation head-on by making "Jill" a priority. The customer service centerpiece and key driver of success in "Jill" stores is the new "Personal Shopping Assistant" service.

"Jill" can make an appointment, either in advance or when she gets to the store, and the "PSA" will help "Jill" from the beginning to the very end of her shopping experience at Best Buy—every transaction and need handled by one reliable person! That's because Best Buy has trained its PSAs to not only have storewide product knowledge but also build relationships with their customers in order to find out what they really want/need.

At checkout time, "Jill" doesn't even have to wait in line at the register but goes to the Personal Shopping Assistant center to pay for her merchandise (which is actually a very nice place to hang out, with comfy chairs, plenty of countertop space, women's magazines, flowers in vases, and even beverages).

And there is Geek Squad service—I love these guys! They are Best Buy's 24-Hour Computer Support Task Force, offering carry-in, on-site, or at-home emergency service for everything from setups and installs to upgrades, 24 hours a day, seven days a week. Geek Squad has even added at-home training services to help customers learn how to use their digital cameras and camcorders. Sign me up!

- **People powered**
  To women, people are the most important, interesting element in any situation. The key to Best Buy's customer centricity success is its focus on the "software" (or *people*) who make the women's shopping experience so much better, not the hardware (or high-tech gadgets) they are selling. Employees don't ramble on about how many pixels or gigabytes there are, but instead are trained to ask lifestyle questions. For a digital camera purchaser, such questions might be:

  - What do you like to take pictures of?
  - When do you take the most pictures?
  - Do you use the zoom for sports?
  - How do you like to share your photos with friends and family?
  - How do you preserve your photos?

A recent insert in the Sunday paper (Figure 5.4, bottom) shows how Best Buy has tuned in to people power (and milestone marketing as well). Instead of focusing on the product, it focuses on the user and features a close-up of a woman holding her baby as she takes her first steps, with Dad using the camcorder to capture the moment. The headline reads "Sharing the magic of every first IS POSSIBLE." Below this big beautiful family photo is a subheadline that reads "Capture once in a lifetime moments. Edit them into a highlight reel. Send them on DVD to family and friends. Let us show you how." Underneath that are small images of the consumer electronics products to use to create this magic. This ad taps into women's focus on the most important people in their life, family, and shows how Best Buy can help them build family connections and preserve family memories. Very insightful!

- **Details matter**
Women are more detail oriented—they notice more, care more, express more. When it comes to "Jill's" shopping experience, she wants things like clean bathrooms, good directional signage, wider aisles, and a kid-friendly atmosphere. Best Buy took notice of the details and customized its retail environments to meet the "picky" needs of Jill. It's the little things that make a difference, and Best Buy made sure that a little thing like a larger sign to show where the bathrooms are located was a top priority. When a three-year-old being potty trained really has to go, "Jill" really has to be able to find the bathroom FAST!

Results:

Customer centricity is paying off for Best Buy, as its customercentric stores significantly outperformed regular Best Buy stores during the most recent fiscal year. According to 2005 results, the 67 stores converted to the new model generated comp store sales gains of 8.4 percent for the fourth quarter (ended February 26, 2005), compared to the 2.3 percent comp store sales increase averaged at the chain's other U.S. stores. Currently, 85 U.S. stores have been converted to the new model.

While Best Buy does not share results of its customer centricity initiative by market segment, Nancy Brooks, vice president, Customer Centricity, will say that "Jill" stores have been very well received. "What we've learned from our initial focus on the 'Jill' target excites us about the opportunity of targeting the women's market. Fundamentally what 'Jill' wants is better service and better attention. When we meet 'Jill's' expectations, everyone in the store wins," concludes Brooks. I couldn't agree more!

FIGURE 5.4 Customer Services and People Power

Best Buy Co., Inc.

Guarantees, warranties, and support hot lines. Studies from several different industries, including cars and computers, have revealed a pattern of women's greater concern with "back-end" product elements that will ensure satisfactory resolution if the product gives women any problems. In fact, a recent Condé Nast/Intelliquest study of computer purchasing criteria found that the two *most* important qualities in women's purchase decisions were warranties and the manufacturer's support and service reputation.[6] By overcoming most women's risk reluctance, offering 100 percent guarantees is likely to win you much more in sales than it will ever cost you in redemptions.

The "samples" above illustrate how to apply the gender insights of the Star to the marketing elements of the Circle, with the ultimate goal of affecting the woman consumer's purchase decision. Let's combine these two concepts into the GenderTrends Compass and take it through the stages of the Spiral Path, which represents women's decision-making process. On this path, you'll see that men and women continue to diverge, which generates some additional implications for how you market to them. Then, having completed the third component of the GenderTrends™ Marketing Model, you'll be ready to start applying it to enhance every aspect of your marketing plan.

CHAPTER 6

The Spiral Path

How Women Make
Purchase Decisions

Gender culture affects a woman during every moment of her life. What *you* care about, though, are the moments when she is thinking about *your* product—or your competitor's product, heaven forbid—because those are the moments you're trying to influence. The final component of the GenderTrends™ Marketing Model, the Spiral Path, captures the way in which her purchase decision process differs from that of the boy next door.

To start with, let's simplify the consumer's purchase path by illustrating it in five stages:

1. *Activation.* The consumer enters the market for the kind of product or service you sell.
2. *Nomination.* She forms an idea of the brands she plans to check out during her search.
3. *Investigation and Decision.* She checks out the brands by scanning ads, reading articles, visiting Web sites, going to the store or showroom, handling the merchandise, kicking the tires, talking to the salespeople, and more.
4. *Retention.* Now a happy customer, she returns to your brand for subsequent purchases.

5. *Recommendation.* In the meantime, she recommends your product or service to everyone she knows.

In Chapter 8, I'll go through this five-stage decision process step-by-step and present the most actionable strategic and tactical approaches for each stage. For now, though, I'm just going to focus on what makes women's decision process substantially different from men's.

From start to finish, women and men seek, search, and research differently. In GenderTrends terms, not only is the Compass different (i.e., gender culture and reactions to marketing elements), but the path the Compass travels, the decision purchase process, is different as well. There are four key disparities in how women and men advance through their purchase path:

1. Women start the process differently—asking around.
2. Women pursue a different outcome—the Perfect Answer.
3. Women seek more information and investigate more options—the Spiral Path.
4. Women's influence on your sales success doesn't end with their purchase—the Retention and Recommendation stages.

Figure 6.1 represents the Spiral Path, the more complex and detailed decision-making process women go through before making a purchase. With just a glance at the graphic, you can see that men's decision-making process is linear: men tend to move straight through the stages involved in decision making without detours or tangential moves, seeking a good solution as their end goal. Women, on the other hand, tend to advance toward a decision in a series of cycles, often looping back to an earlier stage of the process as they reconsider previous decision factors and integrate new information, seeking the Perfect Answer.

Asking Around: Women Start the Purchase Decision Process Differently

We saw in Chapter 4 that one key gender difference is the way that men and women feel about asking for help. Women are fine with not

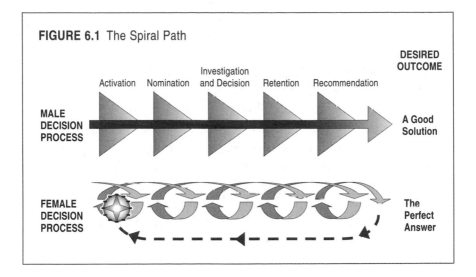

FIGURE 6.1 The Spiral Path

knowing everything, whereas men feel that puts them at an uncomfortable disadvantage and jeopardizes their place in the "rankings." Consequently, when women start up a search for a big-ticket product or service, instead of arming themselves as men do with plenty of knowledge (ads, ratings, Web site reading, etc.) before talking to anyone else about the issue, they ask a lot of *people* for input instead. Not only do they get the benefit of others' experience and opinions by doing so, but they also see the inquiry as a relationship-building gesture. What says "you matter to me" better than asking someone for his or her wisdom and insight?

Women look for opinions and insights from sales staff as well as from people they know. In line with their greater orientation toward people, women are often more interested in getting their information from *people*, whereas men prefer to get it *from impersonal sources* such as written material, instructional videos, computer screens, and the like.

In a case study reported by Paco Underhill in his book *Why We Buy*, male customers were observed coming into Sprint Cellular's retail stores, perusing the phone models and brochures, and leaving the store without speaking to anyone. When men came back, they were ready to sign up for service. Women customers, however, walked right past the wall of phones and brochures to the sales desk in the back of the store and wanted detailed interaction with the staffers to answer their questions.[1]

The male search tends to emphasize the *facts and features* of the product or service under consideration. Men are more interested in the *things and theorems* of a purchase to begin with, and facts and features are exactly the type of social currency men like to exchange with each other. Conversely, the input sought by women includes a more contextual and impressionistic gestalt of other elements as well, such as their friends' and advisors' opinions as to whether a featured detail matters or not, a reaction to a selling environment or salesperson, or a general observation about company reputation.

The Perfect Answer: Women Pursue a Different Outcome

When embarking on a new purchase, men go looking for a good solution, whereas women set out to find the Perfect Answer.

We started this discussion in Chapter 4, but there are a couple of additional points to add in the context of the shopping process: how she thinks about what she's looking for and the "due diligence" process it takes to decide when she's found it.

As you may recall, the gender principle at work here is one of the Focus Strategies: single-minded focus versus multiminded integration. Men define the product or service they want in terms of the features that are most important to them, formulating a short, focused list of key decision criteria and then finding a solution that meets those criteria. When they find the solution, they buy—they're *done*. Women, on the other hand, start with a more generalized sense of the situation they want to address, factor in additional considerations as they move through the decision process, and keep exploring options until they are satisfied that they have found not just a workable solution but the best possible answer. In shorthand: men are buyers, whereas women are shoppers.

Let's say a man needs a pair of black slacks. He'll define his goal up front in terms of a short list of concrete key criteria: pleated, cuffed, costs less than $100. Off he goes to wherever he usually buys his clothes, and he makes a beeline for the slacks section. The first pair of black slacks he finds that meet his criteria and fit well—sold! Problem solved, mission accomplished, go home and watch the game, right?

With a woman, it's a different story. When she wants a pair of black slacks, she thinks context: *I want black slacks to wear to the office party Friday afternoon.* In other words, she doesn't define her goal by *product features* but by *end use.* When she gets to the store, she looks at the black slacks and gauges how they measure up to that use. She may even try on a couple of pairs that would be just fine for Friday. As she's considering which pair to buy, other considerations start to creep in. Are they dressy enough to wear on more formal occasions? How likely are they to wrinkle when she travels? Do they need to be dry cleaned, or can she wash and iron them at home? In other words, instead of discarding criteria, she is more likely to be adding them.

Now she's got a problem: if the slacks don't meet *all* the criteria she's raised, they're obviously not the Perfect Answer. And why should she settle for a partial solution when the perfect slacks might be just a few stores away in the mall? Better to take a look, because "ya never know." Well, it's true! Maybe they have the slacks that go with the black jacket she bought last month, or maybe there's a great sale at the other store. How will she know unless she looks?

In every presentation I give about the path women take to reach a decision, by this point most of the women are nodding their heads and smiling wryly in recognition, while most of the men are shaking their heads in disbelief. The numbers support what I'm telling you, too: 61 percent of women say that when making a clothing purchase, they visit *several* different stores before deciding what to buy.[2]

There's a funny diagram (Figure 6.2) that was circulating around the Internet for a while. It never fails to draw hoots of recognition from both the men and women in my audiences. I like to include it in my programs because it illustrates not one, but three, of the GenderTrends principles I've been laying out:

1. Women will determinedly go the extra mile to find the *Perfect Answer.*
2. *On the way* they will take advantage of opportunities to get a few additional purchases and errands taken care of (a new lamp for the guest room, socks for her husband, a new winter coat for next fall that's 40 percent less expensive if bought on sale today).

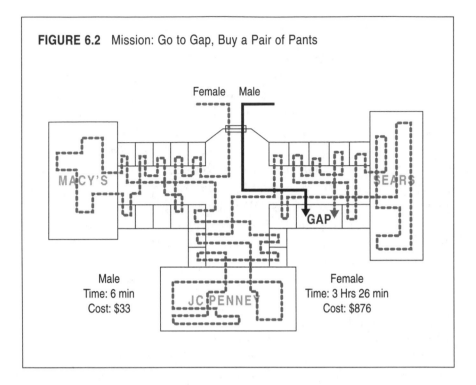

FIGURE 6.2   Mission: Go to Gap, Buy a Pair of Pants

Female   Male

MACY'S

SEARS

GAP

Male
Time: 6 min
Cost: $33

JC PENNEY

Female
Time: 3 Hrs 26 min
Cost: $876

3. On occasion, they buy for their "*tribe*" as well as themselves. ("My sister's been looking for a pair of cobalt blue boots for years!")

Let me ask you: $876 or $33—Who would you rather have as your customer?

One thing to keep in mind, fellow marketers, is that women are very rarely going to buy early in the decision process. In the Sprint Cellular case cited earlier, while men were ready to buy in two visits to the store, with women it averaged three. Women's search for perfection renders them reluctant to buy until all possible options have been explored. The marketer's challenge is to overcome this decision reluctance by assuring them that they have indeed found the Perfect Answer.

Oddly enough, it appears as though men's and women's clicks-and-portals shopping patterns are the inverse of their bricks-and-mortar habits. In the online environment, it's women who stick to the list, go for the goal, and get out, while men tend to take a little more time to browse around. Maybe it's because there aren't any interfering sales-people asking, "Can I help you?" (As if a real man needs or wants any help!)

The Spiral Path: Women Seek More Information and Investigate More Options

The search for the Perfect Answer is the main reason the woman's purchase path is shown as a spiral instead of a linear progression like a man's. As she continues to get more information from her research, and to welcome additional input from others throughout the decision process, she often loops back to previous stages in the purchase path. Maybe she thought she wanted to buy a car, but now she realizes a min-ivan would better suit her needs—back to Stage I, Activation. Perhaps she picked two brands of phone service she was interested in learning more about; then a neighbor raves about her new service and she de-cides to add or substitute that brand—back to Stage II, Nomination. Or she might make it all the way to Stage III, Investigation and Decision, and walk into a computer store with three specific laptop models in mind—and see a brand she's never heard of before. No problem—let's add it into the mix as long as we're here.

Men, meanwhile, are looking to *eliminate* options, not add them. Go-ing back and reconsidering decisions that have already been made is off-strategy. Worse, it's moving *backward,* not forward toward the goal.

Women figure they're bound to learn stuff along the way in any pro-cess; just because *they didn't know everything* when they started shouldn't keep them from being open to better options as they find them.

Each gender is baffled by the other's behavior: To women, men may look mule-headed as they stick tenaciously to their original path even after an obviously better alternative appears. To men, women are indecisive or "fickle," as they say—because they seem to change their definition of what they want and seem unwilling to make up their mind and close the discussion.

When you consider the fact that she's got a longer list of criteria in the first place and add in all this rethinking and looping back, it's not surprising that a woman's decision process takes considerably longer than a man's. Case in point: One study found that women spend *40 percent more time researching* a mutual fund before they invest.[3] While men see this depth of research as unnecessary overkill, women view it as due diligence, what any responsible person should do. To arrive at a decision, women have to be sure they have gathered enough information to know everything that's out there.

Retention and Recommendation: Women's Influence on Your Sales Success Doesn't End with Their Purchases

Marketers' consideration of a woman's purchase path should not stop at the purchase. Because women do so much more due diligence up front, several "side effects" occur as a result. Two postpurchase considerations—loyalty over the long haul and sharing the wealth—have a tremendous impact on a woman's customer value to the marketer.

Loyalty over the Long Haul: Trust Is a Many-Splendored Thing

A woman has a more *personal loyalty* once she has established rapport with a salesperson. Part of what weighs into her decision is a guilty, wincing feeling if she awards her business to someone else after establishing an initial connection with a salesperson who has served her well. So even if a competitor has a slightly better product or service, this connection will prevent her from defecting until, and unless, the competitor's advantages are really overwhelming. Compared to men, who tend to weight the product a little higher and the personal connection a little lower, women are more loyal and less likely to defect.

Streamlining Subsequent Interactions

If it's the kind of relationship that involves regular contact (e.g., a financial advisor), assuming all goes the way it should, women will become increasingly comfortable relying on the advisor's recommendations without nearly as much due diligence involved in each transaction. Once she gets experience with the salesperson's competency and develops confidence that he or she is truly acting in her best interests and not just trying to sell more product, she becomes more open than a male customer to the consultant's advice and recommendations.

As we saw in Chapter 4, whereas men resist being influenced by others, seeing it as compromising their autonomy and framing them as One-down, women actually seek out advice and welcome the opportunity to learn from someone with greater expertise. This streamlines the decision process for subsequent purchases; she trusts the person she has selected as advisor and realizes that the advisor knows more than she does. This relieves her of the need to do all the research herself. She can shift the duty of due diligence onto the advisor—who then brings her the Perfect Answer instead of requiring her to find it for herself. This means fewer hoops to jump through and fewer loops to recycle.

The same holds true for trusted brands. Even if the relationship is not with another person but with a brand, women will continue to use that brand if they've had a satisfactory first experience because they have already done the due diligence to get to the Perfect Answer. Finding the right brand to meet her needs means she won't have to search again, and this is a key part of the Retention stage.

In short, for the initial decision, women will often invest more time and undertake a more comprehensive process than men as they seek to qualify both the product or service and the seller. For subsequent decisions, the emphasis is often reversed, with women relying more on personal trust, whereas men continue to do more of the product/service assessment on a case-by-case basis.

> To American Airlines, women are not just the *only* growing segment of business travelers and the fastest growing segment of American's top tier flyers—women represent their most loyal customers as well.
>
> The percentage of women saying that American's overall service was "excellent" is much higher than that of their male counterparts.
>
> - American's women customers rate its "Value for Money" much higher than men do.
> - The percentage of women who say they would "definitely recommend" American to others is higher.
> - The percentage of women who state that American is their preferred airline is higher.
> - And among AAdvantage® members, women said they spent a higher proportion of their airline travel dollars on American than did men.
>
> As American Airlines has seen, it pays to develop women's business and therefore secure their loyalty.

Referrals: Sharing the Wealth

Roper ASW has been tracking U.S. consumers' reliance on word of mouth in decision making for the past 25 years, and in that time, it has become an increasingly important factor. In 1977, 67 percent of Americans agreed that word of mouth was an important source of information and ideas for them. By 2003, a staggering 92 percent had come to feel this way. And according to Frederick F. Reichheld in the December 2003 *Harvard Business Review,* in most instances there is a strong correlation between a company's growth rate and the percentage of its customers who are promoters.[4]

Not only are women more likely than men to *ask* for opinions from friends, family, coworkers, and others, but they are also more likely to *volunteer* both good and bad purchase experiences with this same circle of people. Women are a medium unto themselves—I like to call it the word-of-mouth media multiplier. According to *People* magazine's research, 79 percent of women have recommended three or more products in the past 12 months; 57 percent have recommended five or more products.

People magazine reported the following products were most recommended by women (and therefore can benefit the most from serious word of mouth marketing!):

Restaurants	66%
Movies	61%
Retail stores	49%
New food items	44%
Cosmetics or hair care products	43%
Cleaning products	41%
Hotels or vacations destinations	38%
Over-the-counter medications	37%
Cell phones or providers	26%
Cars	24%

And the word-of-mouth conversion to sales is remarkable. See Figure 6.3.

Because they've done more homework up front, they feel more confident recommending their choices to friends and others. Conse-

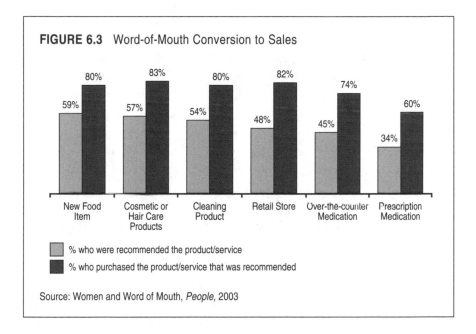

FIGURE 6.3 Word-of-Mouth Conversion to Sales

Categories: New Food Item; Cosmetic or Hair Care Products; Cleaning Product; Retail Store; Over-the-counter Medication; Prescription Medication

- 80%, 83%, 80%, 82%, 74%, 60% — % who purchased the product/service that was recommended
- 59%, 57%, 54%, 48%, 45%, 34% — % who were recommended the product/service

☐ % who were recommended the product/service
■ % who purchased the product/service that was recommended

Source: Women and Word of Mouth, *People,* 2003

quently, what a woman does in the Recommendation stage of the purchase path can have a tremendous impact on a huge number of people. When you convert a male prospect into a male customer, you get a new male customer. When you convert a female prospect, you get more: not only her own greater purchasing role but also a lifelong string of referrals.

Marketing/Sales Implications of Women's Different Decision Process

We've discussed a number of the sales and marketing implications of gender differences in male and female decision-making paths. Let's close the chapter with a summary of what marketers need to do in order to gain the fullest advantage from these differences.

First, one of the biggest misunderstandings about women's "influence" in the purchase process comes from the fact that they are only visible in Stage III, the Investigation and Decision stage, or the face-to-face sales stage. Female heads of households in fact lead *four* out of the *five* stages of the big-ticket purchase process. Women drive Stage I, the

Activation stage, and make the initial decision to buy. Women lead Stage II, the Nomination stage, and determine which brands to consider. Men actually do the driving in Stage III, the one stage that the salesperson sees. And women get back in the driver's seat in Stages IV and V, the Retention, or relationship maintenance, stage and then Recommendation, or referral, stage. Don't overlook her input in *all* stages of the buying process.

Second, it's essential to *leverage word-of-mouth tactics.* Word of mouth is frequently how women begin their purchasing process (in the Nomination stage), and it's also how they pass along their findings to others (in the Recommendation stage).

Third, *provide plenty of information.* The more information you make accessible to her, the more you prime her with what she needs to make a decision. Through communications materials, such as printed information, Web sites, collateral media, and retail merchandising, you can appeal in multiple dimensions—a strategy to which women respond well. You can also provide a great deal of information through a well-trained sales force that understands and respects how much information women frequently already have when they reach the sales floor because of advance data gathering.

Fourth, *use tactics that overcome decision reluctance as a woman tries for the Perfect Answer.* Do the comparison shopping for her by finding out what her needs are and by presenting three options with pros and cons of each. Emphasize the benefits of making a decision *now,* one that can be fine-tuned later by adding a warranty, as an example, or options that can be purchased separately.

Finally, *prepare salespeople for the reality that the initial selling process will take longer* with women customers—and that it's well worth it to hang in there because of the greater payoff in repeat business and referrals.

The Ultimate Outcome: Spiraling to Success

The GenderTrends™Marketing Model shows a woman's purchase decision process as a spiral for a specific reason. A man will proceed fairly linearly from one stage of the decision process to the next. A woman, however, is open to more information and input at every stage of decision making and purchasing, often circling back to previous stages in the process. This is all about women's search for the Perfect Answer—good enough and even "just right" *aren't* perfect. *Perfect* is the goal when women are holding the purse strings and calling the shots. Remembering this will take you a long way toward assessing your market accurately and strategizing the best ways to get to that market, which is where we're headed now.

In the competitive race to marketing success, the choices you make are all about winning, keeping, and increasing your market share, so lace up your running shoes, get out on the track, and be on your mark.

Practical Applications

Strategies and Tactics

On Your Mark

Market Assessment

A View of What's Ahead

Now that we have examined the strength and scope of the women's market and the differences between men and women, as well as the implications of those differences as illustrated by the GenderTrends™ Marketing Model, the material will come together in a new and powerful way. In Part III, the value of the model we've just examined will become apparent, illuminating the entire process of marketing to women as we *apply the model* to actual examples from marketing. With a clear sense of the high impact and untapped potential of the women's market and a detailed understanding of the woman consumer, Part III will explore how to translate these insights into intelligent action and impressive results.

Chapter 7, on market assessment, leads you through the disciplines of market analysis, consumer research, and measurement requirements, with an eye on what needs to change when you're talking about the women's market.

Chapter 8, on tactical planning, shows you how to put together your marketing plan and tailor it to your objectives, depending on which stage of the consumer's decision process you have chosen as your focal point.

Chapter 9, on communications that connect, gives you key considerations to review as you are signing off on recommendations for media buys or communications materials, including packaging, broadcast or print advertising, brochures, merchandising materials, on-site event signage, and Web sites.

Chapter 10, on face-to-face sales and service, lays out essential elements of the interpersonal parts of the process, with special emphasis on providing your sales force with the insights and ideas they need to build their business with this lucrative market.

By the time you finish reading Part III, which begins here with Chapter 7, you'll not only have the full complement of information you need to embark on an effective program of marketing to women, you'll also have seen it in action. Let's get to the action, then, by applying the model step-by-step to existing opportunities and real-life examples.

In order to assess your market and strategize about how best to reach that market, there are three primary areas you need to consider:

- *Find your market.* Define the business case and locate the holes in the competition.
- *Understand your consumer.* Conduct the research that will give you the insights you need to create and articulate your brand's most powerful positioning.
- *Measure your impact.* Find out for a fact what's working and what isn't.

Finding Your Market

Defining the Business Case: *Cherchez la Femme!*

Cherchez la femme means "seek out the woman." It's pretty easy to find women. They're all over the place. In fact, there are too many of them—from a marketer's point of view, I mean. But as I pointed out in the introduction, it is remarkable how many marketers manage to overlook this huge population as they're casting about for new opportunities.

You haven't—that's why you're reading this book. So, let's talk about what you need to do to bring the rest of the organization onboard.

The two fundamental questions you'll need to address in preparing your business case for marketing to women are: "Why women?" and "Which women?" Your mission (and your challenge) is to marshal the troops and prod them out of their comfort zone. It may not be easy, but it will definitely be worth it.

Why Women?

Find out the facts. As I've noted earlier, historically it has been men who bought the big-ticket items. Cars, computers, and hi-fi components have always seemed to hold more fascination for men than women—"It's a guy thing." Women don't talk about these categories much, because they don't *care* about them the same way men do. You don't find *Cosmo* and *Redbook* full of articles on these topics; and I'll bet that women are a pretty low percentage of the subscriber bases of *Road & Track* and *Wired*. My guess is that, like most marketers, many big-ticket marketing managers base their assessment of "best prospects" on a certain amount of gut feeling: It's obvious who the real enthusiasts are (granted), so it's "obvious" who should be the target audience for the company's marketing efforts (Whoa! Not so!).

Just because women don't make a hobby of these products doesn't mean they don't buy them. As we saw in Chapter 1, *women are the majority buyers* in many unexpected areas, including, I might note, new cars and computers—two of men's biggest enthusiasms! Once you've done the analysis, the only thing that's "obvious" is that you need to change your marketing approach for a large segment of your buyer base. For men, a purchase in one of these categories is *fun;* for women, it's *functional.* Two completely different mindsets—two completely different marketing appeals.

This next case study is a great example of "finding out the facts." You'll be surprised to find out in which category "the facts" have led to some pretty radical changes.

Home Improvement

Opportunity:

The home improvement industry has taken notice that Bob Vila has given way to Martha Stewart and adapted its marketing accordingly. Yes, the building business with its macho beginnings has shown some real leadership in recognizing who wields the wallet and some real savvy in reconfiguring their product and marketing mixes to suit. Both Lowe's and Home Depot report *half* of their customers are women.[1] Women initiate 80 percent of all home improvement decisions, especially big-ticket orders like kitchens, flooring, and bathrooms.[2] According to a study conducted by Ace Hardware, they spend 50 percent more per average purchase than male customers.[3] Amazon.com reports that sales of power tools on Mother's Day are roughly *equal* to Father's Day[4]; in fact, more cordless drills are sold for Mother's Day than Father's Day.[5] Single women own almost twice as many homes as single men (22 percent vs. 12 percent).[6] A Sears survey revealed that if given the choice of an hour of free advice from home-repair pro Bob Vila or popular psychologist Dr. Phil, 63 percent of women would chose Vila.[7] As my friend Tom Peters would say, "Do the Math!"

Strategies:

This is one of my favorite industry success stories, and Lowe's is one of my favorite marketers. Home improvement is a macho muddy boots and hard hats category—yet Lowe's recognized the power of its female customers way back in the '80s, long before anyone else caught on. Lowe's has been at the forefront of marketing to women: from store design to advertising, from friendly sales staff to community outreach programs (the Lowe's Heroes), from innovation to inspiration, we applaud them. Lowe's has not rested on its laurels but continues to improve with women in mind—check out the new line of kitchen and bathroom faucets styled by Michael Graves. And the Lowe's Web site is chock-full of home improvement ideas and interactive tools to get them accomplished.

Insights that the home improvement retailers tapped into:

- **Details matter**

  Lowe's revolutionized the home improvement industry by reconfiguring its store design with women in mind. Stores are neat and clean, lights are brighter, aisles less cluttered, fewer boxes are stacked to the ceiling, plumbing fixtures are more stylish, and paint and home-decorating departments are larger. It even widened its aisles to help eliminate "butt brush," as Paco Underhill calls the uncomfortable contact that can occur as consumers navigate the aisles and something that women particularly disliked. It was a pioneer when it added a home decor department, which became *the* destination for women. Details inspire women, and Lowe's gets that. Just walk into a Lowe's sometime—you will feel the difference immediately.

- **People powered**

  Advertising for Lowe's, The Home Depot, and Ace has made a dramatic shift away from cataloging products and prices and now builds its messages around people. Settings and scripts show lots of people—employees and customers—and I'd venture to say the majority are women. Moreover, the primary message has moved from "house" to "home," and from construction to creativity.

- **Lifelong learning**

  Women seek advice both for its immediate content and for the learning it provides for future reference. They also like learning in a group setting, being around others, and get satisfaction from collaborating on common goals. "Women are information gatherers—they want the stores to be inspirational," says Lowe's spokeswoman Julie Valeant-Yenichek. In the fall of 2004, Lowe's introduced "recipe cards" that explain various projects that can be accomplished in a single weekend. And The Home Depot's Do-It-Herself Workshops have been a resounding success, attracting 40,000 women in the first six months alone.[8]

Results:

In a 2004 newspaper article, top executives from both Lowe's and The Home Depot acknowledged stronger than projected results, which they attributed, at least partially, to their ongoing efforts to market to women.[9] We applaud these pioneers in marketing to women and look to this category as a great example for other "manly" industries.

Figure out your share among women. Compare it to your share among men. If your brand has the same share among women as it does among men, that just means no one else in the category is doing anything either. (Otherwise, *they'd* have a higher share among women than among men, and because they'd be taking it from you, you'd be scrambling to catch up.)

With so few companies doing serious marketing to women, any company that exerts itself enough to make a determined effort can expect to capture a disproportionate share of the women's market. Goal: higher share among majority of buyers. It's hardly news to you that, these days, most categories are fiercely competitive: two or three companies dominate the category, and attracting an incremental share point or two is a major marketing triumph. It's much easier to attract incremental share among women simply because nobody else is trying to! So the end result is a higher share among the people who buy most of the product—accomplished at a lower cost because of less competitive clutter and a higher marginal rate of return!

Think about it: Suppose you are a French manufacturer with a French brand of widgets (except they're pronounced "we-ZHAY"), and your market research revealed, much to your surprise, that 60 percent of all widgets sold in France were being bought by people who primarily spoke Korean. Up to that point, all the marketing communications in the category—from you and your competitors—had been delivered solely in French. What do you think would happen if the smartest competitor in the category suddenly converted most of its marketing effort into Korean? (Remember, this is the language spoken by the *majority* of the buyer base.) That brand would gain a sudden and significant share advantage, don't you think? Because *for the first time* somebody is talking to them in their language. They *understand* what you're saying, they respond to your message instead of picking among some equally featured products that they don't have any particular preference for one way or the other.

That's a mighty close analogy to the current situation with the women's market: You'd be surprised how much of your sales are to women customers; and neither you nor your competitors have been speaking to them in their language. *You'd be surprised,* because it's just never occurred to most companies to look at their market opportunity by gender. And *you delivered all the marketing communications in French,* because you speak French and you assumed your best prospects did too.

Someone asked notorious bank robber Willie Sutton why he robbed banks. Puzzled by the question, he answered, "Because that's where the money is." The next time someone asks you "Why women?" the same answer will work for you just as well.

Which Women?

Vary the segmentation variables. I can't tell you whom to target, obviously; that depends on your product and your marketing objectives. If you're in the car business, are you selling Mercedes or Hyundais? Sports cars or minivans? If you market health care, do you represent the maternity ward or the cardiology department?

However, there are two segmentation variables that, if you've been accustomed to marketing mostly to men, may not be on your radar screen: marriage and kids. When's the last time (or the first time, for that matter) anyone ever segmented the men's market by married/single or kids/no kids at home? Probably never. But for women, these two criteria make an enormous difference, as we saw in Chapter 4 under "Milestone Marketing." Each time a new person enters a woman's household, it expands the "tribe" in her head, her day-to-day workload, and the people she assumes planning responsibility for—all of which affect her buying decisions.

On the other hand, there is another variable I frequently see used to segment the women's market that I think may *not* be particularly productive: working/nonworking. The new nomenclature for "non working" is "women who don't work *outside the home*"—the point being to clarify that all women are working women, just working at different locations. Although articles in the media for years have reported on "the mommy wars," an alleged animosity between women who work at home and women who work somewhere else, I've never seen a single skirmish and neither have any of my friends. I think it's because both "segments" of women recognize that each is working hard, making their own contribution in their own way, encountering stress from different sources but still coping. There's just not that much difference between them. From a marketing point of view, the distinction

will still make sense in some categories, but in others, different segmentation variables will yield far more insight.

Throw out age bias. Keep your eye on the baby boomers. I've said it
before, and I'll say it again in Chapter 11, for two very good reasons:
First, it's remarkably difficult to break our culture's absolute conviction that young consumers are every marketer's best prospects. Second, they're not. And until we all get that through our heads, we're
going to continue to miss some major market opportunities.

The focus on young consumers evolved in the days when marketing
was maturing beyond brilliant copywriting and simple ad placement
to a more sophisticated discipline based on target audience definition
and analysis. This occurred largely in the 1970s when, coincidentally,
the leading edge of the baby boomers were entering their 20s: buying
and furnishing houses, forming and feeding families—in short, buying
a lot of stuff. The people creating marketing theory were mostly
young. The people executing it now are mostly young.

But hold on a minute. People in the baby boom population bulge
are entering their 50s. The U.S. Census Bureau predicts a 72 percent
increase in adults 50-plus between 2000 and 2020 and a slight decrease in adults under 50. Adults 50-plus control 77 percent of the
country's assets. Per capita spending is 2.5 times the national average
in 50-plus households.

The numbers are absolutely inarguable. Yet advertisers remain astonishingly indifferent. Networks continue scrambling to develop shows to
deliver audiences in the "highly coveted 18–35" demographic. There's
a glamour and excitement to youth, and a cultural aversion to aging, that
trips us up when we need to be making smarter decisions about who our
consumer really is, what she wants, and how we can bring it to her.

Mark my words—popular culture will soon transition from a youth-
driven mode characterized by more male-oriented values like strength,
speed, and success to an "older and wiser" mode more aligned with female values like understanding, harmony, and giving back to the community. The marketing money will follow the baby boom, and the
savviest marketing money will lead the trend.

The Situation Scan: Finding Holes in the Competition

Smart companies know that to be effective, they have to put together a strategic effort that delivers their message to women in a comprehensive way. But *comprehensive* is a big word; there are dozens if not hundreds of possibilities to improve what you're currently doing and/or to add some terrific new initiatives. No one has the budget or staff to do it all. So where do you start, and how do you figure out where your money will do the most good?

It's important to keep in mind that in most categories, marketing to women—like marketing to men or marketing to anybody—is essentially a *share* game. Women are already buying most of the cars and most of the personal computers—the goal is to get them to buy *your* brand of car or insurance. So the answer to the question—and the foundation to a strong marketing-to-women program—is to know where your brand stands in the marketplace relative to your competition and to be clear about what you've got to work with.

You can usually get a pretty good idea of this fairly quickly. Some people call the process an Opportunity Audit, and some people call it a SWOT Analysis (for Strengths-Weaknesses-Opportunities-Threats). At my company, The TrendSight Group (http://www.trendsight.com), I call it a Situation Scan. The core concept is pretty simple (see Figure 7.1).

Not only is the concept simple, but what you're looking for is simple too:

- How do the operations elements of your brand compare to your competitors'?
- How do your marketing communications compare when assessed against the four key criteria of female gender culture (Social Values, Life/Time Factors, Focus Strategies, and Communication Keys)?

Although in theory you could conduct a Situation Scan internally, this is one stage of the process where you should consider bringing in an outside resource. When someone internal handles it, there are just too many vested interests and too much politics to get an objective viewpoint. Whether this subjectivity is conscious or unconscious, it exists. In all fairness, how can you expect someone who has been running your marketing program for the past three years to tell you he or she hasn't been

---

FIGURE 7.1 The Situation Scan

	My Brand/Company	Top 2–4 Competitors
Offerings and Operations		
• Product/service		
• Retail channels/environment		
• Selling approach		
• Customer service		
Marketing Communications		
• Packaging		
• Advertising		
• Public image		
• Collateral and merchandising		
• Web site		
• Sponsorships		
• Event marketing		

---

doing as good a job as the competition? It's not gonna happen. In fact, I can tell you right now what the findings of the analysis would likely be: "With the exception of one brochure we did last year and a newspaper campaign we have running in the Southeast, everything about our marketing is better than our competitors'." No one means to be deceptive, and it's nobody's fault that the assessment of the status quo is always so positive; it's just normal organizational dynamics. But if you want a true read, you're going to have to step outside on this one.

Operations Elements

This is the lesser of the two areas you need to consider as you work toward maximizing your leverage, because, as we have seen, you rarely have to create new products and services for women. In fact, as we've also discussed, it's usually not even advisable. However, you (or your competitors) potentially have a strength or weakness in how well your product/service, retail environment, and so on, are aligned with what women look for and react against. And there is certainly the *opportunity* for you to enhance what you sell and how you sell it, as well as the *threat* that your competitors may be in development on something already.

The primary tools for the operations element of the Situation Scan are consumer research and "mystery shopper" research.

Consumer research. The next section of this chapter outlines qualitative and quantitative research techniques designed to generate meaningful feedback from women customers. Adopt these techniques and customize them for your company, your product or service, and your sales force. For purposes of the Situation Scan, focus on the fundamentals relating to your operation: Have your customers (or prospects) tried your product? What stood out as good or bad? How about your competitors' products?

"Mystery shopper" research. Send women "shoppers" to interact in person, on the phone, and on your Web site with sales, service/repair, and customer service representatives—both yours and your competitors'. This is qualitative, of course, but make sure you budget for *at least* three to five contacts within each department at each company, so you can get a reasonably reliable "feel" for any good or bad consistencies.

Communications Elements

This is the area that offers you the greatest number of opportunities. It's also usually faster to change communications initiatives and materials than to implement new product features or employee behavior patterns.

At this point, you collect all the current marketing communications you can get your hands on—from both your brand and your competitors'. For most Scans, I try to include TV, radio, and newspaper ads; retail signage, branch layout, and customer service procedures; in-store merchandising materials, brochures, and counter cards; Web sites, e-mails, and, if you're a bank, even ATM receipts. After you've collected all the materials, have them analyzed by someone who is well versed in communications strategy/execution and well briefed on the four Star Points of female gender culture—and preferably with no vested interest in validating the status quo.

Although a Situation Scan or SWOT Analysis is a familiar device to many marketers, it's generally not undertaken in the context of how your brand and the competition align with female gender culture. This new way of looking at things may yield some results that surprise you.

Take a look at the case study for ACTON, a marketing firm that serves small banks. Compare and contrast the bank advertising before ACTON employed gender-savvy principles and after.

ACTON

Opportunity:

"The Power of the Purse" also means the power of the credit card, the stock market, the checkbook, and all other financial instruments. Women are truly the financial services industry's most important customers.

- In 85 percent of U.S. families, women handle the checking account.[10]
- Women handle 75 percent of family finances.[11]
- Credit cards are carried by 76 million women and 68 million men.[12]
- 70 percent of investment club members are women.[13]
  - The National Association of Investors Corporation also found women excelled over men in investing. Their ten-year study showed all-female investment clubs outpaced all-male investment clubs by racking up 23.8 percent average compounded lifetime annual returns compared to 19.2 percent for male clubs.[14]
- Women control or influence 53 percent of family investment decisions.[15]

Strategies:

ACTON Marketing, a company that creates direct marketing packages and promotional materials, and acts as a consulting firm to banks, enlisted my help a couple of years ago when it realized that all bank direct mail looked alike. "We were searching for a way to distinguish our banking clients' mail in the box among all the look-alike clutter," ACTON CEO Lynn Leffert said. "When we discovered Marti Barletta's marketing-to-women ideas, we not only found our new look, we also found a new way of looking at the market." ACTON wanted to lead the way and leverage "the power of the purse"—just as it set the standard when it introduced the Free Checking and a Free Gift strategy in the early '80s. ACTON's strategy was to develop a whole new "marketing-to-women approach" for financial organizations, and I worked closely with the design and sales team to help them create the most gender-savvy communications materials, from direct mail to face-to-face training manuals.

When we did a Situation Scan, we saw that all of the banks' direct mail featured lots of stats and facts, interest rates in big bold type, pictures of random irrelevant free gifts, and comparisons of all of their checking accounts with small and confusing differences. Not at all female friendly! Now let's take a look at what we did to realign their marketing materials with women's values.

Insights that ACTON tapped into:

- **People powered**

  To women, people are the most important, interesting element in any situation. Banking, insurance, and other low-involvement industries need to wrap their heads around the fact that women would be much more involved in their businesses if they just showed people and focused on the benefits to people. ACTON did just that, and you can see from the examples that ACTON's direct mail materials will definitely get opened more often because women will see relevant, familiar, empathetic faces. They also communicate what's in it for the customer (*"It's all in one . . . you have your own lifestyle and your own ideas what a checking account should do for you. That's why you get so many convenient features packed into one checking account—free online banking, online bill pay, free telephone banking, Visa® debit card, etc."*)

- **Storytelling/testimonials**

  Women's social currency is stories and personal details. Using these creates commonality and connections. Rather than focusing on facts and features, ACTON incorporated storytelling and testimonials into its direct marketing materials. ACTON also focused on telling a "you" story (about the customers) rather than an "us" story (about the banks themselves). These changes resulted in drawing more women into the message and ensured that the banks' points registered on the female radar screen. (See Figure 7.2.)

- **The Perfect Answer**

  Women will go the extra mile in order to make the absolute RIGHT purchase—in order to find the Perfect Answer. Women have a longer list of criteria when it comes to the purchase process—they want all the same things as men . . . and then some! ACTON is helping its clients create just the right banking approach to women by developing female-friendly "free gift" offerings such as digital cameras, gift cards, even fashionable trendy purses. Furthermore, ACTON is helping to simplify the decision-making process by training its bank clients to communicate "the right account for you" (Perfect Answer) instead of confusing potential customers with a myriad of checking accounts with minor differences. Listen and learn. And then give her the Perfect Answer.

- **Corporate halo**

  Women expect the companies they do business with to be good community citizens. And banks, who are charged with some of the most important responsibilities and therefore need to earn tremendous trust, should be especially assertive when it comes to doing and communicating their good deeds. ACTON developed some wonderful examples of corporate halo marketing materials for their banking clients to use. They created relevant corporate citizenship ideas tied into fiscal matters—such as setting up a foundation to help low-income families afford housing (and mortgages!) and helping low-income families celebrate the holidays with donations to Toys for Tots. They also focus on helping schools, as children are a top priority for moms and therefore for banks as well.

Results:

"Our first mail project using the new creative approach for one of our bank clients surprised even us," Leffert said. "The marketing vice president told us they opened 12 percent more accounts during that mail cycle than they did during the same time the previous year. We learned that women want more information than men, presented so they can make a decision in the way that suits them." Leffert summarized the program, saying, "This gives banks of all sizes the ability to get their message to the biggest and best audience using the best possible communications and measurement methods. After all, that's what marketing is all about." I have been thrilled to be a part of ACTON's trendsetting marketing approach and am currently working with ACTON on not just getting women in the door but keeping them happy with their current bank.

The outcome of a Situation Scan is a report detailing the findings of the analysis and recommending five to ten action initiatives for pulling ahead of the competition by improving your standing in the women's market.

Once you have this report, you need to pull together a task force with representatives from all the key departments. This is essential to ensuring that your initiatives are well integrated. Given women's predisposition to absorb and assess everything in context, it is critical that the communications that grow out of the Situation Scan and subse-

FIGURE 7.2 ACTON: Before

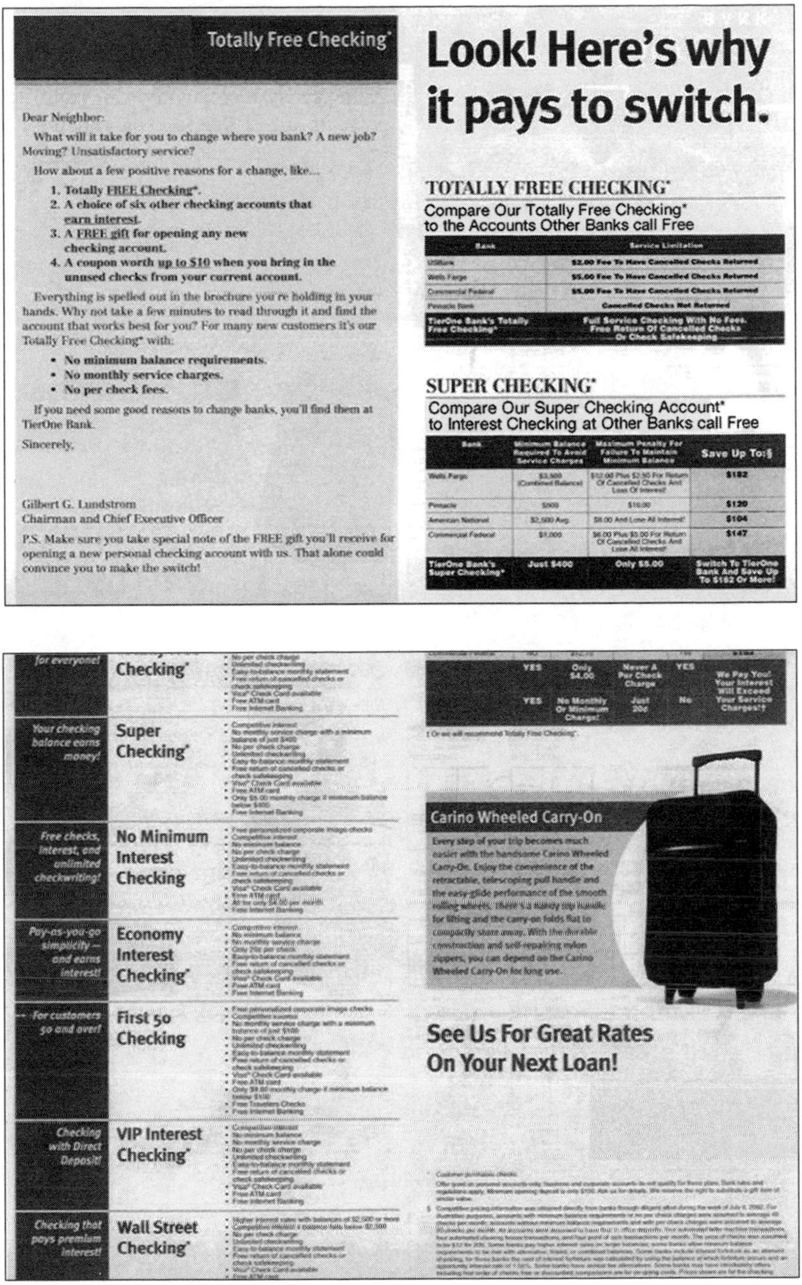

ACTON Marketing LLC

FIGURE 7.2 ACTON: After (Continued)

"We're glad we found this account."

Simply Free Checking

"We're not really a two-income family because I switched to part-time work after our daughter was born. That's made it tougher to keep a minimum balance in our checking account, so Simply Free Checking is perfect for us. We stay away from those expensive service charges and fees, which means more money for the really important things in our life."

- No minimum balance
- Unlimited check writing with no per check fees
- No monthly service charge
- No-fee Direct Deposit available

"It's everything I want and more."

Simply Better Checking

"Free checks. That's what I like about this account, and that's why I opened it. But there are a lot of other reasons this is my checking account. It pays interest on my balance. Plus, all the added benefits I get like no-fee money orders and travelers checks. And free $10,000 accidental death life insurance. I get it all for just $12 a month."

- Free personalized checks
- Unlimited check writing with no per check fees
- Earns interest
- Plus many more exclusive benefits — ask for details

"It's a great checking plan."

Freedom Checking

"I never thought much about my checking account until a friend pointed out how much it was costing me. That's when I switched to Freedom Checking. Because I keep the minimum balance, the account is free — no service charges. I even get some extra cash because of the interest this account pays on my balance."

- Earns interest
- Unlimited check writing with no per check fees
- No-fee Direct Deposit available
- No monthly service charge with minimum $1,000 balance

"A smart move for us."

Investors Choice Checking

"My husband and I saw it was necessary to learn how to handle our money the best way we could. We even took night classes together so we could learn more about finances and investment. Our goal was to find a checking account that pays higher interest when we keep a larger balance. The higher balances pay off another way — no monthly fees make this free for us."

- Earns higher interest
- Unlimited check writing with no per check fees
- No-fee Direct Deposit available
- No monthly service charge with minimum $25,000 balance

ACTON Marketing LLC

FIGURE 7.2 ACTON: After (Continued)

ABC Bank helps fuel student learning

West Elm Middle School

When the school's furnace gave out in November, something needed to be done immediately. ABC Bank stepped in and donated $2,500 to help replace the old unit with a new natural gas heating system. It's another way ABC Bank makes the community's needs — especially those of our children — a top priority.

ACTON Marketing LLC

quent task force have "one look, one voice" and that they build on each other.

Make sure that the task force is roughly 50–50 men and women. Without the women you won't have the "insider's insight" you need to ensure that the work is on point. Without the men you won't have the credibility you need to ensure the organization's full commitment and support.

Understanding Your Customer: Research— Believe It or Not

Once you've *defined* your market, your next step is to *understand your customer.* As is now clear, the "same old, same old" just doesn't cut it when it comes to really "getting it" with the female purchasing population. So let's look at new ways of using research to get the inside insight on Freud's plaintive question: What do women want?

Qualitative Research: Permission to Speak Freely

New research techniques recognize that when women "talk amongst themselves," the dynamics are very different than conversations among a group of men. Women become more communicative when interacting freely with each other and when allowed to "multitalk" in a female-friendly style. Sure, I know it's more efficient to talk or share information in a facilitator environment with a carefully timed and structured discussion guide, *but you will never unearth the underlying insight that way*—not with women. Get women talking with each other instead of *at* the moderator and get them laughing and building on each other's thoughts. What you're looking for are the mutual moments of "Ohmygosh, that's *exactly* what I do!" Then you won't be able to get them to *stop* giving you observations, opinions, and insights, all of which will help you improve your product and sharpen your marketing.

Women-only groups. Even for gender-neutral products, conduct your focus groups for "women only." Why? As we saw in Chapter 4, male and female communication styles are considerably different. Sociolinguists like Dr. Deborah Tannen have found that groups of mixed gender default to male patterns of conversation and interaction. Women become more reserved and less participatory. They don't buy into the competitive "game" that prevails when men are expressing divergent opinions, and because they are less likely to interrupt, hold the floor, or insist on their opinions, they simply won't offer as much information.

And you need that information. While men can give you the big picture, the broad brushstrokes about a product or marketing response, women can give you something different—and more helpful. As we know, women are more likely to perceive detail and nuance and to think in the context of people and lifestyle. And the details that are *important* are the ones that relate to people and lifestyle, not technical specs or performance stats. In these days when every marketer is trying to differentiate his brand from a host of very similar products and services, it's the details that make the difference. And if you structure your research to let them, women can give you feedback and ideas to help you improve your product, merchandising, store environment, delivery, customer service, and Web site. Talking to women—or rather, listening to them—is the best way to provide yourself with the points of difference that will make or break you versus the competition.

Because *make* is definitely preferable to *break,* let's look at three nontraditional research approaches designed to tap into women's energy and honesty when they're talking to each other.

Girlfriend groups. Developed and refined by the LeoShe division of the venerable Leo Burnett advertising agency, these girlfriend groups are like a new millennium version of the Tupperware parties of old. The researcher meets with a group of women who all know each other at the home of one of the group's participants. A familiar environment and a known group make the members more relaxed; they feel more able to be themselves rather than focusing on delivering answers to a moderator.

In addition, in the home environment women are closer to the point of usage of the product—and therefore more likely to be in touch with the details that make a difference. Say you're hosting a girlfriend group on kitchen appliances at Robyn's house. "Come to think of it," Marcia says as she refills her water glass, "one thing I've never liked about my refrigerator is how noisy the ice maker is. Plus, none of my glasses fit under the dispenser in the door, so I end up with water dripping all over the floor every time."

Because they all know each other, they keep each other honest. Admit it: If you believed everything you heard in a conventional focus group, you'd think no woman ever fed her child those "evil" sugared cereals. (So who buys them—the little Irish elf on the box?) But if Betsy hears Jane saying that she always feeds her kids the recommended servings of fruits and vegetables, Betsy's likely to call her on it. "Oh, please," she'll laugh. "You may be *serving* Alex two helpings of vegetables each night, but he eats dinner over at my house with Simon two or three nights a week, and I guarantee you he isn't *eating* them. In fact, the story I hear is that he hasn't laid eyes on a vegetable in two years." *That's* when the researcher finds out that Jane's been "hiding" the vegetables by pureeing them into spaghetti sauce, salad dressing, and even waffle batter—an interesting idea, if you're a food company looking to build share among moms.

What we learned from Oprah. This type of group is a provocative and highly effective new format developed by Mary Lou Quinlan, founder/president of *Just Ask a Woman*. Modeled on a television talk-show format, 35 to 40 women in the target segment are recruited to be in a mock television audience. Mary Lou Quinlan hosts the show herself, leveraging her lively wit and sparkling personality to charm the candor out of her guests. The show is taped, just like a broadcast, and edited to highlight the key revelations that come out of the session. In this way, the "folks at home"—whether that means the sales personnel in the field or the senior executives at headquarters—can hear what their customers have to say "in person" instead of on paper.

Brand champion focus groups: brand fans talk to nonbelievers. Another excellent and innovative way to learn the language and priorities that women bring to your brand is to turn the tables for a change. Find a group of women who *love* your product and put them in a room with people who either haven't heard of it or are predisposed against it. Give them a little time to get to know each other. This is important, because without some points of commonality (i.e., a chance to play a little "same-same"), your enthusiasts won't have a feel for where to start or what to emphasize.

After some time together, switch the group dynamic from "tell me" to "sell me." Ask your brand champions to talk about how they heard about the product, why they tried it, and what happened the first time they used it. Let the "prospects" ask questions and raise objections— and listen to how your advocates answer. This insider's look at women's word of mouth will help you develop communications content and approaches that are compelling and on point with the reality of women's interaction with your brand. In effect, your group will tell you how to overcome resistance to your product or service.

Women online. As we saw in Chapter 5, women are the majority of the online audience, and this is growing rapidly. The five key components of the Internet—communication, content, commerce, community, and convenience—appeal even more strongly to women than to men. Leverage this appeal to gather information from your consumer. It may not be a scientifically representative sample (although the online population is getting more mainstream all the time), but the upside is substantial in that it's very fast and very inexpensive.

Surveys and quizzes. Women love surveys and quizzes, which is why all of the women's magazines run them so often, even using them as part of their audience draw. Take a look at the cover of *Shape* or *Ladies' Home Journal* and you're likely to see headlines like "America's Favorite Day Spas—Tell Us Your Favorites" or "Creative or Pragmatic? Rate

Yourself with Our Kitchen Makeover Quiz." They're fun to fill out, you learn something about yourself, and it's interesting to see how you compare to others in the results. Use this appeal to gather information on your product, your positioning, or a promotion you're thinking about running by delivering a survey via e-mail or through your Web site. Use *quizzes* to gather consumer lifestyle information and *surveys* for product/category feedback.

Keep it fairly short; remember the time crunch! You're better off separating your topics into six surveys of 10 minutes each instead of three surveys of 20 minutes each.

As for incentives to participate, whereas focus groups usually require a cash payment of $25 to $75 per respondent, online research is as cheap and simple as sharing the results, which can be tabulated and shown instantly. Remember, whereas a man is relatively more interested in telling companies what he thinks, women are relatively more interested in learning how other people see the situation.

Run a chat group as a megafocus group. Publicize an online session that provides good information on a relevant topic. For example, a company like Volvo might offer a miniclass online about safe driving in winter conditions, featuring a panel of driving experts to answer audience questions. The interaction will be fast and furious with customer input coming in from all over at once, definitely a chaotic experience in "real time." But if you capture the questions and read the transcripts later, I guarantee you'll have snared new perspectives and valuable thought-starters to run with.

Quantitative: Questioning the Questions

Quantitative research also offers some opportunities for significant improvement. Because research designers don't know, and haven't factored in, that women shop and buy differently than men, their questionnaires contain errors and oversights that may *look* unimportant but can drastically affect the validity of the response. In an effort to understand the needs and attitudes of their consumers, companies routinely commit hundreds of thousands of dollars annually to large research studies. Based on some of the questionnaires I've seen, they'd get a much higher return donating the money to charity. They could at least leverage that investment via publicity to generate some goodwill for the company.

Make your questions specific, not generic. For example, I recently participated in a phone survey for an apparel chain, and the list of questions was laughable. "On a scale of one to ten, how important is quality to your choice of retailer? How important is fit? Service? Selection? Price?" I honestly didn't know how to answer. What does "quality" mean? Sure, I'd rather have an Armani suit—but that doesn't mean I'm willing to *pay* for it. Does that mean that I *do* care about quality (because I want the suit), or that I *don't* (because I'm not willing to buy it)? And how about "fit"? How could fit *not* be important? Do some people really say they don't care if the clothes they buy are too small or too large? As a marketer, all I could think about was the thousands of dollars that the retailer was spending to get answers that were utterly meaningless. Instead, the questions should have been designed to get at women's perceptions and decision trade-offs: *How do you assess quality? Please rank: fabric, sewing, details, designer name. Do you usually prefer to buy clothes to last a lifetime or a season or two?*

Yes, the questions are more complex, making the research more costly to tabulate and difficult to interpret. But unless your research gives you useful information, what's the point of doing it at all? You're better off trying to make your way through a maze with trial and error than with a meaningless map that misleads with random directions.

Capture all the criteria on women's longer lists, not just the "most important" benefits. In a previous example, I told you about a colleague of mine who chose a Nokia phone because it came in Ocean Blue. Was that the most important criterion she applied in choosing a cell phone? No, of course not—not by a long shot. But it *was* the *deciding* factor; she made that clear as she recounted her decision-making process and ultimate purchase. Remember, women have a longer list of considerations. If you use the "forced choice" methodology so popular with phone surveys (asking the consumer to rank the three most important criteria on a list, for instance), you are short-circuiting her decision process. This means that the answers you're getting don't really reflect the way she buys.

Your answer choices should show that the sponsoring company understands how women buy apparel in this case and provide some options that really would actually enter into real women's decision considerations. Don't ask, "How important is fit (or quality, or service, etc.) in your choice of a retailer? Very, somewhat, or not at all important?" (This is meaningless, because every single question will elicit the same response, either all "very" or all "somewhat," and nothing will emerge as a point of differentiation or a focus opportunity.) Or "Which are the three most important criteria in selecting a retailer: quality, fit, service, selection, or price?" (Again meaningless, because you can't shop anywhere without having "enough" of all of these.) Instead, structure your questions to give you some insight into *what she means* when she talks about these criteria or how she weighs her decision among them when push comes to shove. *If a jacket costs about 20 percent more than you want to pay, rank-order the reasons you might buy it anyway:*

- *Gorgeous–Fell in love with it, had to have it.*
- *Bargain–60 percent markdown too good to resist.*
- *Worth it–Higher quality than usual for this price range.*
- *Sold on it–Friend or salesperson I trust said it looks great on me.*
- *Need it–Out of time to shop further for upcoming event or trip.*
- *Other?* _____

On written or online questionnaires, *always* provide a few lines for write-in answers. You'll get criteria you never thought to ask about, and sometimes they're the ones that will cinch the sale. If you think about it, the *best* research study is the one that surprises you—where the consumer tells you something you didn't already know. And if you've already preprogrammed all the answers and limited her ability to give you input, how is she going to help you identify the differentiating details that will cause her to choose your brand, not your competitor's?

Beware of Bias as You Interpret the Results— Both Theirs and Yours

Self-reporting. By definition, *self-reported attitudes and behavior* are likely to be influenced by gender culture differences. For example, consider a couple of financial services studies: all asked whether re-spondents were willing to take substantial risks in order to earn sub-stantial gains. In one 1995 poll by Prudential Securities, 45 percent of men said yes, compared to 26 percent of women.[16] However, when a separate study analyzed portfolios of men and women of similar ages, income levels, and work status, the ratio of stocks to bonds was found to be nearly identical.[17] The caveat? Male culture encourages men to see themselves as independent, bold, and shooting from the hip—so they overreport their risk tolerance. Female culture, on the other hand, is more careful and more information based—and so women un-derreport their risk tolerance. The difference, however, is about how they see *themselves* rather than how they make actual product choices.

Subconscious bias. If you're not careful, *your own subconscious biases* may creep into how you read or report the data. To continue the topic above, another financial services company surveyed women and men about their attitude toward financial risk and released a report that said, "If given a choice, more men (72 percent) than women (62 per-cent) would rather take risks in life than play it safe."[18] What I find in-teresting is the phrasing of this quote: it *positions* women as less inclined to take risks, whereas the *facts* are that almost two-thirds of the women respondents indicated they would prefer to take risks than play it safe.

We'll talk a great deal more about strategic options and tactical in-itiatives in the next chapter. First though, let's close the loop on mar-ket assessment by talking about measurement.

Proving Your Point: Measure Everything—Men Too

Executives can experience great frustration as they attempt to se-cure and hold on to management support for their marketing-to-women programs. In large part, this is because of the lack of evaluative information and valid tracking systems that prove that the initiative is working. Because most companies haven't marketed this way before, most are not set up to track responses by gender. Instead, many track-ing systems are set up to measure "household" response. And despite the fact that the woman head of household is most often making the purchase decisions, corporate databases generally default to the man's name. For example, for bank and investment accounts, both John and Jenny Doe may be joint account holders. Unless a conscious effort is made to record which of the two account holders opened the account, there would be no way to distinguish if this account could be attributed to Jenny's response to the new marketing-to-women initiative or to John's response to something else.

However, the fact that the results of a program are difficult to measure should not lead to the conclusion that the program is ineffective. In fact, nothing could be more foolish. (See the McNamara Fallacy below.) The measurement challenges exist as a by-product of the women's market being overlooked or thought of inaccurately, and until marketers take note of the women's market as the powerful force that it is, those challenges will continue unabated.

The McNamara Fallacy

(Attributed to Robert McNamara, former U.S. secretary of defense and former president of the World Bank)

- The first step is to measure whatever can be easily measured. This is OK as far as it goes.
- The second step is to disregard that which can't be easily measured or to give it an arbitrary quantitative value. This is artificial and misleading.
- The third step is to presume that what can't be measured easily really isn't important. This is blindness.
- The fourth step is to say that what can't be easily measured really doesn't exist. This is suicide.

Charles Handy, The Age of Paradox, *Harvard Business School Press,* 1995, page 221.

Do not let yourself or your company off the hook on finding and following through on a way to measure response to your marketing-to-women efforts lest you collectively fall into the trap of assuming that what can't be easily measured really isn't important or doesn't exist. You don't want to be either blind or suicidal, now do you?

Results Speak for Themselves . . . and for You

It is imperative to capture the results that validate your program's impact. Insist on building in measures that track the impact of your women's marketing initiatives on customers. Tracking systems are not always easy and hardly ever free, but they are essential to overcoming corporate inertia whenever you're leading the team toward something new. Tracking must be comprehensive and should include elements such as brand preference, sales, repeat purchases, and customer satisfaction—*men as well as women.* Remember, many companies fear that by reaching out to women, they may alienate men. But as we've discussed, the opposite is true: improving effectiveness to women tends to boost customer satisfaction among men. *Track it and prove it.*

Because women's decision cycle is longer than men's, it's likely that you will see presales indicators from female consumers, such as *increased awareness, more favorable perceptions,* and *increased requests for information and sales materials,* before you notice a strong improvement in actual sales. Given the pressure companies face to deliver quarter by quarter, your ability to sustain this program throughout the ramp-up time you will need to build and execute it may well depend on your ability to demonstrate preliminary movement in the right direction using these "stand-in" measures. Quantitative surveys conducted via phone, mail, online, and mall-intercept are a great way to track changes in women consumers' awareness of, attitude toward, and interest in your product at the expense of your competitors. Given that the competitive future of your company may well depend on its ability to market successfully to women, it would be a really good idea to put those tracking systems into place right from the start.

As a side note: I have heard from more then one marketing executive that for reasons they can only speculate on, senior management at times seems to hold marketing-to-women programs to a higher standard of proof than some of the company's other marketing investments. Their programs somehow became the poster child for the company's new resolve to insist on greater accountability, measurability, and ROI (return on investment). One savvy executive persuaded management to be more reasonable by proposing to adopt whatever ROI calculations the company was using to evaluate the precise return on its golf sponsorships.

Kaizen: Seeking Continuous Improvement

The Japanese term *kaizen* means "continuous improvement." Just as with any unfamiliar new endeavor, don't expect to get marketing to women perfect on the first try. No matter how much prelaunch research you do, the consumer will always teach you something just when you least expect it. (Remember New Coke?) Your research results are essential to *kaizen*. Without feedback, you can't know what to flaunt and what to fix.

Successful marketing to women requires gender-savvy tactics aimed at the five stages of the consumer-planning process—*activation, nomination, investigation and decision, retention,* and *recommendation*—which we'll discuss in more detail in the next chapter. Without concrete strategies for each stage, the female market will either remain ignored or slip through your grasp. Don't let it get away. With a strong product or service enhanced by gender-savvy communications, you will ensure that the women's market is knocking on your door instead of on your competitor's.

CHAPTER 8

Get Set

Strategy and Tactical Planning

In the previous chapter, we examined how to identify your market and gain a meaningful understanding of your consumer. In this chapter, we will build upon that foundation and apply the principles of gender marketing to each of the five phases of the consumer's decision process. You will learn how to

- connect with a consumer who is in the market for the products you sell.
- ensure that your brand is on the short list of purchase candidates.
- give your consumer what she needs to decide in your brand's favor.
- generate a higher return from every woman customer by using specific marketing tactics employed in the right way at the right time.

First, however, we need to spend a little time on a topic that spans all five phases of the consumer's purchase process: positioning.

Defining Your Platform: Beyond Positioning to Persuasion

Creating a Brand Identity

The word *positioning* describes how target consumers view a certain brand, relative to other brands in the market. One classic, frequently used positioning format goes like this: *To erstwhile soccer moms whose kids have gone off to college, Jaguar is the brand of luxury car that lets her indulge her long-deferred longing for a car with comfort and style.* The positioning statement is made up of three elements:

1. *Your target consumer ("erstwhile soccer moms")*. This is a shorthand statement and should be backed up with a wealth of insights on the market opportunity gleaned from the Situation Scan and an in-depth understanding of the consumer, revealed through the female-friendly research techniques we discussed in Chapter 7.

2. *The competitive set in which your brand competes ("luxury cars")*. This choice has a major impact on how you define your positioning. For instance, Jaguar could position itself as either a luxury car, where it would have to define its advantages versus Lexus, Lincoln, and the like, or as a performance car, where it would be up against BMW, Porsche, and Corvette. With respect to the women's market, it's important to realize that some options are going to be more relevant/appealing to women than to men. No doubt, there are *some* mature women (the target consumer has "college-age kids," remember?) who care about performance attributes like torque, acceleration, and maneuverability at high speeds. But there are plenty more who feel they've earned the luxury of relaxing in comfort and style.

3. *The differentiating point that sets your brand apart from the competitive set you've chosen*. If you have a product point of difference that's perceivable and important to consumers, more power to you. More often in these days of product commoditization, though, the differentiating points *are created through communications* platforms. These platforms describe how you would like consumers to think of your brand, even before they retain anything specific about it. All luxury cars are going to offer comfort and style. The differentiating point in this positioning statement is its recogni-

tion of the consumer insight, "indulge her long-deferred long-ing," which communicates to your target audience that you understand how she feels and what she's looking for.

Defining the Product

Properly done, positioning is a brand-defining process that aligns consumer needs/wants, product design, and marketing communications in terms that are relevant and appealing to your target audience. The two key dimensions to explore in making your product and packaging more appealing to women are utility and styling.

Utility. Although I'm sure it's not true in every category, I think it's safe to say that in *most* categories, women are more pragmatic than men. With less interest in the one-upsmanship of novelty, less interest in the inner workings of tech-mech products, and more time pressures than men, women just want products to work easily and reliably.

The Ford Motor Company capitalized on this insight with great success when it introduced its new minivan, Windstar, several years ago. The vehicle was designed by a team of 30 female engineers and automotive designers, most of whom were also mothers. The innovations they came up with clearly reflected their own experiences and lifestyles and elicited an enthusiastic response among women customers. The new features included easy-to-open tailgates, adjustable pedals (that could be adjusted for shorter people), easy-to-clean interiors, a secure place to stash a handbag, an overhead "baby sleeping" cabin light that could be set to stay dim when the door was opened, and many more. As you can see, most of these features might not have occurred to male engineers and designers, because men rarely concern themselves with any of these issues. But they were seen as important differentiators by women customers. The pragmatic appeal of the vehicle, combined with Ford's astute use of the "female engineering team" design story in their marketing, won Ford a significant share response to the Windstar launch.

Styling. As companies recognize that women have different style preferences and are more responsive to styling enhancements in general, there is a growing awareness of the opportunity this creates to expand their consumer base and pull in additional share. For example, Nokia cleverly took a cue from Swatch and began offering interchangeable faceplates for their cell phones. By taking "styling" in a completely different direction than anyone else in the category, they were the first to move a serious "business" product (cell phones) toward fun and transform a utilitarian device into something that lets the consumer express her own personality.

Similarly, while all of the conventional notebook computers were still encased in chunky black plastic, the Fujitsu Lifebook and the Sony Vaio came out with sleek, matte silver casings that really stood out. They set themselves apart in an instantly perceivable way—*and* attracted all the laptop customers interested in styling because they were the only options available.

But where are the stylish *desktop* computers? The only company to give any thought at all to aesthetic appearance is Apple. This company continually leads the category in design innovation, having introduced color choices (neon orange, green, blue) and nonboxy shapes long before any of its competitors. (And now Apple's iPods have raised the styling bar even higher). And what about home electronics? Oddly enough, although the portable products are often sleek and self-expressive, the products that go in people's living rooms, which logically have much more of a décor element, typically still come only in black or steel. (No wonder everyone always hides them in media cabinets!) Even washers and dryers are coming out of the closet, in stylish new colors from Kenmore such as Pacific Blue, Sedona, and Champagne.

What about taking a page from the Target success story and bringing in a contemporary designer (Target works with Michael Graves) to add some grace and beauty to these products? Sony has already teamed up with Target to create the Sony Liv line which features stylish home appliances for the kitchen and living room, meant to complement, not clash, with your décor. Is it going to complicate your life, add design time, and require new manufacturing processes and packaging? Sure it is. But think of the payoff.

First, it would make your brand stand out and serve as a differentiated basis for brand preference, bringing in more customers. Second, it would create a distinctive look and family resemblance across your product line, motivating the customer to buy *all* her components from you. Finally, you could probably sell these distinctive products for a premium price, covering not only added costs but also providing higher profit. More customers, more sales per customer, and more margin—isn't that what marketers dream of? And all from adding some style to your product and female appeal to your message.

I am extremely proud of this next case study for Volvo, who took the risk and explored utility and styling with women in mind, in the all-too-male auto industry.

Volvo

Opportunity:

If you look at the auto industry in general, it's a sorry sight. In ad after ad, the auto manufacturers talk about cylinder volume, cam shafts, and torque. And then they show pictures of a car on a mountain top in a left turn or a car in a desert in a right turn. No people in sight anywhere. Certainly no families in the picture. And definitely *not* a woman! But who drives these cars?

A note to the Big Three: Women Drive the Car Industry! Women buy 60-plus percent of all new cars[1] and 53 percent of used cars.[2] They influence 80 percent of all new vehicle purchases[3] and spend $300 billion annually on used car sales, maintenance, repairs, and service.[4] Among couples, Ford Motor Co. reports that women have 95 percent veto power over vehicle purchases.[5] Sixty-five percent of women take their own vehicles to the repair shop for service (some industry experts estimate the average is closer to 80 percent).[6]

Strategies:

Volvo recognized the power of women in the auto industry and set up an internal team to leverage the fact that 52 percent of its customers in the United States are women. In fact, I was invited to visit Volvo for a series of workshops and shared one of my key insights that became its rallying cry: "If you meet the expectations of women, you exceed the expectations of men." Hence was born the YCC (Your Concept Car) and my moniker of "godmother" of the new car. Started, inspired, and managed by an all-women team of designers and engineers and blessed by Hans-Olov Olsson, president and CEO of Volvo, the YCC team said women customers in the premium segment want everything that men want in terms of performance, prestige, and style, but they also want more!

Insights that Volvo tapped into:

- **The Perfect Answer**

  Women will go the extra mile in order to make the absolute *right* purchase—in order to find the Perfect Answer. Women have a longer purchase process and also a longer list of criteria when it comes to the
  purchase decision. The female team at Volvo created the Perfect
  Answer in many ways, including smart storage solutions. They developed a capacious central console with an upper level for keys and
  coins, which slides back to reveal generous space for bags and laptops.
  They also made the back seat better for storage by providing cinema-
  style seats, which fold up when not in use, creating a spacious back
  seat slot for extra shopping bags or a second set of golf clubs.

  And because women don't like to fumble with hoods, they don't
  have to with the YCC. Windshield washer fluid, like gas, is added
  through a neat valve in the side of the car—and the only people who
  get to look under the hood are the service engineers, after the car has
  politely told the driver that it is time for a service.

- **Details matter**

  The "diva" is in the details because women want the same things as
  men, *and then some.* The female team at Volvo used technology to create a better experience (what *she* wants), and in the process got a
  sleeker look as well. They wanted a car that is easy to get in and out of,
  so they made it gull-winged (sporty enough for a man!), with doors that
  go up and drop-down sills that descend. The driver's seat also slides
  back automatically when the door is opened and the steering wheel
  moves up. Better yet, the doors don't just unlock, they also open automatically at the press of a key. A welcome asset for the mom (or dad)
  with arms full of shopping bags, sports equipment, and backpacks.

- **People powered**

  To women, people are the most important, interesting element in any
  situation. But are cars usually designed with people in mind? Or with
  speed, torque, and RPMs in mind? The Volvo female team certainly had
  the driver in mind—for maximum visibility, the designers lowered the
  hood so the driver can see the fenders. And they evolved an "Ergovision" system, which scans the driver's body into a computer (how very
  James Bond!) and then programs the car to set its seat, steering wheel,
  seat belts, pedals, and head restraints to the dimensions of the driver.

For drivers who are looking for fashion (or just whatever's clean!), they created interchangeable interior seat pads and carpets, so color schemes can be altered—and washed.

Results:

Volvo officials say they have no immediate plans to mass produce the YCC, but some of its features such as Ergovision will find their way into future Volvo vehicles. Many other changes have been made to cars in order to meet the expectations of women, and men as well as women will reap the benefits.

For instance:

- Bright new fashion colors
- Hooks on the backs of the front seats for the carrying of groceries or take-out dinners
- Thinner steering wheels
- Increased (often ingenious) storage space
- Larger door pockets
- Compulsory cup holders
- More common arm rests set lower down
- Hoods far easier to see over
- Seat elevation, making it easier for the driver to read the road
- Parking distance sensors to aid in reverse parking
- Radio and other controls on the steering wheel
- Visor mirrors
- Luggage webbing
- Drink coolers

"I am convinced male buyers will love this car," said Volvo CEO Hans-Olov Olsson at the vehicle's unveiling. "This is not a boxy pink family car with lots of child seats." "Men saw the car and said they didn't expect this," project manager Camilla Palmertz said. "They saw a good exterior and good interior solutions and said: 'This makes sense.' But women saw the good exterior and liked it, then saw the good interior solutions and said: 'Finally!'"[7]

Additional sources: Samela Harris, *The Official Australian International Motor Show Guide,* October 2004; Luigi Fraschini for *Driving Today,* 2005

FIGURE 8.1 Defining Your Platform: Styling

Volvo YCC

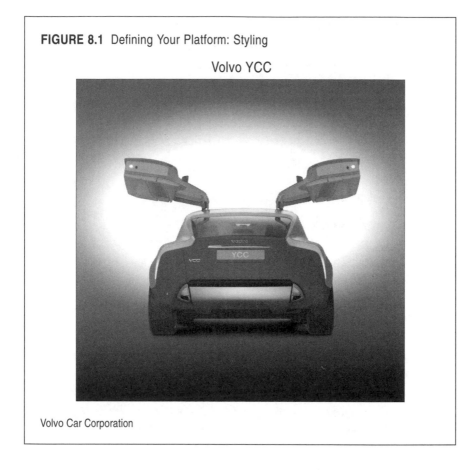

Volvo Car Corporation

Positioning: What Resonates with Women

The importance of positioning in any marketing plan has generated several dozen books devoted solely to that subject. In this abbreviated format, I'll focus on the top four topics on which most marketers are likely to need "corrective" perspective when directing their positioning communications to women: relevance, emotion, corporate halo, and getting clear.

1. Relevance—speaking to today's woman. The 1980s are *so* over. Marketers need to align with *contemporary* female gender culture, not the self-delusional supermom who is frazzled and stressed out from trying to have it all. Today's woman is improvisational: She copes with chaos

more or less cheerfully, recognizing that something's got to give. She picks what's important and doesn't worry about the dust bunnies under the beds until they're scaring the children. She's been coping for 20 years now and has gotten pretty confident about her abilities. So instead of positioning your product to bail her out of a bad day, show how it helps her make a pretty good day even better by delivering benefits like free time, extra ease of use, relaxation, fun, or family time.

2. Emotion—making her care for your brand. While it's true that women are generally more pragmatic than men, they are also more emotional and therefore likely to tune in to emotional benefits over functional ones. It's not that utility doesn't count; she has to know it's functional first. However, what can set apart one car that starts over another car that starts isn't always more cargo space. Sometimes, it's just a warm and fuzzy feeling.

For instance, for years both Volvo and Ford have been positioning their brands on safety. Volvo's ads convey a heritage of caring; Ford's ads focus on crash-test ratings. Volvo's ads create a consumer bond; Ford's fail to create anything much beyond awareness ("five stars!") and skepticism (everybody's claiming five stars). Michelin tires tuned in to an emotional appeal when they switched from advertising their tread depth to advertising with babies. Their sales skyrocketed, and it's a pretty sure bet it had a lot to do with a consumer gut response to what driving safety is really all about.

Remember that women's gender culture is geared toward *empathy* rather than *aspiration*. A small but effective example is the ad for an automatic coffeemaker with a "start brew" timer set for the next morning that says sympathetically: "Finally, someone who gets up before you do."

Also, remember that women emphasize *warmer* over *winner*. They're about affiliation, and hierarchy is a concept that doesn't ring their chimes. For instance, take the premium sports car ad that appeals to the winner orientation with this message: "'Follow the leader' is only fun if you're the leader." Women get it—but not with the emphatic "You got *that* right!" feeling it inspires in a man. Similarly, advertising for a large American SUV says: "Our 270 horsepower engine can beat up your . . . Wait, you don't have a 270 horsepower engine." That "rub it in your face" spirit just doesn't deliver the same satisfaction to a woman as to a man. Take the same product, though—a Jeep, also a large American SUV—and try a different message: "Think of it as a 4,000-pound guardian angel." Now that's a feeling a woman can relate to: the car that cares about the people it carries.

3. Corporate halo—letting your light shine. If you've got an obvious superiority over, or point of difference from, the competition, go for it; highlight the hell out of it! But these days, with more competitors and more heavily saturated markets, many products, services, and companies are seen as almost interchangeable. In a situation like this, sometimes the "soft stuff" like good deeds is the only thing that differentiates your brand.

Usually, the corporate halo features are auxiliary points, tiebreakers. For example, Ford's strong commitment to fighting breast cancer via its Race for the Cure sponsorship may not be integral to its positioning as a car manufacturer. However, it gives the Ford company and its products visibility and good vibes via its fundraising presence at Race for the Cure events, heightened visibility at car shows, and a "feel good" focus in Ford's marketing materials.

Timberland used corporate halo to demonstrate its company philosophy of going beyond merely making boots and apparel to making "good" in the communities where its employees live and work. For example, a portion of the proceeds for Chauffer sandals went to Share our Strength, a goodwill organization that supports women and their families. The shoes were displayed with a tag that informed customers of the effort, and a thank-you card inside the box thanked the purchasers for "putting their best foot forward." For Avon, on the other hand, "*the* company for women," its program to fight breast cancer is more than an auxiliary point—it is a pillar of its brand.

Perhaps the most dramatic example of women's responsiveness to corporate halo marketing was created by Anita Roddick, the founder of the Body Shop, who became the second richest woman in England, after the queen, by making good corporate citizenship the premise of her business. (Well, she *was* the second richest at the time. Now J.K. Rowling, author of the Harry Potter series, has surpassed both of them.) Roddick's cosmetic company differentiated and added value to its colors, soaps, and lotions by banning animal testing, providing economic support to indigenous cultures, and contributing actively to environmental causes.

4. Getting clear—painting the brand pink is sure to give your business the blues. The best initiatives targeted to women are not pink but transparent. In virtually every category, overtly characterizing a marketing program as "for women only" will backfire with both genders. Banks that talk about "women's unique financial needs" or computers that are positioned as "a woman's machine" are not likely to be regarded favorably. Why? Not only do they alienate men, who have a horror of anything "girly," they also make women suspicious: *So let me guess: does this mean it will cost more, like women's alterations? Or will it be dumbed down and lower quality, like that lavender set of garden tools?* Think twice before you think pink.

Here are a couple of examples of painting the brand pink that illustrate what I mean. The wine industry is slowly waking up to the fact that the majority of their product is purchased *and* consumed by women. So why not make a wine just for women? O'Brien Family Vineyard makes Seduction, a Napa Valley red described on the label as "a voluptuous wine with sensual flavors and a velvet kiss." The label on Seduction is black, with a large, gold "O" and is packaged in a translucent, burgundy-colored organza sack so that buyers will—as creator, Bart O'Brien, puts it—"have the pleasure of undressing it." He goes on: "When a woman walks into room with a bottle of Seduction, that's a statement of who she is." You probably won't be surprised that most women find this ridiculous. As one woman said, "Why would I serve anyone a wine that looks like it came from Victoria's Secret?"

There are exceptions, as demonstrated by Be Jane, an amazing company that has formed the first community for women's home improvement. Be Jane provides an online community of female DIYers, features home improvement tips and tricks, and showcases inspirational projects done by fellow "Janes." So they are doing a lot of things right when it comes to marketing to women. Imagine my surprise when I found my reaction to their Be Jane-branded rugged leather tool belt—in bright pink leather—was "Cute! I love it!" (Hey, before you make up your mind, check it out on its Web site. The tool belt's adorable, as are the three incredibly impressive, credentialed, and accomplished young businesswomen who founded this fast-growing media empire.) So while I don't generally encourage marketers to paint any-thing pink or make anything "special for women," the big difference is that this is coming *from* women and obviously a group very into the proposition that women can do whatever a man can do. It gives the pink toolbelt a different feel than if The Home Depot handed out a pink toolbelt to all of its Do It Herself workshop participants. It's kind of like the way we women can call ourselves "girls" and "chicks" if we want to, although we would not appreciate that same language from a business trying to market to us. It's one thing when the gesture says "we women . . ." and quite another when it says "you women." Exactly the sort of marketing communication detail you want to watch out for.

Now that we've explored ways to enhance your brand's appeal to women through positioning, let's start through the five stages of the consumer's purchase path—Activation, Nomination, Investigation and Decision, Retention, and Recommendation. Each of the 12 marketing elements potentially affects every stage of the purchase path. An Olympic sponsorship can be leveraged to perform any number of functions: generate awareness, create a corporate halo and favorable attitude, support a promotional incentive that comes into play at the point of purchase, and even strengthen existing customers' commit-ment to the brand. However, to focus this discussion on how to exe-cute each tactical approach to its best effect with women, you'll find each marketing element placed at the stage on the decision path where it probably carries the most weight.

Depending on your marketing objectives and the strategy you select to focus your efforts, you may want to start with the tactics highlighted in each stage as your core. Then you can look into extending the cre-ative concepts built on those tactics to other stages on the purchase path as well.

Activation: Getting in the Game

Before a consumer will start paying serious attention to any market-ing communication, she has to consider herself in the market, whether it's for a new car, a new cell phone, more life insurance, or another product or service. The trick for marketers is to find and reach that prospect right at the opportunity point when she puts her purchase decision into play. There are three ways to make sure you're in just the right place at just the right time: by *hooking her with news,* by *turning on the power of suggestion,* and by *intercepting her on her way.* Again remember that women drive this stage of the purchase process, so it's key to get their attention.

Extra! Extra! Hook Her with News

One way to reel her into the category is to offer her something extra or new—a new usage no one has thought too much about before or a new product never before seen in the category.

New usage. Many women who had been managing just fine without a cell phone in the mid-1990s suddenly put themselves in the market when Sprint suggested new usages to them. Up until then, cell phones had been seen mostly as a businessman's appendage. When Sprint pointed out that soccer moms could use them to manage their families' activities on weekends, or that single women could feel safer if they carried one for emergencies, they triggered the need—and earned themselves a pole position in the race to capture the purchase.

New product. While women aren't into novelty for the sake of novelty, any product that offers them a better twist on a valued benefit is always welcome. In the automotive category, for instance, the OnStar system was introduced as a new high-tech feature via ads featuring Batman, the ultragadget man—an approach that aligns perfectly with men's craving for cool and urge for adventure. However, it wasn't long until women recognized OnStar as a useful convenience that would help them get around without getting lost (safety) and even assist them in making a few calls en route (multitasking). OnStar's current ad campaign is a 180-degree turn from the Batman era. The current print ad features a mom cuddling her children and telling the story of how On Star saved her life. The family had been in an accident, and the mother was unconscious. But the OnStar system automatically located her car, the OnStar advisor's voice soothed her children, and help was sent immediately. The ad is in a multipage format in order to tell the entire story (like a magazine article), highlight GM's continuous safety features, and provide all of the wonderful family safety benefits and On-

Star safety statistics to make women feel good about having OnStar in their car. OnStar is no longer a luxury gadget but a must-have for a lot of women.

Combined with the Sprint cell phone example above, this little observation has substantial implications for marketing most high-tech products. These types of products are developed by tech-happy companies and marketed to tech-happy consumers—men—usually without too much exploration of the product's relevance to less-tech, more-touch consumers—women. On the other hand, with women making up a full 50 percent of the population, it's a market you won't want to overlook. In the two examples above, women find their own way into the category a few years after the innovation has become well distributed among early adopters.

So a marketer can capitalize on this pattern in one of two ways: Plan a "one-two punch" approach to introducing the product, first to men and then relaunched to women a few years later. Or preempt the competition by doing a dual launch, simultaneously targeting men and women with gender-tailored messages. The latter approach is, of course, more aggressive and somewhat riskier. But with the fierceness of global competition these days, consider the advantages of being first to go after "the second half," recruiting women to your brand before your competitors even turn their attention to them.

Communication Notes: Bringing Her News

If you're going to use an innovation to pull your consumer into the market, she obviously needs to know about it. That means:

- **Make a loud noise.** In addition to advertising funds, make sure you commit a healthy budget to publicity. Innovations and new angles like these new usages and new products are just the type of news the media are looking for.
- **Present the human interest side.** Make sure to present the innovation in the context of women's language and lifestyle. Not only will women relate to it more directly and quickly, but the human interest angle will make it much more likely to be picked up by the media than if there is just a product focus.

The Power of Suggestion—Highlight the Need

A more sophisticated version of "Would you like fries with that?" approach, this principle takes note of the fact that many of us don't really even know we need or want something until someone prompts us to consider it.

Consumer education—open her eyes. Consumer education marketing tactics tap into women's greater lust for information. As lifetime learners, they expect and value lessons and advice, whereas men are less likely to appreciate advice and sometimes resist it, seeing it as an attempt to one-up them and co-opt their autonomy. Often, it's simply a question of providing information the consumer may not have had before or creating awareness of a real need she'd just never thought about.

For instance, many women assume that if a woman's income is lower than her husband's, she doesn't need as much life insurance. When someone points out that if she were to die, he and the kids would not only lose her income but they'd have to hire someone to do all the cooking, cleaning, and child care, she realizes she may not have thought this through. To cover that added expense, in addition to the loss of income, a woman actually needs *more* insurance than a man of the same income.

The insurance company or agent doesn't create the need but rather raises awareness of a need that already exists. This type of information could be delivered by the company via a brochure or a PR news story, or by an insurance agent in a client phone call or community seminar—all are forms of consumer education that use the power of suggestion to activate the consumer's purchase process.

Seminars and workshops. Seminar selling is a very popular technique with financial services companies like American Express and Merrill Lynch, who have used it for years. Now, marketers in other categories are turning the technique to work for them. For example, The Home Depot recently began offering remodeling classes for women, covering topics like how to build a deck or how to lay tile. Once the "handywomen" know they can do it themselves, they have to buy tools and materials for their project, of course—which their host is more than delighted to provide.

FIGURE 8.2 Sur La Table: Seminars and Workshops

Sur La Table

Learn. Eat. Laugh.
Celebrate the pleasures of
life in our *convivial*
culinary classes.

The Home Depot execs initially worried that women might deem "women-only" classes to be offensive. In fact, the classes have been tremendously popular and have drawn a great response. One reason: women like the chance to work with other women, free from apprehension about men being impatient, competitive, or condescending as the women ask questions.

Tomboy Tools has taken this concept and created a business out of it. Tomboy Tools hosts in-home tool parties (think Tupperware) that emphasize interactive demonstrations, last about two hours, and include an overview of the company's tools. Tool parties have become so popular that the company launched an associate program to train women to run them.

Sur La Table differentiates itself from competitors in the high-end retail food and cooking category by offering a culinary program in a fun and relaxed setting with highly skilled chef-instructors from a wide variety of culinary backgrounds. Their ad (see Figure 8.2) makes the classes seem like so much fun!

Articles. If well associated with the individual and company providing them, articles in women's media can offer almost as much benefit as delivering a seminar. Of course, the face-to-face experience is always going to result in a higher conversion rate. But articles reach a lot more people and are a lot less expensive to develop.

Communication Notes: Consumer Education

When undertaking a consumer education tactic, keep these points in mind:

- **Know your market.** Don't assume you're talking to beginners unless you have some evidence of it.
- **Tailor your communications.** Remember the way women absorb and process information. Add context, lifestyle implications, and stories to the facts, charts, and blueprints you need to get through the materials.
- **Be sure to tell her to "bring a friend."** The social aspect will increase the appeal to her and double the audience for you.
- **Don't sell. Don't.** I know you've gone to some trouble to offer all this free learning, and you feel you've earned the right to put in a plug for your company and your products, but women seem to find this more distasteful than men do. Unobtrusive mentions of the examples you are most familiar with (namely, your products) are fine. But when the presenter shifts over into sales mode, women's reactions are to pull back—and the rapport you've worked so hard to build is broken.

Intercept Marketing: Arouse the Want

Another way to tap into the power of suggestion is to place the product in her path—and let nature take its course. Sometimes, "what you see is what you want." You weren't really planning to upgrade your laptop until next year, but then you saw the new Sony Vaio, and . . . *well, you really did sort of need a new laptop, and why wait until next year?*

Intercept marketing is about placing the product in your consumer's daily life and letting her generate her own impulse to acquire it. Unlike men, who are disinclined to interrupt their progress toward the current goal to explore something that's not on their task list, women are willing to make a short stop "on the way" to their destination and take a look at something that intrigues them. And sometimes, that's all it takes to start the buying juices flowing.

Go where the women are: "out and about" placement. Some companies like to be in the middle of large numbers of women, and the mall is usually a great location for that kind of event marketing. Such was the case when Buick Regal, partnering with retail giant Sears, brought its car models right into the mall for perusal up close and personal. Hyundai has taken that one step further and now has dealerships located inside malls. Sony is setting up shop next to the likes of Tiffany in upscale shopping malls to give consumers a more intimate shopping experience with a special effort to attract more female shoppers. Lifetime Television created a "spa on wheels" nationwide mall tour, where visitors got samples of soaps, body washes, and skin analyses in addition to advice on nutrition, fitness, beauty, and fashion. Fitness demos, style shows, makeovers, and other live performances drew crowds, and the event also highlighted Lifetime's advocacy efforts for stopping breast cancer and violence against women. At the tour's end, Lifetime had intercepted and shared its message with more than 120,000 women.

Go where the women are: sponsorships and alliances. Other companies prefer a more targeted, personalized approach, like Apple, which was one of the sponsors of a motivational conference attended by 10,000 women in middle management. In addition to the visibility and goodwill it earned as a sponsor, Apple outfitted its booth with ten demonstration models of a new laptop for these high-potential prospects to test drive. An example of partnership marketing that suggests a purchase through proximity comes from HEB, the leading grocery store chain in Texas. It created store-in-store concepts with partner retailers such as Verizon Wireless, Payless Shoes, and Wells Fargo Bank so that its female customers can multitask and get more shopping done during just one trip.

Go where the women are: bring the women to you. Use borrowed interest to attract women to your own events. Although one wouldn't expect a high turnout from an invitation to a minivan test-drive event, Oldsmobile Silhouette's marketers learned that hosting a women's golf clinic—and bringing along some minivans for the ride, as it were—generated curiosity, test drives, and ultimately several sales among clinic attendees.

Taking Action on the Activation

Once you've activated the consumer's buying process, make sure you provide a way for her to act on her impulse. The whole point of targeting the Activation stage is to be the only brand present when she experiences her first inclination to buy. But you have to *be prepared to capitalize on your advantage.*

Have plenty of follow-up information available. At the seminar, in the article, on location at the event, offer an abundance of brochures, videos, Web site links, and the like that are easy for the consumer to get to. Make sure the information is well branded and spells out how to get easy access to the seminar leader, article author, or company consumer services group.

And be ready to follow up with an appropriate consumer contact immediately after she's "met" you. Many companies include a contact-generating effort at events they sponsor—usually an offer or prize that motivates consumers to leave their business card. Most companies never do a thing with those valuable lists of consumer leads—because they haven't prepared ahead of time.

At the very least, have a letter prepared in advance to go out the following week, reminding her of your "meeting" at the event, communicating why your company was a sponsor of the event, and suggesting a next step that may be of interest to her, based on her attendance at the event. The connection can be tenuous, but you are trying to find a way to communicate "same-same," that you have something in common.

For example, I've spoken at a number of women's leadership forums in various cities, many of which have attracted automotive sponsorship. A hypothetical follow-up letter from BMW might say something like: *Thank you for stopping by our exhibit at the Women's Leadership Forum last week. BMW is proud to have sponsored that groundbreaking event as part of our ongoing commitment to support women in our community. Another of our programs that supports women is our Drive for the Cure initiative to raise funding for breast cancer research. This program has several facets, including our pledge to donate a dollar per mile for every test drive (up to $X). We would like to invite you to participate in this program and would welcome your call to schedule a test-drive. By the way, as part of our effort to make life easier for busy women like you, one of the services we offer is to bring the car to you at your office or home. Please give us a call so we can schedule a test drive at your convenience.*

Don't just dump the stack of business cards on the corner of some poor salesperson's desk for cold calling. Instead, use a well-planned follow-up to convert a *buying activation* into a *brand opportunity.*

Nomination: Surviving the First Cut

Influencing this stage of the purchase path deserves particular consideration when marketing to women because of a basic household truth. Even if a given purchase is unequivocally a joint decision—as it probably is, for instance, when the family is deciding where to go on vacation—it's the woman of the house who does the preliminary round of research.

She starts her shopping process by looking around for options that offer what she's interested in. In other words, she nominates some candidates to the short list. Differences in male/female priorities, process, and marketing response often result in different brands making the first cut. And when you think about it from a marketing point of view, the first cut is the unkindest cut of all, because it is where most of the brands in the marketplace get tossed out.

> The three deciding factors that determine whether a brand will make it on to that short list are:
>
> 1. **Top-of-mind awareness.** She can't consider your brand if she's never heard of it. Actually, it's more than that: your brand has to come up as a candidate more or less spontaneously before she's even started to do any serious research.
> 2. **Relevant differentiation.** Your brand has to stand out from other similar brands in some way that's relevant to her needs or preferences.
> 3. **Brand likability.** This is the Sally Field factor: "She likes you, she really likes you!" (Or at the very least, she's got nothing against you.)
>
> You can address all of these deciding objectives together through programs delivered via word of mouth, milestone marketing, and/or brand/image communications.

Word of Mouth: Worth a Mention

As we saw in Chapter 6, women are much more likely than men to start their purchase search by asking around. This is especially true when the benefits of the product are "invisible." In other words, the benefits can only be assessed through direct experience—for example, cell phone service, computers, and financial planning advisors.

In these typically "male" categories, a woman prospect will ask men their opinions, because men are assumed to be more experienced and knowledgeable in these categories. But she will *believe* women more for two reasons: First, she knows that another woman will better appreciate what elements are important to her. Second, she knows that when asked directly, men will have a tendency to overrate the product or service they use. They're concerned that if they admit it's not terrific, it would reflect poorly on their judgment in purchasing the product in the first place, which is—to men—a clear sign of weakness! Women, on the other hand, with their "full disclosure" and "let me help you" inclinations, are more likely to flag any areas of dissatisfaction that warrant notice. The marketer looking to maximize the *credibility* of his referrals will make sure his women customers are happy first.

Companies have even been formed to turn women's word of mouth into a business. BzzAgent harnesses word of mouth to turn loyal customers into a unique marketing and research channel that is powered by real brand evangelists. The company develops word-of-mouth programs that help clients market *with* their customers as opposed to *at* them. BzzAgent gives its network of more than 60,000 volunteer brand evangelists—or BzzAgents—the opportunity to experience a client's product or service firsthand. BzzAgents are then asked to form their own honest opinion and share it with others in natural conversations. They are awarded BzzPoints for every interaction they report, though more than 70 percent of all BzzPoints issued are never redeemed. Bzz-Points have no cash value. Not surprisingly, 70 percent of the agents are women. Tremor, a word-of-mouth operation that is a division of Procter & Gamble, has an astonishing 240,000 volunteer teenagers spreading the word about everything from toothbrushes to TV shows. A spin-off, Tremor Moms, is in the works.

Milestone Marketing: Finding the Receptive Mindset

Finding the receptive mindset means knowing *when* she is most likely to be looking. As we saw in Chapter 4, life events trigger new needs, and most of these needs fall into the woman's bailiwick to address.

Two of the most obvious life events are marriage and children, both of which affect a household's purchasing patterns very noticeably—and both of which affect female purchasing behavior much more dramatically than males'. Furniture, apparel, place of residence, choice of car, number of appliances, a desire for insurance . . . prospects for all of these major purchases can be found at the altar or in the maternity ward. And your understanding of her roles and her mindset within the context of these life-changing circumstances can turn the key to get you in the door at these critical times. Conversely, your lack of understanding can lock you out.

For example: Engaged women are big spenders—and not just at the bridal registry. Sure, they're buying veils and rings, but they're buying a lot more, too.

There are lots of media vehicles for reaching brides. Magazines like *Modern Bride, Bride's,* and *Bridal Guide* are all examples, as are Web sites like TheKnot.com, WeddingChannel.com, and Bridalzine.com. These vehicles are loaded with ads for dresses, flowers, china, jewelry, and honeymoon trips, but none shows ads for insurance, cars, cell phones, or financial services. (One major exception: Citigroup's Women and Co., which has done a brilliant job creating highly engaging ads for the *New York Times* wedding pages.) What a missed opportunity! Here's a segment of the women's market that's ready to buy, but only the dressmakers and wedding suppliers are talking to them. Remember: First in, first win. You're not just getting a newlywed; you're quite likely getting a customer—an entire family, eventually—for life.

There are plenty of other major life events that trigger consumer needs as well. And women, if approached appropriately, can be grateful for some help in these areas. They include buying a new house; starting, buying, or selling a business; or sending a son or daughter off to college. Similarly, a divorce, an inheritance, retirement, the death of a spouse—*all prompt women to spend money.* Some of these are joyful events, some are traumatic; all require a sensitive approach. In most cases, you'll find communications from the "expected" industries at these points. Your opportunity is to be the first in your industry to do the *unexpected.*

Special interest media. There's always an advertising vehicle aimed at people making one of these life transitions. New mothers are deluged with "care packages" in the hospital; people moving into a new neighborhood often are greeted by Welcome Wagon packages from local

FIGURE 8.3 Engaged Women Buy Big-Ticket Items

Women in their 20s	Past 12 months (%) Single	Engaged
Buy/change insurance	31	43
Buy/lease new car	13	41
Open new bank account	20	36
Change cell phone	14	24
Buy stocks or bonds	12	20

Source: Study by *Modern Bride*/Roper Starch, reported in *Marketing to Women* newsletter, Feb. 2001, pp. 1 and 3.

merchants; graduation from high school generates a rash of direct mail contacts. A little research will locate the delivery vehicle.

Positioning hook. The power of this approach is that you may well be the only one in your category connecting with this audience in this vehicle. (Remember, just because no one else has thought of it *doesn't mean it doesn't make sense.* Look at the numbers in Figure 8.3 for the percentage of engaged women who buy/lease a new car and explain to me why there aren't any car ads in bridal magazines.) Nonetheless, because you are presenting your brand in a very specific context here, it would strengthen your message to make the connection to the context.

Making a Good Impression

To make the first cut, it's not necessary for the consumer to have a lot of detailed information yet. What drives this stage is a general feeling that this is "the right kind of brand" for her, not solely from a product quality point of view but also from a positioning that puts it in her competitive set and from a favorable overall corporate reputation. Your best bets at affecting this "general impression," in addition to word of mouth, are brand/image advertising and public relations.

Brand/image advertising. This kind of advertising should put its power behind one of three objectives (all of which overlap to some extent, but let's look at them separately for purposes of discussion):

1. *Establishing what "class/type" of product it is.* The consumer may not know anything about Mazda cars, except that she starts humming "zoom ZOOM zoom" every time she thinks Mazda, which tells her it's a fun car to drive. If that's what she's looking for, that's enough to get Mazda on her initial short list.

2. *Communicating who the user is.* You could do what Mitsubishi's been doing lately. In an effort to add youthful appeal to its brand, it's been running a slew of TV ads with teenagers or very young adults in the car listening to the latest tunes and doing something self-expressive: dancing, singing along, and so on. Gap communicates it's not just for kids anymore through ads celebrating diversity of age, gender, race, and lifestyle.

3. *Creating a distinctive brand personality.* These ads don't communicate much about either the product or the user; their goal is to make the brand/company *likable.* You know who's done a fabulous job with that? Brawny paper towels. Its Web site, http://www.brawnyman.com, offers 10 to 15 30-second tongue-in-cheek film vignettes, all featuring a real-life Brawny man, whose rugged, manly appearance harbors the soul of every woman's dream: a guy who asks about her day, compliments her new hairstyle, listens attentively, rubs her tired feet, brings her tea and all things perfect. Brawny Man is attractive and touching because he is so sincere and tries so hard . . . but in each vignette there's a sly, wry tweak to the story. The cumulative effect as you get to know this adorable guy through the series of vignettes (I clicked through each and every one—they're addictive!) is so hilarious you'll find yourself laughing out loud. Likable? You bet. (For the love of this Web site alone, I swear I'll never buy another brand of paper towels).

Public relations: good deeds and disasters. This is a secondary, less-flexible approach than brand/image advertising, but it warrants your consideration here for two reasons. First, public relations (PR), as distinguished from product publicity, is an image medium. If you can get out the good news about your company's commitment to customers, commitment to employees, community support programs, and other good deeds, this all contributes to building a brand or company personality that matters to women.

Second, and conversely, if you're not ready with a contingency plan to quickly address any PR disaster with integrity, you're going to hear the sound of women's wallets snapping shut so fast you won't know what hit you. I can tell you, though: It's the reverberation of the sound of "no"—*no more of my time, no more of my consideration,* and *no more of my money.* The good news is that women do take the good news seriously, but the bad news is that they take the *bad news* like a ton of bricks.

Investigation and Decision! Crossing the Finish Line

OK. You've got a horse in the Derby—that's great news! You're not over the finish line yet, though; now you've got to figure out how you're going to win. Interestingly enough, the marketing mantras for this stage of the consumer motivation process are completely different from those for the previous one.

Perceived Product Advantage

The subtitle says *perceived* because perception can be influenced as much by skillful *communications about the product* as by the product itself. Given two identical products, the marketer who can best illustrate how the brand delivers the benefits the collective "she" wants, and do so in language she can relate to, will win the sale. And the word *advantage* is to emphasize that no matter how good your product may be in the absolute, she will not be ready to make a decision until she has compared several options. Your brand will be one in a lineup of options, and you have to have some edge if you want to be the chosen one. This has implications for what you include in your product/information communications, as you'll see below.

Included within the idea of perceived product advantage is the concept of *value*. The price she's willing to pay is a function of whether she feels the item is "worth it." If she sees more benefit in one option versus another, she's willing to pay more for it (up to a point). So, net-net, on the product dimension the brand that delivers the most advantage for the best value will win the Perfect Answer prize.

Product/Information Communications: A Voracious Need to Know

Nobody really knows why, but everybody pretty much agrees: women want more. They want more facts, more answers, more access. Maybe it's the shopping training we get from girlhood or the gatherer instinct from prehistoric times, but when we're making a serious purchase decision, we want to make sure we've checked it out, inside and out, backwards and forwards, and upside down if necessary. Men don't do it that way. Men focus on "the important stuff," the "high, hard ones." (I guarantee you: no woman came up with *that* expression!) Men prefer their communications streamlined. The point to take away here is this: if you design your informative communications for men's minds, women will find them lacking.

General Motors continues to innovate and recently launched its "Women in the Driver's Seat" Web site to educate, inform, and empower women making major automotive buying and servicing decisions. The site gives readers straightforward information on buying a vehicle, servicing a vehicle, and safety on the road. The site includes checklists with detailed information on what a prospective car buyer needs to know when going for a test drive, negotiating a price, or taking delivery of a vehicle. The data are also available in printed guides, which can be picked up at participating GM dealerships and at GM Auto Shows in Motion held around the country.

- *Make sure the benefit emphasis is female friendly.* Translate the raw product feature information into women-relevant lifestyle benefits (e.g., instead of only saying "The car accelerates from 0 to 60 in seven seconds," complete the thought by adding, "which gives you the power you need to safely merge into freeway traffic").
- *Deliver the message using the precepts of women's Communication Keys.* Context, stories, and personal details will draw women into your message and ensure that your points register on their radar screen.
- *Provide comparisons with several key competitors.* At first, this will seem counterintuitive: Why would you provide your prospects

with information on your competitors? But look at it this way: she's going to do the comparison anyway. And she's not going to buy until she's done the due diligence to her satisfaction. By providing her with the information she wants, you both direct her perspective and accelerate the decision process.

Suppose you offered this feature on your Web site: she can select the model she's interested in and can include three competitors. Then she clicks on the criteria she wants comparisons on. The site presents the information in easy-to-compare chart form—and it also provides editorial comment. Mazda provides just such an electronic comparison device with a kiosk located at one of its new dealerships where customers are encouraged to step right up to a kiosk to research sticker prices. The kiosk is part of Mazda's new retail strategy still in the early stages of implementation, which hinges on the high degree of power the customer now has when shopping for a car. Enabled by the Internet, the customer has new expectations and bargaining power and, in many cases, has made the purchase decision online. Mazda dares to compare, which will allow women to research their options right there in the Mazda dealership, which in turn will speed up their readiness to decide. The benefit to Mazda is the opportunity to respond on the spot to any questions or objections that may arise during her research, before she leaves the dealership.

Personal Interaction

Sales are not made by product alone. Because of her predisposition toward people and relationships, a woman will find herself inclined to buy from the salesperson who is most successful at creating a rapport. The desire to award the business to "the better person" will weigh more strongly in her considerations than in a man's.

Face-to-face: make it or break it. Women appreciate being told, but they hate being sold. What's the difference? Mostly it's in the point of view of the salesperson. Women want to feel they are partnering with an advocate, not resisting an adversary. I'm not saying it will cinch the sale if a product isn't satisfactory, but it will definitely break the sale if the personal interaction is *not*. Chapter 10 is devoted entirely to spelling out the selling skills that are most likely to motivate women, so we won't spend much time on it here. For now, let's just cover one warning signal that tells you your presentation is coming off the tracks.

She's not buying it. Watch for head nods and little "mm-hmm" sounds of acknowledgment. When they stop, *you stop*. Head nods have a whole different role in male and female conversation. For men, head nods mean agreement: the listener agrees with the speaker. For women, though, head nods are how they encourage participation; they mean "go on" rather than "yes, I buy what you're saying." So men are confused when they get head nods from women and then are told "I hear what you're saying, but I don't agree with it." Again, what they should be watching for is when the head nods stop. In woman-speak, that means "I've heard enough, but because it's your turn, I won't interrupt you." When that happens, it's time to take a breath and ask a few questions: let her have her say so you can learn more about what she's looking for.

Retail Environment: Don't Waste Her Time or Yours

Remember, women give more consideration to context and greater sensitivity to their surroundings. When a woman walks into a car dealership, a doctor's office, or a bank, she immediately starts receiving and assessing signals that will factor into her overall impression of the product and the company. What a golden moment to send her a message! Instead, many companies let her stand—or sit—*waiting*.

Waiting time. Studies show this is *overwhelmingly* the single most important factor affecting a shopper's opinion of store service.[8] It's likely that it affects women even more than men, because multitaskers feel they're being kept from moving ahead on several additional projects. To "unitaskers," waiting, though frustrating, is still on task and still oriented toward that sole goal they're pursuing. A few principles of retail design, office décor, and even common courtesy can go a long way toward overcoming her sensation of wasting time—and your mistake of wasting opportunity:

1. *Reduce waiting time for routine tasks by providing alternatives.* An example would be check-in at a business hotel, where there are always long lines around 3:00 PM when rooms become available. Instead of having customers wait in line to obtain a key from a front desk clerk, why not set up kiosks in the lobby? Guests could insert a credit card and receive an e-key plus directions to the room.

2. *Make waiting time more productive.* Some places, like Jiffy Lube and doctors' offices, have waiting time built in. In that case, help her make good use of it. Jiffy Lube, recognizing that 65 percent of auto repair/maintenance visits are handled by women,[9] is experimenting with offering free local phone calls and Internet access to customers waiting for their car.

3. *Offer some modest amenities and courtesies.* Jiffy Lube, as part of its very savvy program to capture the women's market, has redesigned its waiting rooms to make them more appealing to women by including CD listening stations, new furniture and color schemes, general interest women's magazines, Starbucks coffee, and satellite TV. Feedback has been very favorable; in a recent survey, 54 percent of the respondents who visited one of the remodeled sites in Chicago stated that the appearance of the waiting area "improves the likelihood" that they will return to Jiffy Lube.[10]

One of my favorite case studies is for MinuteClinic (see Figure 8.4) because it shows that someone has finally figured out an answer to the "waiting" conundrum at the doctor's office.

MinuteClinic

Opportunity:

The answer to many a mother's prayers! MinuteClinic is based on the premise that certain simple health problems can be more quickly and inexpensively diagnosed and treated at a walk-in clinic than in a doctor's office or an emergency room. The idea for the company came about in 1999 when Steve Pontius and two business associates were meeting to discuss a medical Web site they wanted to launch for physicians. During a break, the men complained about the hassles they encountered in taking their children to the doctor for simple ailments. As a father of four, Pontius says "you just know" when it's an ear infection, but waiting several hours to be treated is a huge hassle. As they swapped stories, Pontius soon realized he had stumbled onto a market niche, and the idea for MinuteClinic was born.

Strategies:
MinuteClinic employs nurse practitioners supported by software that helps them diagnose and treat a handful of medical conditions, including strep throat, ear and sinus infections, pink eye, bronchitis, bladder infections, and the flu. They also offer back-to-school vaccinations and flu shots as well as screenings for thyroid, glucose, and the like. Because no visit takes more than 15 minutes and there are no appointments scheduled, MinuteClinic is an ideal solution for professionals and working parents who cannot afford time away from the workplace. The result is a convenient care system that saves patients, employers, and insurers time and money. Interestingly, although MinuteClinic was originally the brainchild of a group of men, its benefits accrue primarily to women, who are more often the "designated parent" when it comes to doctor visits.

Insights that MinuteClinic tapped into:

- **Multitasking/"On the Way"**
  A major component of MinuteClinic's strategy is to locate the centers near places people go anyway, including universities, office complexes, large employer headquarters (e.g., Best Buy) and retail stores, like Target, Cub Foods, and CVS. What could be more of a time saver than having health care in an in-and-out convenient retail location that is open for extended hours so that you can get a checkup, shop for household items, and fill the prescription right then and there? At Target and Cub Foods, MinuteClinic even offers its customers beepers, so they can shop and then be called when it's time for their appointment. To make it even more convenient, MinuteClinic is now offering the capability to get in line (as there are no appointments) from the home or work computer or even by phone.

- **Word of mouth/surprise and delight**
  Women are a marketing medium unto themselves. The word-of-mouth phenomenon takes place every day among women, and they have the power to make or break a brand. MinuteClinic's rapid success is a result

of word of mouth—50 percent of new customers come from satisfied referrals. To quote the CEO, Linda Hall Whitman: "This really is viral (pardon the pun) marketing at its best." The fast, friendly, inexpensive, and high-quality service certainly speaks for itself. But MinuteClinic has also employed a wonderful "surprise and delight" tactic—each customer gets a handwritten Get Well card within a week after the Minute-Clinic visit. How thoughtful!

- **Milestone marketing**
  Milestones often create changes in a person's health and health care, and MinuteClinic has tapped into this truth in its first TV campaign, which is about a bride about to be married who experiences pain in her ear and can no longer ignore it. So she dashes off to the Minute-Clinic to get her ear examined and medicine to clear up the problem, and she's back in time to gracefully sweep into her wedding and then sail off into the sunset, happily ever after (see Figure 8.4).

Results:

Under CEO Linda Hall Whitman, the company changed its model to target insurers and large employers that pay their employees' health care costs directly. The move has paid off handsomely: since inception in 2000 and based on projections through the end of 2005, MinuteClinic will tally over 300,000 patient visits and will have saved uninsured individuals, self-insured employers, and health insurance companies over $15 million and countless hours of wasted time.

What's more, MinuteClinic is adding sales to its partners' bottom line, as 55 percent of customers buy general merchandise, 40 percent buy OTC drugs, and 95 percent fill their prescriptions at their MinuteClinic locations.

Hall Whitman concludes: "MinuteClinic found a fundamentally better way to diagnose common illnesses and provide the right remedy, quickly and conveniently. But more importantly, we have been able to fulfill an unmet consumer need for more patient-centric health care. The secret to our success is based on our desire to help consumers, especially busy women, which has translated into our 99 percent customer satisfaction rate."

We hope to see MinuteClinic succeed (and can't wait for there to be one in our neighborhood!). Hall Whitman expects expansion to more than 350 clinics in 20 metropolitan areas by 2008.

FIGURE 8.4 MinuteClinic: Multitasking/"On the Way"

MinuteClinic Inc.

FIGURE 8.4 MinuteClinic: Milestone Marketing (Continued)

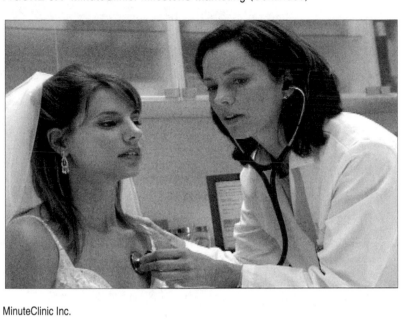

MinuteClinic Inc.

Sensory reception. Women are more receptive on all five sensory channels, meaning they are more appreciative of the nice touches and more repelled by the not-so-nice. Let's take a car dealership as an example to illustrate ways to respond to this difference:

- *Vision.* Environs will be noticed as much as the inside of the showroom. For instance, landscaping, attractive signage, and orderly displays all contribute to an overall impression of a well-run establishment, whereas salesmen loitering outside the front door smoking will not.
- *Colors.* Don't just settle for white walls. Use colors to create a sense of energy and enthusiasm in the showroom (e.g., vivid red), alertness and organization in the finance office, and relaxation and calmness in the service area (soft blue).
- *Hearing.* Use environment-appropriate music the same way as color. Make sure the music isn't too loud for her more sensitive ears. I once visited a small shop that sold elegant, upscale paper products—gorgeous textured invitations and beautiful leather-

bound journals. The young sales clerk, who was solo in the store, had elected to play what was evidently her preferred style of music—disco. I tried not to care, but it was impossible for me to savor these lovely products while bombarded by the BeeGees. As I escaped, my parting thought was, "My goodness—I hope the owner finds out what's driving her customers away before she goes out of business."

- *Touch.* Women are more tactile. A study conducted in Sprint Cellular retail stores revealed that whereas men were content to examine the phones behind glass, women wanted to handle them to assess weight and "hand feel." Women also prefer more texture in the environment: softer fabrics on furniture, textured finishes on walls, thicker carpeting, and the like. Sephora has revolutionized the beauty industry by taking cosmetics out from behind the glass, as it is typically sold in department stores.

- *Smell.* Women prefer areas that feel and smell clean, so service areas can be unpleasant for women. The best of them look dingy; the worst look and smell dirty. Clean up the grime and add a little shine.

- *Notice/Recall details.* Even tidiness can make a difference. A few small things out of place—the retail equivalent of a dirty dish or a pair of socks on the floor—will get noticed and create dissonance for women.

Incentives: There's More to Motivation Than Money

Traditionally, the role of incentives has been to *influence brand choice:* by giving the customer a discount, or some added value, the company is giving her a reason to choose one brand over another. While that dynamic is still alive and well with women, there's also another reason to provide incentives: *to break through women's Spiral Path decision* process. Deflect the urge to pursue "the perfect decision" and encourage her to make a good move *now.* And that leads to different offers, different timing, and different language. As incentives, offer what women want:

- *Services instead of money.* Customer service is a given now in any retail situation. Companies that say "what makes us different is our service and our knowledgeable, helpful, kind, and courteous people" are kidding themselves and not keeping an eye on their competitors, who are all saying the same thing! But customer *services* that save women time would be a huge hit. One enterprising stationery store in my neighborhood defended itself against the "big box" office/school supply giants with an innovative promotion aimed at saving moms time during the busy season. They got the supplies list from every teacher in the district and would prepack a shopping bag for you. All you had to do was call up in advance and say "Mrs. Burgess's Class" and an hour later, you could waltz in, pick up your bag, pay, and waltz out three minutes later. When I had young babies and found myself hauling mass quantities of diapers, wipes, and formula into the house each week (all while managing an infant and toddler, mind you!), I used to dream about a retailer who would bring it to me in a weekly delivery. Would I have signed a six-month contract? You bet. What's a few dollars compared to that kind of convenience?

Current car dealership promotions are universally the same: a cacophony of cash offers focused on financing and discounts. You can't tell one from the other, which makes you think they must all be ineffective. A car dealership seeking to capture a high share of the women's market could run a promotion offering special service to everyone who buys during the promotional time frame: free car pickup and drop-off at the office or at home for regular maintenance checks and repairs. Or a car company could offer a chance to win one year of unlimited access to a driver/ errand runner who could chauffeur the kids, meet you at the airport, pick up prepared meals, handle any little driving errand that comes to mind. Actually, a really cool prize would be to offer women a one-year contract with a "rent-a-wife" service that could handle *all* those errands. I've so often heard women wish they could delegate to someone.

- *"Sharable" prizes.* Fly her with her husband, kids, and one more adult (Mom or babysitter) for two weeks in the Bahamas; or let her invite four friends to Montana for a "girls' getaway" soft adventure trip. Timberland sponsored a three-week long sweepstakes in conjunction with Macy's/Dillard's stores that celebrated the "endless possibilities" of being a woman by offering the chance to win an enriching life experience for herself and a friend or friends. The grand prize winner received her choice of private cooking lessons for herself and a friend with Chef Traci Des Jardins of the Acme Chophouse in San Francisco; a collaborative community service project for the winner and 30 friends; or a retreat at Red Mountain Spa in Ivins, Utah.

How You Benefit from Women-Oriented Promotions and Prizes

Women-oriented promotions, which are basically female-oriented offers with a time-limited deadline, will benefit your business in three ways:

1. **Attract attention to your brand.** Female-friendly prizes like those above are new and different, a great way to distinguish your brand from the competitive pack.
2. **Extend awareness and participation.** Word of mouth will travel. Unusual approaches like these are fun and worth a mention, which will not only drive awareness and participation but also keep the memory floating around a lot longer than a run-of-the-mill, business-as-usual offer.
3. **Shorten decision time.** If a time-sensitive promotional offer gets her to close the sale faster, then its work here is done.

- *"Chick" prizes.* These are things women love and just never get enough of. Give them flowers (a fresh bouquet each month); foot rubs or a full body massage once a week for a year; or a library of chick flick videos and a year's supply of popcorn for four. They'll respond to your promotion and tell their friends to enter too, and if they win, they'll never stop talking about your company. Even if your end users are mostly men, don't forget who the buyer is. One of my friends went into a local store called "Bleachers Sports," which focuses on sports memorabilia in the form of baseball cards, collectibles, and such. During this visit, the friendly owner came up to her and said he was running a "Moms only" NCAA basketball pool—he entered everyone's name into a random pool, assigned random teams, and if your team got into the Final 4, you won a prize. And not just any prize—first place was a $100 gift certificate to Miss Behave, a sassy women's clothing store just down the street. And second place was a gift certificate for his store, which of course would be shared with the kids. My friend will definitely patronize his store more because he appreciates his "mom" clientele.

Retention and Recommendation: Making the Most of Current Customers

Once the customer has bought a brand, she converts from being a "prospect" to being a "customer." Given women's greater loyalty after the initial purchase, they're basically yours to lose from thereon out. As long as you don't do anything too egregious (she's forgiving but only up to a point), she'll keep coming back. For this stage, the marketer has two objectives:

1. Build the customer relationship and enhance her sense of brand commitment, so she returns to the brand for any subsequent or related purchases.
2. Motivate her to become an enthusiastic brand ambassador and recommend the brand to her family, friends, and acquaintances.

Unfortunately (for themselves), at this point most marketers drop the ball and turn their attention to the next prospect. The reason for this is actually understandable, though still not forgivable from a business point of view. Marketing and salespeople are generally charged with developing *sales revenue,* whereas focusing on current customers boosts *profit.* Focusing on current customers may get smaller incremental sales revenue per customer, but each dollar of revenue takes so much less time, communication, and effort to generate that it's more than worth it from a profit point of view. Nobody really tracks it that way, however, until all the different departments' operational costs hit the bottom line in the corner office. As a result, nobody really gets credit for it—and as a result of *that,* nobody really cares (except the customer and the stockholders, of course!).

When you ignore your current women customers, you're leaving a lot of money on the table—more than you realize. We're talking not only about her own future purchases but also those of her neighbors, her friends, her family, and so on. In life insurance, over the lifetime of a customer women provide an average of 28 referrals compared with 15 from men. This means that each and every woman customer brings in a lot more money than hers alone—and a lot more than her male counterpart does.

Help Your Customer Take Care of You

Most discussions of customer relations focus on how you and your company should take care of the customer—certainly an essential point in marketing, as you know. For the moment, though, let's reserve our consideration of customer care for Chapter 10. Here, let's discuss *how to help your customer take care of you.*

GenderTrends Genius: Dori Molitor

President, WatersMolitor, Marketing Brands to Women; (952) 797-5000; dmolitor@watersmolitor.com

Turn Women Consumers into Brand Enthusiasts
Everyone says they're targeting women, yet most women don't feel understood by marketers. According to the Yankelovich Monitor, 59 percent of women feel misunderstood by food marketers, 66 percent in the area of health care, 73 percent in automotive, and 84 percent in investing!

Imagine: 60 to 80 percent of women consumers feel misunderstood by the marketers who depend on them for their survival. Now that's an opportunity!

Traditional marketing's failure to understand women illustrates its inability to look beyond functional and attitudinal motivators for the deeper sociological, cultural, and psychological underpinnings of women's true purchase behaviors.

Learn the three critical steps to creating a bond with women consumers that translates into cash register rings. (Continued on page 300)

Make it easy for her to send you more customers. Make it easy, not only for *her* to shop in your store or on your site, but also for her to *send her girlfriends and family* there. One marvelous device, pioneered by Amazon.com and now used on a number of the more sophisticated shopping Web sites (even The Home Depot has one), is the wish list. Like bridal or baby registries, wish lists "institutionalize" shopper referrals. When asked by her best friend what she wants for Christmas, the wish list holder can say, "Oh, I don't know. I've got a wish list on Amazon, if you want to take a look at the kinds of things I like." Wouldn't the husband be just as grateful as the wife if the response to the annual dilemma of the perfect birthday present were, "Well, you could check my wish list at Tiffany"? (Oh, all right, at Target would probably be more realistic for most of us.) Every wish list brings in 5 to 25 new shoppers per list holder. And the next step is to enhance the service with event reminders, like those used by Proflowers, Harry & David, and Red Envelope.

Make it easier for her to come back to you than to try out one of your competitors. For example, one program pioneered by Cary Broussard, the highly innovative and dynamic leader of Wyndham Hotel's initiative to focus on women business travelers, is the Wyndham by Request registered customer profile. The profile keeps track of which newspaper she prefers, what she likes to have in her minibar when she arrives, whether she prefers a foam or feather pillow, how many extra towels she needs, what kind of juice she likes with her breakfast, and a host of other personal details. So whenever she's traveling and needs a hotel, naturally she's going to check Wyndham first, because she knows things are going to be just exactly as she likes them when she arrives, saving her a handful of calls to get set up in a new hotel. Incidentally, when Wyndham launched its women's initiative in 1995, women constituted 19 percent of its guests, same as the industry average. In 2001, that figure roared ahead to 35 percent of total guests, while their competitors' ratios stayed the same. Women now account for 50 percent of all Wyndham travelers and 35 percent of Wyndham's business travel base. And because the number of male guests has grown, too, it's plain to see that Wyndham's women are all incremental customers bringing in lots of incremental dollars.

Make it easy for her to give you more of her business. *Cross-selling* means persuading her to buy additional related products from you. *Up-selling* means either convincing her to buy more or to buy the enhanced/premium version. Focusing your marketing dollars on prospects who are already buying from you and therefore more receptive than average is a highly efficient way to boost your marketing ROI. Think of it as twice the sales for half the price. There are two key opportunities for cross-selling and up-selling to women.

Initial purchase—multiple items that go together. The first opportunity is *at the initial purchase* and draws on women's inclination to view any individual item as part of a larger context. Department stores have this figured out: whereas men's apparel is usually organized by type (shirts, jackets, slacks, etc.), women's apparel is usually organized by outfits. Women who come in intending to buy a new pair of slacks generally leave with a coordinating blouse, sweater, and perhaps a jacket as well. Catalogs are able to take this a step further and integrate the belt, shoes, and jewelry into the outfit.

The same principle is being applied in other retail contexts as well. For example, home improvement stores have taken a strong interest in women customers over the past several years. These traditionally male environments are starting to merchandise their bathroom and kitchen fixtures and décor items as coordinated "collections." The big idea? Find ways to group related products together, both "anchor" items and accessories. You will find women willing and interested.

Another industry that could do this is banking. Consider a "new mover" package for out-of-towners moving into a new neighborhood: in addition to the mortgage, the bundle could include banking, checking, and investment products. Similarly, a "college loan" package could include a loan for the parents to help with tuition plus checking, savings, and a credit card for the kid. Think of the incremental business that will fall into your lap simply because you thought to suggest it to someone who was buying from you anyway. (McDonald's has been masterful at drumming this into their order takers.)

Current customers—offering more of the same and trading up. The second opportunity is to *focus more of your marketing efforts on following up with your current customer.* It is a marketing truism that *sourcing* more of your sales from current customers is more efficient and therefore more profitable. The reason is that it requires fewer marketing dollars and less sales effort, because current customers already

know and like your brand, store, salesperson, and/or company, so there's not as much convincing required.

Women customers are likely to be even more receptive than men for two reasons: First, as we saw in Chapter 6, women put so much more research into their first purchase that they are inclined to amortize their investment by staying brand loyal on subsequent purchases. Second, women weight relationships more heavily than men do, so they are inclined to award their business to the person who served them well in the first place.

Reach out to your current customers by creating and maintaining direct marketing databases that help you keep track not only of your customers' contact information but also of their purchases and preferences. Offer them additional items related to what they own (which you'll know, because you'll track this information in your database). And after enough time has elapsed for them to be in the market again, give them a special offer on the premium model of what they bought last time. With this strategy, you will get a higher response rate from a more focused marketing expenditure. Moreover, you will make your current customers feel special, which will reinforce their commitment to your brand.

Maximizing Your Impact: Leverage a Strategy, Not a Tactic

So many tactics, so little–time? money? strategy? So little *strategy!* When marketers introduce a new advertising campaign, launch a new product, or sometimes even just add a product improvement, *it's a big deal.* It changes everything: the message, the media, the motivational dynamics. The change permeates every element of the company's communications· television, print, the sales materials, in-store signage, collateral.

Oddly enough, though, when marketing to women, some marketers seem to think that they can put a picture of a woman in one of their print ads and call it a day. That's not strategy; that's just plain ineffective. You might as well know up front: If you're not ready to make a commitment to this market, don't expect it to come running into your arms. One delightful date is not enough to make a marriage. And it would be foolish to think you can woo the women's market with a single contact, a tentative program, or a short-term outlook. Only a comprehensive program, integrating several different tactics and creating numerous communication opportunities, can build the kind of brand presence you need to persuade a person. This is especially true when that person is a woman because of women's drive for context and search for the Perfect Answer.

The role of strategy is to make it easier to choose which tactics will return the most bang for your marketing buck. There are millions of programs and communications you could use; the trick is to choose the ones that will do the most good. Start by figuring out which stage of the woman's decision process offers the most opportunity for increasing your business. Concentrate most of your tactical efforts on that stage rather than spreading your initiatives across the decision process. Nobody has enough money to do a good job across the entire process.

You need to avoid spreading yourself too thin. Use your strategy as your screener. There are lots and lots of impressive and interesting marketing tactics in the world. Unless a tactic has a laserlike focus on the purchase path you decided would do your brand the most good, don't bother with it. It will only diffuse your message and defuse your marketing efforts.

Figure 8.5 is a reference chart to help remind you of which strategies and tactics offer the most leverage at each stage of the woman consumer's purchase path. Only someone with an in-depth understanding of your market conditions, your marketing objectives, and your consumers can decide where to put your focus and how you should allocate your resources.

The discussions in this chapter showed you how to tailor those tactics to make them most effective with women consumers. Chapter 9 will highlight communication considerations to keep in mind as you are signing off on specific media buys or the copy and visuals for your marketing materials.

FIGURE 8.5 Marketing Contacts along the Consumer Purchase Path

DECISION STAGE	ACTIVATION	NOMINATION	INVESTIGATION & DECISION	RETENTION & RECOMMENDATION
DECIDING FACTORS	Awakening the Need	Awareness Relevant Differentiation Brand Likability	Perceived Product Advantage Personal Relationship	Brand Commitment Customer Relationship
TACTICAL KEYS	**Extra! Extra!— Bring Her Some News** • New Product, New Usage • Advertising & Publicity	**Word of Mouth** • Asking Around • Credibility	**Info Communications** • Print, Web, Collateral, In-store Communications • Comparison Shopping • Value	**Take Care of the Customer . . .** • Service & Support • 1-1 Continuous Learning Database • Problem Resolution • Surprise & Delight
	Power of Suggestion • Consumer Education • Workshops & Seminars • Article Placement • Intercept Marketing • "Out & About" • Sponsorships & Alliances • Proprietary Events	**Milestone Marketing** • Special-interest Media • Positioning Hook	**Shopping Experience** • Salesperson Interaction • Retail Environment	**. . . and Help Her Take Care of You** • Making It Easy • Cross-/Up-selling • Referrals
		Making a Good Impression • Image Advertising—TV, Print, Out-of-home • Public Relations— Good Deeds and Disasters	**Incentives** • What Women Want • Why You Should Give It to Them	

CHAPTER 9

Go! Communications
That Connect

You know whom you're targeting and have a strong understanding of how she thinks about your product and your brand. You've chosen your tactics and know what kinds of communications you need to develop. From Chapter 9 you will learn how to

- get the most out of your media budget when targeting women.
- frame your brand's message within the context of female gender culture.
- watch for executional details that can make or break your communications materials.

Media/Delivery Vehicles: Seeing Past the Numbers

Conventional media planning starts out as a straight numbers game and then quickly turns into a matter of opinion. Using sophisticated computer models and highly segmented demographic information, good media planners can develop a hundred different media vehicle combinations that deliver about the same number of people in the primary target audience. Then they apply judgment and experience to point out qualitative differences and recommend which is a better fit with the overall feel of the brand, tone of the campaign, or advertising objectives. Here are some additional considerations that should be factored in when developing media plans to motivate women.

Word of Mouth

We've talked about the prevalence and power of women's word of mouth, but consider this interesting idea: *women as a human medium.* Why not recognize and take advantage of this uniquely female phenomenon to stretch your media dollars? Once you've met your primary media goal, take a second look at the numbers and give some weight to the "chat factor."

Circle of influence. When choosing among plans that deliver equally well against the primary target definition, men or women, take a minute to compare how each delivers against women overall. The more female spillover you have, the more aunts and mothers and neighbors and coworkers you have on your communications team.

Dual audience: tip toward women. Some media plans are developed against a dual audience demographic, often expressed as something like "Adults, 25–49." When comparing options in this case, don't overlook an internal check of the female/male ratio in the plan. The higher the ratio, the farther your message goes.

Image and Information: Split the Message

An ongoing tension in advertising is the dual need to create a strong brand identity, while at the same time communicating enough specific product information to sway an immediate buying decision. Women's greater response to both the image and the informational components could be viewed as a stalemate—or as a strategic opportunity. The solution? Split the job.

For *brand/image communications,* you need media vehicles that can offer a rich message in a short amount of time. TV, magazines, and radio are able to bring imagination and emotion to your message, components that are often key to creating brand/image advertising that sticks. The proliferation of highly targeted cable channels makes broadcast affordable, even for smaller media budgets. And you may not always think of it right away, but *outdoors* (billboards) can be effective here as well. They're sort of like the haiku of advertising: very short format, very little time to make your point, but if you get it right, tremendous punch.

For conveying *product information,* particularly in the depth that your women prospects are seeking, you're going to want to use media that accommodate long format copy. For advertising, this means magazines and newspapers. Sometimes, say in financial services, women will want even more information than you can cover in an ad, so be sure to make it easy for them to access it by offering brochures via a toll-free number or by directing them to your Web site. And don't forget to make the most of your in-store presence by posting informative merchandising materials and take-one collateral right there at the point of sale. In addition, three new technologies that didn't even exist five years ago are rapidly evolving, making it ever easier and more cost efficient to quickly distribute just the right information to just the right customer at just the right time: Web sites and e-marketing, electronic in-store merchandising, and increasingly sophisticated database management.

"Connecting" versus "Reaching"

Although *editorial context* is not a new concept in media planning, women's greater sensitivity to context and emotion has been undervalued relative to the more easily grasped quantitative considerations. And yet the difference between "reaching" a prospect and "connecting" with her hinges on these very dimensions. To avoid that oversight in the future, after your creative has been developed and decided on, ask your agency to more deliberately weight editorial context by assigning a contextual value to the various media vehicles under consideration.

Media Units: Optimize for "Effective Impact" instead of "Effective Reach"

In Chapter 4, we saw that women appreciate more context and communication richness in advertising. We hypothesized that women may well respond better to more of an immersion approach to advertising rather than to the traditional single-minded "topline" approach. If this is so, we should reexamine our thinking about media units as well. The logical inference, particularly for high-involvement big-ticket purchases, is that women will respond proportionately more to larger media units that permit more richness and flexibility in the communication: for instance, two-page spreads instead of half-page ads, TV :60s instead of :30s, and so on.

Traditional media planning is often based on the principle of "effective reach." The goal is not to maximize the total number of people in the target who see the advertising but rather to maximize the number who see it *at least X times.* X is the minimum number of times the consumer must see the ad for it to be effective—in other words, for it to generate the intended effect: awareness, recall, persuasion, and the like. For women, experiment with the principle of "effective impact" instead. Determine the *minimum media unit* needed to fully capture women's attention, elicit their emotional response, and otherwise have a strong impact. The goal is not *exposure frequency* but *dramatic impact and engagement with the message.*

While this may sound radical at first, in concept this is second cousin to the strategy espoused by marketers who advertise infrequently but only in the top-rated programming, like the Super Bowl (Master Lock is famous for this), Academy Awards, or Olympics. *If you want them to notice, go big.*

Be a Maverick: Women Will Welcome You

Consider "unconventional" buys that take advantage of your pioneer status. To see what I mean, look through the pages *of Architectural Digest* or Oprah's magazine *O!* Both are full of ads for exactly what you'd expect: lifestyle products and high-end jewelry in the one, anti-aging face creams and a few financial services ads in the other. Where are the cars, the computers, and the consumer electronics? Women buy over 60 percent of the first two categories and about 55 percent of the third, so why are they totally invisible in two of the publications for which certain women's segments express the strongest fondness?

They're probably missing for two reasons: First, advertisers are trying to straddle the difference by running their ads in dual-audience books. Second, advertising agencies are recommending media vehicles based primarily on efficiency. But agencies are the first to insist on the value of innovation and ability to break through the clutter when it comes to creative executions. Why not apply that thinking to media choices as well?

Messaging: What Works and What Backfires

The four compass points of gender culture in the Star—*Social Values, Life/Time Factors, Focus Strategies, and Communication Keys*—will direct you to executional approaches that women find engaging, meaningful, and motivating. This section is organized into two perspectives:

1. *What you say.* These are in the realm of ideas and communication premises you can use to catch her eye, engage her imagination, make her smile, and win her heart.
2. *How you say it.* These are specific points on visuals and language that you need to be aware of: some to use, some to refuse.

The GenderTrends™ Marketing Model is a rich source of ideas for different ways to address your women customers, ways that are more relevant and effective for this target than are the conventional approaches directed at men. Before you start creative development, use these checklists to suggest ideas as you're deciding on creative approaches to explore for your advertising campaigns and secondary communications materials. Then once the creative is finished, be sure to review the "how you say it" list to scan for pitfalls and opportunities as you're signing off on recommended copy and visuals.

What You Say: Meaning and Motivation That Break Through

People First

Tap into women's orientation toward people as the most important and interesting element in life. Show people in the visuals and let us hear their stories in their own words. Talk about how your brand benefits people by making life easier, lovelier, or more fun. Especially in some categories, where many products are difficult to differentiate without exhaustive explanations, and *everybody's* ads look alike, this is a great way to break out of the pack and boost your sales by a few million bucks. One of my favorite print ads that truly breaks through clutter in its category is the one for Hokanson rugs shown in Figure 9.1.

User focus trumps product focus. While men may be interested in the widgets and gadgets of cars and high-tech, a woman's eyes glaze over and she starts looking around for someone to talk to. What the product means to the person who uses it is far more likely to seize her attention and hold her interest. Play your cards right: just as in poker, the cards with people on them will beat the numbers cards every time.

Personalize the brand. There are also other ways to bring human interest to your communications. You can use an engaging spokesperson or even an engaging spokesproduct. For example:

Swedish Covenant Hospital in Chicago has been running an interesting ad lately: A fairly handsome doctor-type gazes out at you under the headline "Mom called it. My oldest brother became the fireman. My baby brother became the lawyer. Me? I'm the heartthrob." And the subhead continues "Mend a few broken hearts and your patients forget you're just a heart surgeon." To tell the truth, I didn't even know there was a Swedish Covenant Hospital—but now I do. And I know they have great cardiac facilities, and maybe the doctors are even nice. Mission accomplished.

When's the last time you heard a computer called "adorable?" How about *Apple's iMac* desktop? Staring back through the display window at a human admirer, the anthropomorphic little machine starts to

FIGURE 9.1 People First

Source: Hokanson Designers and Manufacturers of Custom-made Rugs and Carpets

mimic him; they even stick out their "tongues" at each other! *Adorable.* My parents bought a new Apple just because of that ad. And I've personally heard of three men who bought it as the family computer (that would be on display, in effect, in a kitchen or other high-traffic area) because their wives thought it was cute.

Why aren't cars doing this? Cars are "badge" brands, which means people see their car as an expression of who they are. We anthropomorphize cars, personalize them, even *name* them! My first car was a Dorothy, and depending on their reliability, subsequent ones have also had some cute names—and some names I can't print in polite press. This has all the makings of *a relationship waiting to happen.*

Warmer Wins over Winner

Several dimensions of women's "other orientation" offer opportunities for marketers to drop a hook.

Group hug versus top dog. Remember that autonomy and winning don't have the same pull for women as for men. Not that she doesn't like her "flexibility" and sense of personal achievement, but the warmth and interaction of "belonging" are more important to her than to a man, and to her ear, "solo" can have kind of a sad sound to it.

Others matter. Not only that, but helping someone else, which isn't mission critical for most men, is a plus for women. This isn't necessarily in a mushy, nurturing way; it's more that it makes her feel useful, appreciated, and powerful. Honda has a scholarship program to *help young women athletes* go to college; Aetna helps her *take care of her employees* by offering 401(k) plans; an ad for life insurance points out that insurance isn't for the people who die; it's for the people who live (Figure 9.2). Appeals on how the purchase can help her *help others* fit well into her female frame of reference.

Make the world a better place. The mirror corollary of the principle above is that she thinks *you* should help others, too. BP gas stations have taken an unusual approach in that their advertising (not just PR) focuses on their environmental initiatives. In a market with numerous well-established competitors, this new contender distinguished itself on a criterion I care about. Next time I see one, I intend to stop in.

FIGURE 9.2 Others Matter

Copyright 2005. Life and Health Insurance Foundation for Education. All rights reserved.

She Prefers a Peer Group to a Pyramid

Use characters, spokespersons, environments, and situations that emphasize *affinity* instead of *status*. Brand images should reinforce "so much in common" and "she's like me" rather than "I wish I were like her."

Dig for the differentiator. As we saw in Chapter 4, she has a longer list, and sometimes the detail that makes the difference is pretty far down on that list (like the Ocean Blue on my Nokia phone). Make sure you find out what it is, and then, even if your primary communication stays focused on the "headline criterion," make sure the differentiator gets through somewhere—even if it's just in the picture or a note in the corner. Women pick up on the details, but you have to give them something to go on.

How You Say It: Context, Stories, Language, Humor, and Other Essential Elements

The Cast: How You Portray Women

Beyond "respect" to "understanding." Articles about communicating with women cite countless studies, surveys, and anecdotes, revealing that women feel marketers and salespeople don't view them or treat them with respect. While that may be true, the term *respect* is so overused and underdefined that it is generic and meaningless. What women mean by "respect" is not about being put on a pedestal and kowtowed to (and it's a good thing, too, since that is utterly antithetical to male culture!). It's simply about being listened to and being accorded as much response as if the communication were coming from men: men who speak up for what they want and matter-of-factly expect to get it.

Better real than ideal. For the last 20 years, in survey after survey, women have told advertisers that advertising offers little for them to identify with. Female culture is all about commonality and empathy, not differentiation and aspiration. She's looking for that flash of recognition that sparks a connection between her and the real people, real situations, real product usage, and real reactions that tell her you get who *she* is.

Coping with chaos. Today's woman copes cheerfully with chaos (usually). She has to. She normally has a full-time job, primary responsibility for managing her household, and plenty of church, school, and community activities to amuse her in her "spare time." The part a lot of advertisers haven't caught up with is that women no longer feel torn with guilt at not being supermom. Their houses aren't spotless, their kids are sometimes mouthy, and more often than they'd like they have a bad hair day. And that's OK: they're fine with it. It's advertisers who apparently live on Planet Perfect, and when women visit there, they don't recognize a soul.

Cast more women who aren't 20-year-old glamour goddesses. Grey Advertising's study showed that 82 percent of women wish advertisers would recognize that they don't *want* to look 18 forever. Eighty-two percent is not a small radical fringe, folks! Forget ditzes like Jessica Simpson; instead, look at *Judging Amy, Law & Order, Crossing Jordan,* and *The West Wing.* They all have attractive, normal-looking women with a brain in their head—and they don't seem to be collapsing in the ratings. In fact, the last I looked, they were doing pretty well.

Choose your spokeswoman wisely. When choosing a spokesperson for your brand, keep in mind that for women's role models, the key dynamic is empathy, not envy. In fact, women seem to like a role model better if she (or he) isn't perfect. Oprah is one of the most widely admired women in America (and probably the most influential), and one of the things women like about her is that she struggles with a lot of the same things they do. In other words, less Miss America, more Miss and Mrs. Real.

Reflect the new definition of beauty. While advertisers have become very conscientious about including ethnic diversity in their communications materials, only a pioneer few are even beginning to show the age diversity and size diversity women are looking for. Sara Lee's Champion apparel and the Lands' End catalog spring to mind, with their real-sized models. One of the cornerstones of female gender culture is in-clusion, and women resent the rigidity of one standard of attractive-ness. It's time to let go of the "blondes have more fun" (and better looks, more money, higher status, and better men) approach to beauty.

Tap into the "girlfriend factor." Savvy advertisers seek to create implicit bonds with their customers by delivering their messages with warm thoughts and positive associations. Until recently, most advertisers ne-glected one context that is very important to women: their relationships with their women friends. Togetherness is a fundamental premise of fe-male gender culture—it is a society of "constellations," not "stars."

The depth and meaning of a woman's friendships are among the most treasured elements in her life. According to the Grey Advertising study cited above, 74 percent of women would like to see advertising show more women doing things together with their girlfriends, sisters, and moms. Yet based on what I see in the media, this is almost uncharted ter-ritory for advertisers. Personal disclosure, constant contact, and emo-tional expressiveness make up the core of the girlfriend factor, and each creates opportunities for emotional association with your brand.

DeBeers provides an interesting look at what happens when you talk to the female target in a completely different way than has been done historically in this category, and girlfriends are a big part of it. See the next page for a case study about their innovative campaign.

The Setting: Presenting the Message

Stories. As you'll recall from Chapter 4, one of the Communication Keys of women's interaction is sharing anecdotes from their daily life. A recent TV ad for a home improvement retailer is built on this very premise. "If this house could talk," the ad says, "the stories it would tell . . ." and as a result it evokes the personality of the house and the peo-ple who have lived in it. In home improvement, you've got a category that's as manly as they come—construction, contractors, heavy tools, and muddy boots—but the reality is that these days *women are undertak-ing almost half of DIY (Do It Yourself) projects* and, on average, spending more than the men. So this company had the savvy to jump in with a female-friendly campaign that's bound to make women feel comfort-able and welcome—*and* that's bound to pull them in to buy.

The Diamond Trading Company

Opportunity:

Though it's a $45 billion a year industry,[1] diamond sales were flat in much of the '90s.[2] Rings' share of diamond jewelry sales had slipped, and only 14 percent of diamonds were self-purchased.[3] Ken Gassman, a diamond jewelry analyst, summarizes the opportunity thus: "There are more career women with money to spend, but they just haven't been spending it on diamonds."[4] No longer willing to wait for a man to propose on bended knee or for an overworked husband to remember an anniversary, the Diamond Trading Company has convinced women of the world that they should be treating themselves to diamond jewelry.

Strategies:

The Diamond Trading Company, a subsidiary of the international diamond company DeBeers, launched a campaign designed to get women to buy a diamond ring to be worn on their right hands—signifying independence and power. The trend has quickly caught on, especially on the red carpet. Stars like Sarah Jessica Parker, Jennifer Lopez, Debra Messing, and Madonna have all been spotted wearing magnificent right-hand rings. Focus groups revealed "a sort of superstition" that a diamond ring should only be a romantic gift from a man. Thus the right-hand ring was positioned as a "signature style piece" that "liberated" women from a taboo. How did the Diamond Trading Company market this right-hand ring to women in a motivating way? How did it break the taboo?

Insights that the Diamond Trading Company tapped into:

- **People powered**

  To women, people are the most important, interesting element in any situation. So instead of showing a big picture of the rings all sparkling and aglow, the Diamond Trading Company instead focuses on the user, the woman, the powerful and independent female who deserves this right-hand ring.

- **Empathy**

  Most women don't want to be looked up to any more than they want to be looked down on. Female gender culture is not founded on competition and aspiration, as male culture is. Women prefer to belong and to be understood rather than be admired and envied. The latest print ad installments feature "real" (not celebrity) women who have two sides—the "people powered/romantic/taking care of others first" (left-hand ring) side as well as the "independent/intellectual/challenging" (right-hand ring) side. The Diamond Trading Company "gets" both sides of women, both equally strong and now both equally celebrated.

- **Peer group/girlfriends/word of mouth**

  Women's motto is "all for one, and one for all," or "the more, the merrier." This especially applies to their "girlfriends"—you'll always have someone to talk to, to bounce ideas off of, or to share experiences with. And girlfriends like to share their discoveries with each other, like to connect by complimenting each other. The right-hand ring must generate a lot of word-of-mouth buzz among women with the means and desire to have one and to share one. After all, the tag line and call to action of its current marketing campaign is: "Women of the world, raise your right hand!"

Results:

Over the past five years the self-purchase market for diamonds has escalated 41 percent and is reported to be worth a staggering $5 billion a year.[5] Consumer recognition of the "right-hand ring" jumped from 25 percent to 59 percent,[6] and some are predicting higher holiday jewelry sales partially due to increased interest in the rings.

Context. In Chapter 4, we learned that whereas men "see" more clearly when key information is extracted and "extraneous details" discarded, women better absorb information when it's presented in context (e.g., as used in a typical situation). So if you are accustomed to delivering your message via a bulleted list of key facts and product features—which may be an ideal format for men—you need to think about adding a complementary treatment for women, one that places the product within its environment, lifestyle, and feelings.

One of the most innovative and comprehensive uses of storytelling I've seen was Neiman Marcus's 2003 holiday catalog. It is nontraditional in the sense that most holiday retail ads and catalogs focus solely on the products, not the users, and the copy talks about the features, not the human benefits. But Neiman Marcus created a completely different atmosphere by creating family stories around five (very affluent) families and weaving the product messages into its descriptions of their hobbies, needs, and passions. Figure 9.3 shows one of the families. The featured individuals were interesting so instead of just flipping through the glossy big book, this year I spent some quality time with it, coming back to it several times over the course of the season. The people-powered approach succeeded in engaging my interest; created commonalities between the featured individuals and various people I was buying gifts for; presented the products in the context of human benefits; and motivated me to keep and return to this very well produced, expensive marketing piece again and again.

Sensitized population: Marketing 101. "Don't irritate your prospect." This should go without saying, but it doesn't, because men don't have the same sense and sensibilities as women. The result: *irritation,* however unintentional. Numerous ads developed in good faith and certainly meant to appeal to women have unexpectedly (to the advertiser's mind) appalled their intended target audience. One ad for wine coolers showed a wedding cake with a bride-and-groom cake topper on the left, a shapely young lady popping out of a cake on the right, and the headline: *Men and women like different things.* Next to the brand name was the tag line "It's what women like." Well, women may like wine coolers, and they may like weddings, but, parody or not, I guarantee you they did not like that ad.

Show some emotion. Emotion-based advertising has a powerful pull for women. There are *always* people involved. It's generally based on a shared moment and shared feelings—whether it's inspiration, exhilaration, or just sheer wacky happiness. And it has a way of sticking with you: I worked on the Kodak account for four years and still got a lump in my throat every single time I saw the "Kodak moments" reel.

FIGURE 9.3 Neiman Marcus: Presenting the Message through Stories

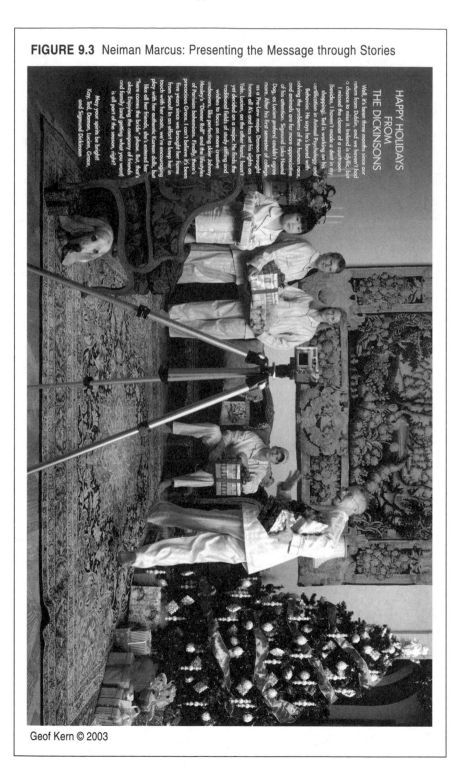

Geof Kern © 2003

The more it's tellable, the more indelible. To make it easy for women to transmit your message, build your case in sound bites, strong visuals, and, again, stories. It's much easier for women to recall and recount an ad with one or more of these elements to anchor it.

The Script: Watch Your Language

Cast not aspersions. Comparative scenarios with one party at a disadvantage or portrayed as inferior make women uncomfortable, and they react surprisingly strongly. Even indirect language with a seemingly innocuous claim can trigger this reaction. For example, in 1999, when my client Wachovia was developing a campaign addressed to women business owners, one of the newspaper ads we tested included the statistic *Women are starting businesses at twice the rate of men.* Would you believe that not one woman, but several women, immediately rejected that language on the grounds that it was putting down men? We changed the statement to read *Women are starting 70 percent of all new businesses,* and it went through without a murmur.

Similarly, when my Allstate client tested a copy claim several years ago that said *Women drivers have 15 percent fewer accidents than male drivers. To women drivers everywhere, we say THANK YOU,* a number of women in the focus group saw that as male bashing, objecting, "That's just as bad as they've always been about us." The moral of the story is that while fact-based *product* superiority claims are probably OK (if they're not too heavy-handed), *user*-based superiority claims are definitely not. No people put-downs are allowed—and that means men, competitors, other women, *anyone.*

Deep-six any bragging and swaggering. These just aren't women's style. Perhaps you'll remember the SUV magazine ad that started off like this: *Our 270-horsepower engine can beat up your . . . wait, you don't have a 270-horsepower engine.* Men and women are both likely to smile at that ad, but whereas men will be smiling admiringly, women will be shaking their heads thinking, "Boys and their toys . . . they never change."

Beware of talking about "women's unique needs." Many advertisers' first inclination when undertaking a marketing-to-women initiative is to showcase their understanding that women are different and to make it clear that they are prepared to treat them differently. The only problem with that is this: women don't *want* to feel different. They just want to feel taken *seriously*. The risk with the "women's unique needs" approach is that unless the approach is done well, with great subtlety and respect, women feel stalked instead of wooed.

Check word meanings. You may not have known that there were two distinct gender cultures, but you were pretty sure you could say for a fact that we all speak the same language here in the United States, right? *Not necessarily.* When client New York Life wanted to recruit more female insurance agents, it started out by asking both male and female agents what they saw as the primary benefits of choosing an insurance career. As the first priority, both men and women said "money." Men elucidated that as "the ability to earn a lot of money," whereas women thought of it as "the ability to get paid what I'm worth." In this example, both genders used the *same word* but with *different meanings*.

The second priority agents expressed was identified by men as "independence," whereas women said "flexibility." If you think about it, they're really saying the same thing, but their word choice frames it in a completely different context—a "mirror-image" example—but in this case one in which *different words* were used to express the *same meaning*.

The moral of the story is that to create communications that women will respond to, you have to be in close touch with women's meanings and word choices. You can't strain them through male perception and assume you'll emerge with the right meaning. It's not realistic to assume that what "makes sense" to men is going to resonate with women in the same way.

How to make a lady laugh. Before we close the chapter, I'd like to spend a few paragraphs on one of the more misunderstood aspects of communicating to women: women's humor. First of all, with politically correct sensitivities to this and objections to that, along with reasonable demands to be taken seriously, it would be easy to lose sight of the fact that women have a great sense of humor. It's just *different* from men's.

Men's humor grows out of men's culture: humor is another way to connect through the one-up/put-down mechanism, and the punch line to a joke usually plays on how some poor guy gets his comeuppance. Not surprisingly, women's humor grows out of female gender culture. It operates on the dynamic of *identifying with* the person in the funny situation—the delighted recognition of a similarity you didn't realize before: "OhmyGod—that is *exactly* the way I am." or "You're kidding, your husband does that too?"

Young creative geniuses, often male, are always pushing clients to dare to be "edgy." Forget edgy—*edgy* means someone gets cut, and women don't like to see anyone get hurt, even for a good cause. For instance, current TV ads for Lipitor, a cholesterol-lowering drug, show vignettes of lovely people, including a well-coifed, gracious, glamorous, silver-haired woman coming up a red carpet as if to the Academy Awards. Suddenly she trips and falls flat on her face. The message is *Cholesterol doesn't care who you are—it can bring even a princess down.* But all I can think is *Oooh, that poor woman! Is she OK?* Frankly, I'm kind of mad at Lipitor for tripping her.

Debra Nichols is senior vice president and director of Women's Financial Advisory Services for banking behemoth First Union. Her role, which she has accomplished with amazing success, is to make sure that women are recognized and addressed as a target audience across every line of business in the bank. At a recent conference, she shared what I think is an enormous learning: When starting a new program directed at women, marketers should allow a longer creative-development lead time to build in a three-round learning curve.

In her experience, the first draft comes out "too pink," with the positioning a little trite, the models too idealized, and the copy too sparse. The second round, after coaching, comes out "too beige," with information overload and still little that is really engaging. The third round, fortunately, brings things back into balance, often hitting the mark, tapping into the meanings and motivations that will connect with the brand's women customers. This dynamic makes it essential to set up a male/female advisory group (the women to comment, the men to learn) to look at the creative and identify any red flags before spending money on production and media.

Question: Can Men Develop Good Advertising for Women?

A recent *Ad Age* survey noted that while 60 percent of agency account services executives are female, the creative staff averages only 35 percent female. This raises an interesting question: Can men develop good women's advertising? After all, if they could, wouldn't it have been done already? The answer to both questions is a qualified yes. It can be done—and even has been. I've seen wonderful creative work by men on many occasions. Here's what it takes:

- He has to be a sophisticated enough communicator that he can work easily and comfortably in the world of women's verbal and visual subtleties and emotional richness.
- He needs in-depth briefings on the specific principles of female gender culture (the Star), how women respond differently to the marketing disciplines he's working with (the Circle), and how this particular target segment of women thinks and feels about this particular product.
- He needs to be open to feedback on his work from women that may not "feel right" to him, at least until he becomes familiar with the new culture he's working in.

Well, as far as *marketing* goes, that's a wrap—we've finished up our discussion of strategies, tactics, and mass-delivered messages. Now, let's turn our attention to *selling*—the face-to-face encounters that will make or break the sale.

CHAPTER 10

Face-to-Face

Sales and Service

The title of this book is *Marketing to Women,* and so far most of the focus has been on *marketing tactics,* or means of mass communication, rather than *selling strategies,* or what needs to happen face-to-face with the consumer. Many companies have learned that one without the other is a pretty lame duck. Some have learned the hard way through a massive marketing initiative that brings 'em in but leaves 'em standing in the aisles unconvinced—and that's not a pretty sight. You can have the best marketing program in the world and deliver thousands of customers into the store, but without the face-to-face follow-through, *you won't get the sale.*

This chapter is for sales professionals. Everything you learned in Chapters 1 through 6 about female gender culture and buying style has direct application to how you interface with your women customers. You'll learn how to

- identify top women prospects and bring yourself to their attention.
- introduce yourself and follow through with relationship-building activities.
- discover what she's looking for in a product and persuade her to consider yours.

- overcome "decision reluctance" and close the sale.
- keep your investment in this customer paying off for you over and over again.

Prospecting

The amount of prospecting that sales professionals have to do varies considerably from industry to industry. People who sell computers, consumer electronics, or telecommunications products really don't need this skill; their customers come to them. Customers come to car dealers, too, but the more sophisticated salespeople take the initiative to actively cultivate prospects on their own. However, the real pros at prospecting are the people in the financial services industries—banking, investments, and insurance. Building up their book of business requires making a very wide range of contacts and having the skill to convert a high percentage of prospects into customers. Let's start with ideas for making contacts among women prospects.

Track 'em Down: Identifying Prime Prospects

When you're in the money business, your best prospects are *people who have a lot of it* (the brilliant conclusions continue unabated, as you can see). OK, so that's no surprise. And presumably, by the time you finished reading the section on women of wealth in Chapter 1, you realized that women actually control the majority of the financial assets in this country. But who *are* these women? And how do you *meet* them?

Affluent women—they're not who you think they are. Most beginners in the high-net-worth women's market assume "wealthy women" is synonymous with "wealthy widows," and so that's the first market—and sometimes even the *only* market—they look to. Certainly, there are wealthy widows looking for financial advice, but they're not the only females with funds. As you'll see, there are actually a number of submarkets of affluent women.

Wealthy widows. There's some logic to the belief that the market of affluent women is composed largely of widows: one of the major themes in this book has been that as the baby boomers age, the amount of money concentrated in women's wallets will grow exponentially, largely because most women survive their husbands by 15 to 18 years. What's more, I heard a startling statistic at a conference recently: Someone from a financial planning powerhouse said information suggested that close to 70 percent of widows change financial advisors within three years of their husband's death.

This surprised me initially, but it makes sense when you think about preboomer generations: Women didn't work outside the home, and they generally didn't get involved with big-ticket decisions. Financial advisors built strong relationships with the man of the house but rarely involved his wife. With no existing relationships to hold them back, the widows walked. The moral of the story is this: When you're working with "married" money, make sure you build relationships with both the husband and wife.

The executive suite. The second place people look when they're seeking affluent women is here, probably because of all the press coverage top corporate women get. (Although their ranks are growing fast, they're still kind of a novelty.) This is a good place to look—but it's not the end of the road. While there are certainly lots of women earning big corporate paychecks (as detailed in Chapter 1), there are two other categories that I would look at as well: women in professional practice and women business owners.

Professional practice. If you work in the high-net-worth market, chances are you already know which are the high-paying professions. But it may surprise you to learn how many of these professions have women-specific associations. In the medical field, for instance, there are American associations of women dentists, emergency physicians, psychiatrists, radiologists, and surgeons. These organizations generally exist to address nonmedical issues (they have access to medical information through the "general" association) and may welcome an offer to provide their members with some worthwhile insight on managing their money, whether at the local chapter or the national conference.

Women business owners (WBOs). We touched on these categories
briefly in Chapter 1, but let me just throw a couple of additional eye-
openers at you: The fastest-growing segment of women-owned businesses includes the larger businesses, the ones with 100 or more employees—and presumably the greatest investment needs. From 1997
through 2000, the number of women-owned firms with 100-plus employees grew by 44 percent, over 1.5 times the rate of all comparably
sized firms. Other factors that distinguish the $1 million women-
owned businesses from smaller women-owned businesses: They are
more likely to use formal advisors such as accountants (40.7 percent
vs. 28.9 percent), lawyers (15.7 percent vs. 6.6 percent), and boards
of directors (13.3 percent vs. 4.6 percent), and less likely to use informal financial advisors such as family or friends (21.7 percent vs. 35.5
percent).

Between 1997 and 2004, privately held women-owned firms (50
percent plus woman-owned) were active in all industries with the fastest growth in construction (30 percent growth), communications and
public utilities (28 percent growth), and agricultural services (24 percent growth). The number of women-owned firms with employees has
expanded by an estimated 28 percent between 1997 and 2004, three
times the growth rate of all firms with employees.[1]

A full 72 percent of WBOs have investments in stocks, bonds, or
mutual funds compared to 58 percent of women employees. As we
said in Chapter 1, these aren't the local Tupperware ladies chatting it
up on Wednesday nights. You'll find them where you find the other
well-to-do business owners—chambers of commerce and philanthropic
boards, but more on that in a moment.

Another advantage of seeking out women business owners is the opportunity to cross- and up-sell to them. The vast majority (86 percent)
of women business owners say that they use some of the same brands
of products and services—such as telecommunications services and insurance—in both their business and their household, and that this is a
conscious decision based on quality, convenience, discounts, and experience with the company.[2]

The point here is that there are lots of prospects out there, and you
know what *the kicker* is? Affluent women are *almost never prospected!*

The kicker. When I started working with financial services companies, I'd been in my career for 19 years, I was a vice president at a large marketing agency, had a nice salary, and had almost never been contacted by a financial services advisor. (If I'd been prospected twice, that was a big year.) When I realized this, I asked numerous female colleagues of similar rank and salary what their experience had been—and it was always similar to my own. Meanwhile, our male colleagues of similar rank/salary got contacted frequently. At least half of the senior executives at my company were women. Thus, at least half of the prospecting pool was being overlooked. Astonishing! Here's the *kicker* to the kicker: One financial services guy *did* contact me that year, and he now has *all* of our accounts.

An even more dramatic example: One of my clients asked me to do a survey among affluent women—those with investable assets over $1 million. A woman I spoke with said that she was one of the eight top executives of a company that had recently been acquired. Each of these eight executives came away from the acquisition with several million dollars for their shares. Shortly thereafter, all seven of her male colleagues were deluged with prospecting contacts from people who wanted to help them manage the huge chunk of money they'd received. She was "deluged" with exactly two. Wow! Obviously someone saw this list (in fact, many people did) and decided that seven of the executives were worth contacting—while the other one, a woman, wasn't. What were they *thinking?* Are you starting to see how easy it is to think faster than your competition when it comes to women?

Choose and Schmooze: Networking

Once you've found the organizations that have high concentrations of the people you're trying to reach, the next step is to network with those organizations and the people within them. Even "general interest" organizations like Rotary, the Optimist Club, professional associations, community groups, local and regional leadership organizations, and so on, while predominantly male, have substantial percentages of female members.

The day-to-day reality of making contacts and building relationships is that people naturally tend to network with others like themselves.

Men network with men, women with women—sometimes it's just easier to talk to someone else who has the same language and customs as you do. But the upshot is something that has important implications for male networkers.

Women in a world of men are invisible.

One of my woman friends, a regional director at a major insurance company, was training a salesman to be an insurance agent. He wasn't fresh out of school; in fact, this man was mature, confident, and fairly seasoned as a worker. During his training he accompanied her to a networking event—a meeting of the local chamber of commerce. At this meeting, she observed that although 25 to 30 percent of the attendees were women, he didn't talk to *any* of them.

After the meeting, she said to him, "I was interested to note that you're meeting and greeting—just not with any of the women." His response? "Oh, were there women there?" She laughed and said, "Sure there were. There were 15 or 20 of them." Apparently, something in his internal software was registering the women in the room as "background noise." Whatever the reason, the point is that even face-to-face with the physical reality, 25 to 30 percent of this networking opportunity was *invisible* to him.

Men in a world of women are apprehensive.

In New York, there is a well-established organization called the Financial Women's Association (FWA). It has about 1,100 members, all high-level women involved in the financial services industry. I was told that about 10 percent of the members of the FWA are men. At one of its breakfast meetings, with 150 people in attendance, I sat at a table with one man and seven women. I heard someone ask the guy if he felt odd surrounded by a majority of women. He acknowledged that at first he had been concerned that he might be, but he'd been attending now for several years and had always found the women to be welcoming and engaging. As a matter of fact, when the woman who was chairing the breakfast meeting welcomed the attendees, she made a special point of welcoming the men.

The truth is that when you're trying to network with women, apprehensions are understandable—but unnecessary. Because female gender culture is inclusive and egalitarian, women are inclusive and welcoming to men in their midst. Their view of men coming into these professional organizations tends to be very positive. Rather than slanting toward wondering what he is doing invading their territory, most women feel: *Finally! Here's a man who is taking us seriously and treating us like any other professional association.* By attending, you're signaling respect. If you make the choice to participate, you won't stick out like a sore thumb; you'll stand out in positive ways—because many of your male colleagues are *not* doing this. You are a pioneer, a maverick, way out in the forefront.

Join the Party

At any networking event, a lot of us find it hard to approach a group of people we don't know and introduce ourselves. With men approaching a group of women, some men feel the added apprehension of whether they'll know what to talk about. What if the women are talking about *shoes and jewelry?* What if they're talking about *labor and delivery?* (And they may well be. Appalling as it may seem to men, women among women can shift from business to personal—from prepping for a big meeting to panty hose that run when you have *no* time to deal with it—and the conversation can get really personal, really fast.) So men worry that if the women are in the middle of some intensively engaging topic, they may not drop it when the men approach. Then what will the men say? They can hardly share their own panty hose war stories, now can they? In fact, it may be true that women won't always instantly change the subject, but they *will* rapidly acknowledge men and eventually find ways to bring them into the discussion. Women are "groups" people and "people" people. If the guy wants to be a part of the group, he will be welcomed in.

Seminar Selling

Like networking, seminar selling is an often-used tactic when you're building up business. The typical way of doing seminar selling is to get as many people into the room as possible, with the expectation that of any given 50 people in a room, 1 or 2 will become live prospects. It's because of this low conversion ratio, of course, that you try to get the maximum number of people into the room.

With women, though, there's a more productive way to go about this: Have *smaller* seminars and higher conversion ratios. Instead of getting 50 into a classroom, go for 10 around a conference table—if the 10 are women. Linda Denny, who rose through the ranks from insurance agent to regional director to corporate vice president at New York Life, came up with this innovation when she was helping regional offices all over the country recruit more women into an insurance career at her company. Ten or so women who had been referred to the local office as interested in learning more about insurance sales were invited to participate with a group of other women in an exploratory discussion about the career. So the size of the group was considerably smaller than is typical.

The second departure from standard practice was this: Instead of Linda talking while the "audience" passively listened, she would start with each person introducing herself and saying a little about why she was there. When Linda talked about her personal background, she made a point of sharing anecdotes illustrating why she had found being an agent such a satisfying career. As each woman introduced herself, she would do the same: Linda asked them to say a few words about who they were, what they did, what they loved about their current job, and what they'd change if they could. She calls this "kitchen table recruiting," because the feeling is a little like a group of girlfriends sitting around the kitchen table with a cup of coffee for a couple of hours.

Very quickly the women in the room get to know each other, and the conversation becomes candid. Linda would keep her ears open for opportunities to comment on how a career with her company provided something the prospect was looking for or resolved a problem at her current position. For instance, a participant might say that she loved being an emergency room nurse because she could help people when they needed it the most. In response, Linda might say, "That's one of the things I love about my job, too; when someone's just had a tragedy, I can come to her door and deliver a policy benefit check so that she doesn't have to add financial worries to everything else she's dealing with at a time like that."

Linda's experience has been that it's not at all unusual to get *three to five interested people* out of only *ten* participants with this approach.

The reason is that she has made it a personalized experience, selling the career by making it relevant to the individual woman in the room.

Instead of *talking* at her, she has *listened* to her and then commented on how the career connects with her life.

It's not hard to translate this approach from recruiting to sales. Instead of sending out direct mail invitations to every woman in the neighborhood inviting her to a seminar on investing in a down market—and hoping that the room is packed—use your contacts and networking skills to invite ten women to a "private investment workshop." Tell each to bring a list of two or three questions, as the workshop will be small and interactive, and you'd be happy to answer individual questions. As you answer, of course, you're learning more and more about what is important to the prospect and, at the same time, demonstrating what a whiz you are and what you would be like to work with. Some consultants set this up as a three-part series, held on-site for a group of participants who work at the same company. The series approach gives you and the participants several chances to get to know each other and further boosts the likelihood of turning a prospect into a customer.

> At my sales training seminars, I'm often asked whether women customers prefer to work with female financial consultants. The answer is "not really." It's true that professional women often like to support other professional women by trying to include them in any search for a new advisor—doctor, lawyer, accountant, and so on. But once she starts interviewing them to decide with whom she wants to work, it's a completely level playing field. Competence and chemistry count a lot more than gender. Your competence in the field is up to you, of course, but I can help you with the chemistry. Read on.

Cultivate the Relationship

Let's say you've identified a number of top prospects who happen to be female. Once you've gotten the business card, how do you stay in touch? Lots of business relationships require a period of time to bring to fruition, particularly those where personal trust is one of the keystones of the relationship. For the really high-dollar accounts, getting to know each other is an important part of getting in the game.

Business entertainment. The methods men use to create one-on-one relationships, which work well with other men, simply aren't as comfortable with women. Relationship building often has a social component, and guys build bonds by *doing* things together, so they might play golf, catch a ball game, or go to a boat show together.

When it's a man and a woman together, the problem is that it *looks* like a date, it *feels* like a date, and so even though both people know that it's *not* a date, they feel awkward. They're just not sure how to behave. The situation is rife with opportunities for miscommunication. Even the little behavioral things get weird: Does he hold the door? Help her with her coat? What is appropriate and what isn't in the business relationship?

An alternative, of course, is to make it a foursome: include the spouses. (This assumes you each have a spouse. If one of you doesn't, then the one-on-one scenario described above gets even weirder.) The good news is that now you're getting to know the husband as well—and it's always good to get to know both. The bad news is that your wife will only want to go out on so many business dates—chances are she has her own commitments, and there are only so many days in the week. Plus, out of courtesy to the two spouses, the outing becomes almost entirely social. Without much chance to even broach the business topic, you've lost half the benefit of business entertainment.

This is all on top of a few simple realities. Although many women play golf, it's not nearly as universal as it seems to be among men. Not as many women are interested in spending an afternoon at a ball game. Men may not be interested, either, but it's part of the expected male culture: men are supposed to be sports fans, and so they go along with it. Women may well go along with it, too—but it *won't benefit the relationship* if she's regretting the loss of the four hours.

So what *do* you do, because obviously you still want to get to know women prospects? Here are several suggestions—not the "right" way, just recommendations for alternative ways to get to know women prospects.

Meet women in groups versus one-on-one. *Join and participate in organizations* where you can interact with women, such as community and volunteer organizations, which are often made up predominantly of women—the PTA, for example. In my hometown, the PTA has 80 committees, 79 of which are chaired by women and 1 by a man: my husband. In situations like this, women feel a sense of comfort and familiarity as you're getting acquainted, and since the focus is on the work you're doing together, the social relationship can develop very naturally without a lot of effort or awkwardness on either side. Soon, word of your particular skill set gets around, people start coming to you for informal advice, and suddenly you've got a prospect.

As it happens, my husband's job doesn't involve prospecting; he volunteered out of a sense of community service. The point is, if he *had* been prospecting, he would have been in the catbird seat. Does it involve a significant time commitment? Sure it does. But like everything else, what you get out of it depends on what you put into it. Your return is a network of female friends and neighbors who know who you are, what you do, and how well you do it. *And* you get a network of women who will be quick to refer business to you at every opportunity.

Make your own groups. Create networking events. Women love to network with each other, and they'll love you for picking up the tab. Why not set up a luncheon to talk about a subject pertinent to women? Invite a group of women to attend a museum event with cocktails and conversation afterward. If it includes a fun event, food, and interesting women to chat with, women will attend. Let's say it's a traveling Impressionist art exhibit—the tickets are limited and hard to get, so you buy 10 or 15 tickets and send out an invitation to a few of your clients inviting them each to bring a friend. The invitations note that cocktails will be served first at the place across from the museum, then the exhibit, then time to chat. Each woman will be delighted to offer her friend this treat; and each woman will be providing a "warm" introduction to another great prospect.

Magnet Marketing: Stand Where They Can See You

(First, let me say that it was really hard to refrain from titling this section "Become a Chick Magnet!" Being female myself, I'm allowed, you know. However, duty calls.)

Personal visibility. Women are more likely than men to volunteer, so one way to create personal visibility is by volunteering in community services organizations, serving on boards of directors, and otherwise participating in the community, as we briefly discussed above. You can also make yourself visible through the media: write articles and provide information that's relevant. Two things make this a great marketing idea. First, you'll get the visibility you want. If you target "affluent women who need a car" as your market, for instance, you might write about how to choose a luxury car and then submit your article to *Chicago Woman* or a newsletter for a women's professional association. Second, there's minimal competition; most of these types of publications are looking for content that is relevant and useful to their readers.

Community visibility. Offer information to groups of women: approach existing organizations or groups and offer to speak on your area of expertise. There's an assumption that you must be good if the executive director or president is inviting you; otherwise surely she wouldn't do so! These are women who already have something in common, if only the group, and also probably know each other fairly well and trust each other already. Therefore, word of mouth spreads particularly quickly and well.

The Sales Consultation: Presenting Your Case

All right, we're done with prospecting now, and those of you who went on break because your sales job doesn't involve prospecting can come back into the room and sit down. It's time to consider the sales presentation. Here's where the four Star points of the GenderTrends™ Marketing Model can really help you. Social Values, Life/Time Factors, Focus Strategies, and especially Communication Keys—all have important insights you can use when interacting with your women clients and prospects.

What every customer looks for in a successful sales relationship is a combination of knowledgeability and trust. We're talking "big trust," as in "with all my worldly goods," and "little trust," as in "do you really know what you're talking about or are you just bluffing?" Men and women develop trust in somewhat different ways. Let's talk about how to build trust with women.

The first and most important thing I can tell you is this: Talking to women involves a good deal more *listening* than most men are used to.

Listen More Than You Talk

No need to strut your stuff. One way men earn each other's trust is to communicate their track record. A guy will talk about how good he is as a way of proving he can do a great job: "Half of my clients are worth over a million dollars," he'll say. Or "I doubled his return in six months." They talk about achievements, drop names, and let you know where they stand in the company hierarchy. I call these "credibility displays," because they remind me a little of a peacock who's very proud of his tail feathers. Don't get me wrong—this is the right thing to do in male gender culture. If you don't, men assume you don't have anything to brag about. But women don't brag. They'll tolerate it quietly, but they won't be impressed. As a matter of fact, rather than building respect, credibility displays are much more likely to ruin rapport.

Listen to her "life story." *Why does she launch into her life story when all she wants to do is buy a car?* The average male salesperson has a tough time not getting judgmental on this one. As she's explaining to him how many kids she has, she is also telling him how *they'll use the car to go to the beach on the weekends and for camping in the fall, so of course that means the dog has to come along . . . you wouldn't believe how dirty a dog can get after an afternoon at the beach . . . but most of the time, she'll just be driving to and from work . . . freeway driving, you know, so it has to be really reliable . . . and she occasionally needs to drive clients around to look at the houses she's representing, so it has to be a pretty decent-looking vehicle.* Ha! Caught you! You were looking at your watch, weren't you?

A lot of salesmen are puzzled by this "life story" thing. When men want to buy a car, they come in and tell you what they're looking for: a four-door sedan with a V-6 engine and antilock brakes. In the immortal words of Lerner and Loewe, "Why can't a woman be more like a man?" Can't she just stay focused on what we're doing here?

Well, she could, but she's trying to *help* you, believe it or not. First of all, she *is* telling you what she wants in a car, because she's telling you what she's going to use it for. As we saw in Chapter 4, women think and communicate in both contextual and people terms. You're supposed to be the expert—now that you know what the qualifications are, which cars should she look at? Second, by giving you all this personal information, she is giving you lots of great stuff to work with to build rapport with her. In her culture, if you're a nice person, you'll make a comment or two on something you have in common—the beach, the dog, driving around with clients, it really doesn't matter what. She's giving you a chance to be friendly, for crying out loud—and you're looking at your watch?

Your Turn to Talk

Present the product. Many corporate sales training programs still teach salespeople to give a canned pitch. There's a set way to present the product, a specific order to discussing its features. The goal is to get in as many good things as you can say about the product before the customer "sidetracks" you with questions. You're missing the point: it's not just small talk. She's given you the selling cues you need to persuade her that your product is what she wants.

Don't use the canned pitch; personalize your pitch based on what she's telling you. Explain how the interior of this SUV is designed to be both stylish and easily cleaned—cleaned of sand, for example. Show her how easy it is for anyone, large or small, to climb into the vehicle (just think about those kids and her women clients). Mention that this model has the best repair record in its class, so she won't ever have to worry about being stranded on a freeway. Not only does this tell her you were listening carefully, but it puts all your persuasive points in a context that is much more likely to motivate her to buy.

Pay attention to nonverbal feedback/language. When talking to each other, women generally face each other directly and watch facial expressions and gestures for the extra meaning behind the words. Guys tend to stand at an oblique angle to each other, both looking out in front of them and checking in with each other over their shoulders once in a while.

When women listen to another person, male or female, they use furthering phrases ("I see . . ."), make acknowledgment noises (umhum), and do a lot of "face work"—smiles and empathetic expressions—to show they're tracking with the conversation and to encourage the speaker to continue.

Think about how a woman sees the body language and nonverbal conventions of male gender culture: Here she is, trying to be friendly, telling you a little about herself, both to build rapport and to give you what you need to help her. And what do you do? Listen in as she tells her girlfriends how it looked from her perspective: *"He didn't listen to a word I said! He just stood there while I was talking, no reaction, didn't even look at me; he kept looking out over the parking lot. And when I was done, he turned and asked me what kind of car I wanted to look at—right after I just told him!"* Now, obviously, she doesn't understand male gender culture any better than you understood female culture (before you read this book, I mean!). But after all, *she* is the customer, and *you're* the one who's supposed to be figuring out how to connect with *her*. It's actually not that hard, once you know what's going on.

GenderTrends Genius: Joanne Thomas Yaccato

President, Women and Money, Inc. (women@womenandmoneyinc.com)

Reading Her Signals Right Can Make or Break Your Sale

We have worked with countless numbers of male salespeople who commiserate that they find it hard to sell to women. One of the biggest complaints men make is they don't have as much success closing women as they do people of their own gender. It generally goes something like this: "I do everything right. I give her tons of good information. I answer questions and I listen. She gives me all the right buying cues, and then I go in for the close. Then she walks out of my office and I never see her again." It's a surprisingly common refrain.

So we ask how he knew the woman prospect was so in sync with his sales presentation. The number one answer is: "She clearly agreed with everything I was saying. She nodded in agreement throughout the whole pitch. That's when I decided to close." And there it is. This is a classic example of communication style misfire.

To find out what went wrong—and learn how to avoid losing the sale—see page 302.

Answer Every Question Thoroughly

Remember, women have a longer list and are voracious information seekers. So no matter how trivial or irrelevant her question may seem *to you,* answer it. I realize from your point of view you think you're helping her by keeping the discussion focused on what matters—you're trying to be efficient and may even be trying to be considerate of her time. But if your response to her question is, "Well, that's really not what's important here," you've lost the sale because you've offended the customer. If she says it's important—and if she's talking about it, that's what she's saying—it's important.

One area I've heard several women comment on is salesmen's unwillingness or inability to answer questions on how the product compares to the competition. When my friend Pam was shopping, she asked one salesman, "Why should I buy this car instead of that competitive make and model?" She took it as a given that anyone doing due diligence on such an expensive purchase would compare several options; and in her mind she was giving the salesman an opportunity to showcase his product's advantages. His answer? "You just can't compare the two." "Why not?" she pressed. Again, he said, "You just can't."

This salesman lost the sale because he didn't know his competition as well as she did—and he tried to make her feel dumb for asking a perfectly reasonable question. Interesting sales strategy. Contrast that with the next dealership she went to where they were prepared to answer the same question with details on their product's advantages compared to the competition: newer engine design, more headroom, slightly better gas mileage, and so on.

Don't Put Down the Competition

There's one important qualification to keep in mind as you're applying the advice above. Because of their egalitarian culture, women see any kind of a put-down as inappropriate—"shady dealings." So while it's good to delineate the differences, don't disparage. "I've heard a lot of complaints about their new model; it just doesn't sound like it's very well made," would be going too far. The key is to keep it neutral, not negative.

Small Courtesies Make Big Points

We've talked about how women are more sensitive to nuance and the underlying meanings, and what this means in terms of her response to seemingly minor oversights. The flip side, as I said, is that the positive stuff goes a long way too: Small examples—but not small to women—include offering to get her a chair if it seems as if she's had a long day, or getting her kids a couple of sodas from the vending machine because it's such a hot day. But at a recent sales training seminar I was conducting, I realized I had to be a little more specific on this point.

A very experienced and *successful* salesman came up to me after the seminar and told me how pleased he was with the seminar and all the new stuff he'd learned. He said it had never really occurred to him to do the small courtesies before, but if "sucking up to the client is what it takes to make the sale, I guess I can do that." I thought he was joking at first, but he wasn't. Coincidentally, later that week I reread a paragraph in Dr. Deborah Tannen's book *You Just Don't Understand!* in which she recounts an instance of a psychologist asking a husband-wife pair of respondents what they thought "politeness" meant. They both happened to answer at the same time: the woman said "consideration for others," and the man said "subservience." I couldn't believe it, but as I asked around among my male acquaintances, it turned out that quite a few men shared this attitude.

Suddenly, I realized that when I was recommending to men that they offer women customers small courtesies, to many of them I was suggesting something completely antithetical to their culture. So now I hasten to add: If you can't do it with genuine sincerity, *don't do it at all.* Women will see right through you, and instead of having gained her appreciation, you'll have lost her trust.

A Sensitized Population

Earlier in the book, I addressed the fact that women have "extrasensory sensitivity" (they are able to register more subtle levels of sight, sound, touch, etc.) and "emotional X-ray vision": they can read nonverbal signals more precisely, including tone of voice, facial expressions, and body language. Here, I want to add an additional and important attitudinal component that magnifies these sensitivities: women are a "sensitized population."

At this point, most women, like many people of color, have had enough experience with being slighted or treated inappropriately in certain business situations that they've come to expect it. Not that they're any more tolerant of it, but forewarned is forearmed, and they've learned to at least be on guard against it. So nowadays, when women have a negative experience with an individual or a business, instead of chalking it up to overall lousy service, they often assume it's *because* they are female.

For example, car salesmen have a reputation of being condescending to women. I'm sure most of them are not, but the fact of the matter is, almost every woman I've met when the subject comes up has a story to contribute. And the stories get around, so car salesmen's reputation precedes them. Both male and female car buyers are going to encounter rude treatment or poor service from time to time. But when men are treated rudely, they don't walk out of the dealership feeling they were treated that way "because they're men." Instead, they think, *That guy's a jerk.* But women often chalk up bad behavior to disrespect for women. And the really bad part is that's what they tell their friends, neighbors, and coworkers about the dealership.

When you consider the dramatic differences in men's and women's interaction styles—credibility displays, rapport-building games based on "one-up" instead of "same-same" and exchange of personal details, different listening behaviors, and so on—and combine that with many men's underlying view that small courtesies are expressions of subservience rather than consideration for others, you can see that the situation is rife with opportunities for misunderstanding. And even innocuous, unintended oversights can easily be perceived by "sensitized populations" to be just one more example of deliberate discourtesy.

I'm not trying to create an atmosphere of "walking on eggshells" here. Rather, I'm attempting to lay out in very concrete terms how and why an extra dose of sincere consideration and thoughtfulness goes such a long way with women. I think many salesmen are genuinely puzzled by women who get upset over a "little" thing like handing the keys for *her* test-drive to her husband. A little extra reading on the topic and a little focused training for your sales force—both can go a long way toward making sure you get your share of her business.

Closing the Sale

The Perfect Answer—A Longer Road

We've discussed it before, but it's critical to closing the sale, so let's talk about it once again and more specifically. Whereas men are looking to *make a good decision,* women are *looking for the Perfect Answer.* As a result:

- Expect a lot more questions from women.
- Expect a longer decision process.

Salespeople are trained to try to close the sale in the initial meeting. That may work with men, because they have a faster decision process, and frankly, "shooting from the hip," that is, making decisions on the spot is one way they communicate their autonomy and decisiveness—the "cowboy factor." But women are marksmen, not cowboys—and if you rush them or push them while they're trying to zero in on what they want, all you're going to do is irritate them.

Women want to consider, compare, and talk it over with trusted advisors. It's not enough for the product or service to meet her needs; it must be the *best* way to meet her needs. It can be frustrating in this respect, but I'd advise you to refocus your attention on what you're going to do to follow up instead of pushing too hard right away. Otherwise, she will start to distrust your motives (you're supposed to be her agent, not her adversary) and destroy all that great rapport I just helped you build up!

Short-circuiting decision reluctance. Emphasize decision benefits. Focus on the benefits of making the decision *now*—she won't have to make another trip to the store, for example; or at least all her money won't just be sitting there in a checking account when it could be earning a return, and so on. Motivate her to decide sooner rather than later.

Minimize her risks. Pull out everything you have in the arsenal that will minimize the risks she sees in making the decision or in making it now. A warranty tells women that the product doesn't have to be the Perfect Answer; it will function as she expects—and if it doesn't, she'll be protected.

Maybe means maybe. Remember, when men say "I'll think about it," it's the polite way to say "I'm not interested." But when women say "I'll think about it," it really means "I'll think about it." Sharon Hadary, executive director of the Center for Women's Business Research, told me she once made this point in a presentation, and an experienced, successful salesman slapped his hand to his forehead and said: "Oh my God, I'm just realizing how much business I've left on the table over the years because I didn't know that."

You need to follow up with women: don't just be prepared for a subsequent conversation; expect and plan for one. Call her and say, "I was thinking about your concerns, and here's another reason that you should make this decision." To women, this signals a level of connectivity that fits right in with female gender culture—and she'll be responsive to it, I can assure you.

Selling to Couples

As I discussed earlier in the book, independence and autonomy are among men's highest values. As a corollary, it should come as no surprise that men resist being influenced—especially by women, especially in public. Whereas in the women's world a suggestion is seen as an offer of help, in men's minds doing as a woman suggests is too closely reminiscent of being obedient to mom.

On the other hand, in the context of a buying decision, the reality is that women's influence is very much a part of the process. In the presence of a salesperson, this leads to some complicated interpersonal dynamics, as both the man and woman are trying to figure out how to get and accommodate her input without the embarrassment of the salesperson seeing him actually listening to her. (Horrors!)

When buying a car, a computer, or an insurance policy as a part of a couple, some women will jump right in with their own questions and observations; but others simply won't talk much in front of the sales-person, holding their comments until the couple is alone. She can raise her objections and express her preferences much more directly without her feeling "bossy" or his feeling "henpecked." From a sales-person's perspective, the big downside is he doesn't get the opportu-nity to hear her reactions and answer her concerns, which significantly reduces his chances of finalizing the sale.

In my sales training seminars, when someone asks me about selling to couples, I suggest:

1. Ask her directly for her questions and reactions, so she can tell *you* what she wants without appearing to be giving direction to her husband.
2. When addressing her, be sure to tap into what you know now about selling to women: listen carefully, use nonverbal signals to show she has your focused attention, position your product in terms of how it fits into her "life story," emphasize people benefits over product fea-tures, answer all questions thoroughly even if they strike you as "triv-ial," proactively provide comparisons to the competition, and so on.
3. Be sure to excuse yourself for a few moments to give them some privacy as they finalize the decision. Remember that private cou-ple decision making is different from public decision making by couples; your observation that she didn't talk much in front of you doesn't mean she doesn't have a major say in the decision. If you let the guy shoot from the hip without consulting with her, she may not have gotten what she wants. She will share her thoughts with him on the way home, and they may well return the item the next day. Think of the paperwork! Also, and no less important, you will have missed a chance to build rapport with her—and the consequent recommendations and referrals that generates.

Service, Support, and Building the Customer Relationship

Standing Behind Your Product

Research shows that women are more interested in, and put more weight on, warranties, guarantees, and customer support hot lines—

the back end or postpurchase features. At this point women are still perhaps a little less familiar with technical or mechanical items like cars and computers—or believe that they are—than men are. As a result, women want to be sure that they have help if they encounter problems with the product. Sixty-five percent of the time, it's the woman who takes the car into the repair shop, and the numbers are similar for other home-related maintenance.

One Person at a Time

A number of research studies have shown that if a customer has a complaint about your product or service, and the complaint is resolved to her satisfaction, the customer will end up being *more* loyal and *more* satisfied than a customer who never had a complaint to begin with! Some marketing and sales executives joke that they should build in a little glitch—with a great response plan ready to roll into action, of course—just to increase the overall customer satisfaction level.

The fact is, there aren't that many companies that truly satisfy customer concerns or complaints. Instead, you often get stuck in an endless menu on the phone, and when you do reach a voice from the Land of the Living, the answer is ultimately that nothing can be done about your problem anyway. For anyone reading this who says, "That's not *our* customer policy," let me say two things. First, *of course* it's not! No one makes a *commitment* to delivering bad customer service. Second, try using your own customer service number anonymously—not from a company phone. I'm afraid that you're likely to discover what most customers discover: *the service is terrible.* That's right; I said it, and I bet you've probably said it, too, about other companies. But most people believe their own press about their company.

I heard of one study that included the question "Would you come back to . . . ?" in reference to the company that had sold the product. Of the people who answered no, not *one* mentioned the product; all of them instead identified a *service-related* problem.

If customer service resolves the problem *and* does so via a caring, intelligent person on the phone who genuinely wants to help reach a resolution, it's surprising and delightful. The companies who actually seem to be getting this, in my experience, are HMOs. For example, I had Aetna as my medical insurance provider, but the sponsoring company recently switched everyone over to United Health Care. Frankly, I dreaded the switch, because Aetna customer service was so good, but to my immense surprise and pleasure, UHC's customer-service people are equally as good.

A customer letter to Geico praising its service and one particular claims adjuster, Mark Newman, recently traveled all the way up the corporate ladder to Tony Nicely, the CEO. What had the adjuster done to deserve it? He'd given his customer his home and cell phone numbers so she could reach him after hours, because it was difficult for her to try to call him during the day. This one small courtesy made a huge difference to the customer, making it immensely easier for her to fit her car problem into her Life/Time. She wrote a thank-you note to the company, CEO Tony Nicely wrote a thank-you note back to *her,* the account was locked in for life, and the customer is now the company's most enthusiastic source of referrals.

Unfortunately, what *usually* happens when a customer calls with feedback—and let's face it, particularly complaints—is *not* delightful, and it certainly doesn't engender loyalty or positive word of mouth. Business relationships can have a great deal of similarity to personal relationships in many ways. Here's what women expect from both.

Recognize me when you see me. One of my pet peeves in dealing with catalog companies is that I have to give them all of my information every time—often before they can even check on whether the item I want is in stock! Coldwater Creek is different, though. They greet me by name as soon as they pick up the phone; they're efficient and helpful as I'm placing my order; and at the end of the call, they run through a quick confirmation check: "Still live at this address? Want to put it on the same Visa as last time?" Now, I know this is basically a really fancy caller ID system, but the net effect is to give me the feeling I would get from shopping in the same small town store for years. When I "walk in the door" somebody looks up and says, "Hi, Martha. How you doin' today?" And these days, that's really rare.

In Stephen Covey's book *The 7 Habits of Highly Effective People,* he talks about the concept of an "emotional bank account." The idea is that when you're nice to people, you're depositing equity in your emotional bank account with them, and over time it grows and compounds. This means that when something goes wrong, the customer gives you the benefit of the doubt and tries to work with you. Is Coldwater Creek's caller ID system the *reason* I shop there? No, of course not—it's their great clothes and accessories. But it definitely puts a couple of bucks in their emotional bank account whenever I call, because they make it easier and more pleasant to call them than to call anyone else.

Stay in touch now and then, even if you don't want anything. Every so often I get an e-mail from United Airlines, which I fly frequently, telling me about new developments I need to know about—and not trying to get something from me. For instance, it told me about an impending strike by mechanics that might affect my flight choices. Similarly, a friend who bought a Ford Windstar got a follow-up call from the dealership a few weeks after she'd purchased it, just letting her know that Ford was there to answer any questions or problems and asking if she liked the car.

Surprise me every now and then with something nice. Out of the blue, for absolutely no reason, I got a letter from Jeff Bezos of Amazon.com. (Well, he signed it, didn't he?) The letter included ten one-cent stamps and arrived just after the price of stamps went up a penny. "We can't replace your refrigerator lightbulb," the letter read, "and we can't make your tuna salad just the way you like it—but we can save you time." It felt as if Jeff himself had taken a peek into my lifestyle and recognized how very busy I am; when am I going to get to the post office for a book of add-on stamps? Jeff did it for me. Cost: ten cents. Customer delight: priceless. You can bet that beats a coupon for return on investment.

Then there was the "Sweetest Day" surprise I got from Peapod a couple of years ago. For all customers who happened to have scheduled a grocery order delivered that day, Peapod included a bouquet of a dozen lovely red roses. It wasn't an incentive, a reward I claimed for ordering more or ordering sooner. It was a sweet surprise, totally unexpected and forever remembered. (Hey, even my husband doesn't give me a dozen red roses unless it's my birthday or something!) These customer relationship marketing efforts are the equivalent of a wife's or mom's tucking a little note into the lunch box—it's the thought that counts, and the unexpectedness is part of the value. To women, who pride themselves on being thoughtful and adding a smile to someone else's day, it's a really nice surprise to have someone think of them that way.

One of the most original "nice surprises" I've heard of comes from a financial advisor at Investors Group, the largest financial services company in Canada. Martin Taylor is among the top five percent of the company's producers, and I have no doubt why. Many of his customers are women. Whenever he gets a new client or significant new business from an existing client, Taylor sends her a jar of homemade apricot jam. The jar even has a hand-lettered label, personalizing it further. The twist on this that I love the most is that his customers often call up and *thank him for the thank-you!* Again, you can be sure they're telling all of their friends about this—and that's how he keeps getting more and more referrals!

Now you've seen how the principles of the GenderTrends™ Marketing Model can enhance the performance, not only of marketing executives, but also of your company's sales professionals. I urge you: Give your sales force the training it needs to be successful. When the sales professionals realize how much money they can make with a new understanding of women and some fundamental but fairly basic changes, they'll be eager to get on board. And their commitment and enthusiasm are critical to the effectiveness of any marketing program you run.

PART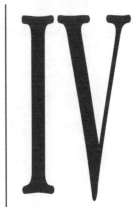

The Bigger Picture

CHAPTER 11

PrimeTime Women™: The Target Marketer's Golden Bull's-Eye

Introduction

Marketing to Women, the book, is now in its second edition. But marketing to women, the business practice, is still in its infancy. In many ways, the key principles and critical lessons that I offer in this book represent only a "first pass" at the topic. The next step is to look more carefully at the many segments within the women's market that deserve consideration in their own right.

Don't get me wrong. I'm not saying that one group of women is so radically different from another that you have to start over with a whole new set of insights—on the contrary. The GenderTrends™ Marketing Model and the strategies and tactics that flow from it span countries and continents, ages, and generations. Yet for each group of women, there are additional insights that can deepen our perspective. And many groups present substantial opportunities that merit additional attention.

African American women, for example, are an overlooked and underserved market whose potential has yet to be fully unlocked. The same is true of Hispanic women. As we move forward in refining our understanding of women from multicultural backgrounds, insights from marketing thought leaders like Pepper Miller and Isabel Valdes will be invaluable.

Understanding African American Women

In order to understand African American women, it is important to first step back and look at how African American culture shapes both Black men and Black women. Marketers need to throw away the thought that African Americans are just dark-skinned white people and understand that African Americans want their differences to be acknowledged and discussed. There is a strong desire for positive recognition of Black Culture and the Black Experience.

The majority of African Americans are "living Black." They are living, worshiping, and socializing exclusively with each other by choice. Diversity, for many African Americans (and most Americans), occurs primarily in the workplace.

African Americans maintain one very distinguishable characteristic compared to any other U.S. cultural, racial, or ethnic group, what I call The Filter™—the psychological baggage of slavery, postslavery, and discrimination. This Filter has had an astounding impact on how others see African Americans, how African Americans see themselves, and is the core of the "Black Experience" for most African Americans.

Everything Marti outlines in this book about the significance of women in the American marketplace is only magnified when looking at African American women. They are the means for reaching the general Black consumer market. According to the Selig Center, African Americans spend $723 billion annually, and Diversityinc.com estimates that African American women alone spend $270 billion. African American women own the largest share of businesses (39 percent) among minorities and these businesses generate nearly $20 billion in sales every year.[1]

More often than not, a Black woman controls how the money is spent in her household. Across many key categories, African American women are more likely than white women to be the primary decision maker in their households. (See Figure 11.1.)

There are some important attitudinal differences about African American women that marketers need to understand. For example, Black women are nearly twice as likely as white women to say brands reflect who they are. And cost is no object when they really want something according to 49 percent of African American women versus 41 percent of white women. Twenty-eight percent of African American women regularly change some aspect of their style (clothing or hair) compared to 8 percent of white women (2003

FIGURE 11.1 African American versus White Females as Household
Decision Makers

	African American Females	White Females
Household appliances	80%	71%
Health care plans	76%	65%
Mobile/wireless phone service	65%	50%
Financial services/investments	62%	51%
Major purchases (e.g., house)	61%	43%
Home electronics	59%	46%
Computer hardware/software	58%	46%
Automobile	58%	48%

Source: Window on Our Women (WOW) Report, *Essence*, 2002.

Yankelovich Monitor, Multicultural Market Study in Collaboration with Chee-
skin and Images USA). In addition, according to two separate studies conducted by the University of Michigan and the University of Missouri, African
American females have a more positive body image than do white females.
Years before "bootylicious," Black women celebrated their curvy figures.

Effective Black Marketing

Queen Latifah's celebrity spokesperson role for Cover Girl Cosmetics talks
to a diverse audience. It also embraces Black beauty and celebrates being
full-figured. She is not hiding behind some prop; it's a full body shot and she
looks sexy and happy. Most women in America, not just African American
ones, can relate to that ad.

In the 1990s Burrell did some really effective ads for Coca-Cola. They really spoke to African American women. The ad is a tight shot on this woman's
face and she's saying "The ad said they were looking for the all-American
girl. What do you think?" Her appearance was the antithesis of the blond-
haired, blue-eyed, button-nose model. She was very dark skinned and had
natural hair. This campaign made a profound statement to the African American community, particularly to Black women, because it said that Black

beauty is recognized, respected, and appreciated. It's a fantastic example of positively celebrating differences.

Tide with Downy ran an ad targeted at African American women that showed a baby sleeping on what was revealed to be a Black man's chest— another smart ad from Burrell that turns a negative stereotype on its head and uplifts the community.

Black women are particularly underserved by the travel, financial services and investments, and auto industries. There is a lot of room for smart marketers to come in and make a big splash with African American women.

Reaching African American Women

African American women do use general market media, but study after study says that they especially look to Black media for product information and for cues on how to live their lifestyle. It's an incredibly effective way to communicate with these women.

Grassroots efforts that uplift the African American community as a whole such as events/conferences sponsored by churches—about three-fourths of Black women are members of a church—are a great way to reach these women. One of my favorite examples of grassroots events is a wealth-building seminar series that Wells Fargo Financial Services did. They brought in known and respected speakers, authors of books African American women know, such as *Girl, Get Your Money Right.* Wells Fargo got 300 new customers out of 1,000 attendees.

The beauty shop is another grassroots way to reach African American women. Black women spend two to four hours per visit in the salon. They go more often and they stay longer. Talk about an environment to build word of mouth!

Source: This sidebar was written by ethnic market expert Pepper Miller, founder of The Hunter Miller Group (1985). The Chicago-based firm helps Fortune 500 companies understand how to market their products and messages to the multicultural consumer market with an emphasis toward the African American market. Ms. Miller is the author (with Herb Kemp) of *What's Black About It? Insights for Marketing to African Americans* and publisher of "Market Snapshot," a monthly statistical ethnic consumer-focused news bulletin. For more information, go to http://www.huntermillergroup.com.

Understanding Latina Women

Latinas are a huge and growing force within the U.S. consumer market. "One in seven persons in America is a Hispanic," states the June 9, 2005, U.S. Census Bureau release. The Hispanic population is 41.3 million and growing annually at a rate of 3.9 percent, compared with the nation's overall 1 percent growth. However, that number is actually low; it does not include the 3.8 million residents of Puerto Rico nor the 1 million U.S. Census Hispanic undercount. A more accurate estimate for the U.S. Hispanic population is 46.2 million.

In addition, Hispanics are adding an estimated 500,000 households per year. There is a constant growth caused by immigration, but Latino births presently outnumber the new immigrants. Once in America, these immigrants need to learn not only a new language and culture, but they also have to deal with an overwhelming number of brands and products, many of these new to them!

Due to U.S. labor demands, this growth is going to continue for many years to come and Hispanics' incomes will continue to grow as well. The Selig Center predicts dramatic increases in Hispanic spending power. In 2000, it estimated that U.S. Hispanics spent $490 billion. In 2007, U.S. Hispanics will spend $926 billion.

And, as you can guess, Latina moms control much of that spending. It is very important to keep in mind that the Latina market in the United States is not a monolithic market. There are differences within this group and more complexities to marketing to them than people often expect. These differences sprout from many sources—the impact of sociodemographics, the level of acculturation, even country of origin and age upon arrival.

Looking at the differences from general market women, Latinas are the key decision makers in their household but often take on what appears to an American observer to be a much more supporting role to the man of the house. Within traditional Hispanic culture, *machismo* is strong, and Hispanic women understand this. They usually want to make their men look good, up front, like he's taking care of everything—even when she's the one really making the decision.

Another difference lies within demographic numbers. Today's Latina is much younger on average than the general market woman. The median age of a Latina in this country is 26 compared to 30 years old for the general market. This age difference has a tremendous impact on Latinas' purchase behavior and the places in the market where you find Latinas. She's actively in child-birthing years. Latinas have a much higher birth rate: 2.9 births per woman versus 2.0 for the United States as a whole. So you've got a younger woman with more children. One in five children under 18 in the United States is of Hispanic origin or descent.

Wow! Where does her money go? Into her house, her kids, a family car, cooking from scratch, and keeping the house clean and beautiful. In nearly every category that has to do with children and food at home, Latinas over-index in purchasing versus the general market.

Another tendency marketers need to understand is the degree to which Latinas focus on the family, the group. This is called *marianismo* and places a high value on serving and taking care of her family. She is not as likely to be individualistic in her pursuits—she is more family centered and leads a more intense collective lifestyle than most white people today. What is most motivating to Hispanic women is improving the quality of life from a family perspective—not an individual one. She is willing to sacrifice to a high degree for her family and children to "make it."

Acculturation is the process of integrating of the values and the lifestyle of the country of origin with the host country. Every immigrant brings what I call an "Invisible Bubble" and gradually begins to adopt and adapt to the ways of the new home country. Sometimes it's testing the waters—she begins to see how American women ask for help from their husbands to take care of the children or household chores, and she thinks, "Hmm, why don't I do that?" Now don't forget that there is a very large part of the Latina market that grew up in the United States and went to school here. They are acculturated already. Whereas more than half of all Hispanics were born outside the United States, 88 percent of those younger than 18 were born here, according to the Pew Hispanic Center. Hence, marketing to young Latinas is quite different from marketing to the traditional immigrant! For example, targeting Latinas does not mean simply translating everything into Spanish—some who are recent arrivals do not speak English, obviously—but merely translating your general market communications into Spanish misses the point. Your brand, product, or service may be unknown to her and thus requires an introductory strategy. For long-time resident Latinas, the issue is to communicate In-Culture™* positioning, perhaps in English or bilingual but not the same as general market communications.

There are several Latina segments today and you need to identify which of them shows the best "high-value profile" for your product, service, or brand. You may not get the expected or potential business returns if your marketing communications program does not take this into account.

U.S. Born (Acculturated)
- Brand, category "mature"
- Have emotional connection with brands
- Retail and shopping savvy

Foreign-Born Recent Arrivals (Nonacculturated)
- Emotional connection with brand known in country of origin
- Unknown brands—lack of emotional connection with most American brands

Differences between Hispanic cultures also need to be recognized. Cuban born versus traditional Mexicans, for example, are quite different—from cooking different types of foods to different lifestyles. Hence, these two Latina segments will be moved by different messages, visuals, and products. Cubanas in particular and upscale Latinas in general tend to be more elegant compared to Latinas as a whole and the general female market in the United States. As a marketer, you need to understand these differences and distinctions within Hispanic culture to effectively communicate with your Latina consumers.

Effective Latina Marketing

Procter and Gamble's "Avanzando con su Familia" program is one of my favorites. The company created a publication in which Latinas can learn more about P&G products, how to use them, and how to make them the best for their family. P&G demonstrates a thorough understanding of these women's mindset and builds an emotional connection that will last. I also think Honda understands the Hispanic culture, realizing that a Latina woman is behind the man who's buying the car. She wouldn't say much at the dealership but she's there all along saying, "this or that car," and "yes, we can do it" to him. Honda ads direct the message to the man, but its emotional communication is directed to the woman. It has done an incredible job of communicating with the heart of the Latina.

Oscar Mayer and Kraft Foods also have done a great In-Culture™ marketing job. They put together a unique grassroots campaign to build emotional connections within the entire Hispanic family. In 2001 they created a talent contest nationwide called "Cantando a la Fama" where kids sang the Oscar Mayer jingle in public locations and broadcast over local Spanish radio; 25 million people heard these contests—an increase of 77 percent from the previous year. Undoubtedly, the participants and their families as well as the Hispanic community will remember the Oscar Mayer jingle as part of their family history.

PepsiCo and Frito Lay understand the level of sacrifice and commitments these Latinas are willing to make for their kids to "make it," or to do better in life. Not only do they donate and sponsor educational programs and scholarships, but they have also created many In-Culture™ programs beyond the typical advertising approach. A few years back, Los Angeles Pepsi enticed Latinas (who grew up with Coca-Cola in South America!) to switch to Pepsi by pledging a few cents per two-liter purchase toward building Pepsi parks in low-income neighborhoods. It was a huge success! And Pepsi succeeded in creating new "loyals" among Hispanic moms. These campaigns are all about making Latinas switch and build emotional bonds with these brands, even though in some cases they didn't grow up with them.

I think nearly every marketer knows that salsa outsells ketchup in the United States and has for many years. Who doesn't eat tacos and burritos at this point? Popular music and the arts in this country are dominated by Latin artists. American culture is becoming more Hispanic every day. Understanding what is important and motivating to Latinas is essential to being a successful marketer.

*In-Culture™ is a term coined by Isabel Valdes.

Source: Isabel Valdes, President, IVC, Isabel Valdes Consulting, an In-Culture™ marketing consulting organization. Ms. Valdes is a pioneer Hispanic marketer and founder of the In-Culture™ approach to marketing. She's a published author of three books and is currently working on the fourth, *Cracking the In-Culture Marketing Code*. (Q2, 2006 Paramount Market Publishers). She's received numerous awards and is a frequent public speaker at trade organizations, boardrooms, and universities in the United States and abroad.

For more information, go to http://www.isabelvaldes.com.

One demographic group in particular occupies what I call the absolute bull's-eye of the women's market: namely, women aged 50 and older. In fact, what makes this category so hugely important is that it lies in the bull's-eye of another "awakening giant" within the consumer world—the so-called mature market. (Not my favorite term, as I will explain below. But it will have to do for now.) As my colleagues David Wolfe and Brent Green (and remarkably few others) have noted, consumers in the 50-plus age group possess a degree of purchasing power that is large, fast growing, and all but unseen by marketers, who, for a variety of reasons, retain an outdated obsession with youth. The movement of baby boomers into this age bracket, which coincides with their peak earning and asset-accumulation years, is only accelerating this trend. And women are leading that charge, financially and otherwise.

PrimeTime Women™ is the name that I've given to this group. I'll say more below about why I've opted to use that term. Here, I'll simply note that 50-plus women are not only in the prime of their life as individuals but also as representatives of a demographic entity that is coming into its prime as a market force to be reckoned with. If women are "the world's largest market segment," as my subtitle for this book indicates, then PrimeTime Women™ are the fastest growing and most salient segment within that market. Indeed, for that reason I have decided to make PrimeTime Women™ the subject of my next book. This chapter offers a brief snapshot—a sneak preview—of my findings concerning this next big market.

In this chapter, you will learn

- where PrimeTime Women™ fit within the broad framework of age and gender segmentation.
- why PrimeTime Women™ are the ultimate bull's-eye for target marketers—for demographic, financial, and biological reasons.
- what factors keep marketers from seeing the "perfect storm" of opportunity that PrimeTime Women™ represent.
- how PrimeTime Women™ think, how they make buying decisions—and how you can reach them.

"Cornering" the Marketplace

First, let's briefly, consider an analytical framework that will place PrimeTime Women™ in the proper context as a target for marketers. What distinguishes these women from other consumers? Two things, obviously: They aren't men, and they aren't under the age of 50. In other words, they emphatically do *not* belong to the group of consumers who have long been the apple of every marketer's eye. For at least as long as I've worked in marketing, younger men—sometimes the emphasis is on "Men, 18–34," sometimes it's on "Men, 18–49"—have consistently won the field's "most coveted" label. It's a cliché, and a very powerful one at that. Younger men have significant earning power, they have lots of discretionary income, they are hard to reach but eminently worth reaching, and they wield a large degree of influence over the rest of the consumer populace. That, at any rate, is the theory behind this reigning dogma.

But what if that theory is wrong? What if changes in society, in culture, and in the economy are in the process of shifting the axes of demographic influence? Earlier in this book, I explained how that shift is occurring with respect to the relation between male and female consumer behavior: If you give women what they want, you'll find you're boosting your appeal among men as well. Add in the elements of asset accumulation and buying power, which are increasing among both women and 50-plus consumers, and you will see that identity of the "most coveted" group starts to blur. Factor in the power of gender culture along with the power of aging—something that affects people of both genders—and the picture really begins to change.

Here, then, is the framework that I propose. Divide the consumer market into four quadrants, marking the division along the lines of gender and age, as follows:

	Men	**Women**
Ages 18–49	Men, 18–49	Women, 18–49
Ages 50-plus	Men, 50-plus	Women, 50-plus

There are countless other ways to segment the marketplace, of course. But these four quadrants correspond to the basic demographic groupings that set the paradigms for marketing today. As you can see, PrimeTime Women™ are in diametric opposition to "Men, 18–49." They have long been the "also ran" group among the four, the group last to be marketed to. They aren't young, and marketers are most comfortable with pitching to the young and impressionable. They aren't men, and marketers have tended (foolishly, as I have shown) to value "the manly money clip" over "the power of the purse." In effect, the thinking has been that younger men occupy the demographic "hot corner" (to use an all-too-appropriate sports metaphor): By targeting them, you also draw in people from adjacent corners— "Women, 18–49" and "Men, 50-plus."

This chapter will turn the tables on that whole way of thinking. It will suggest that winning over PrimeTime Women™ may well be the key to "cornering the marketplace." PrimeTime Women™ will occupy the center of gravity in the marketing world for the next two decades by virtue not only of their preponderance in the population, but also of their consolidated weighty wallets. And as gravity tends to do, PrimeTime Women™ will draw toward themselves the values, priorities, and purchasing practices of the rest of the world. Where they lead, the other quadrants will follow. As women mature, the social values, focus strategies, and other aspects of gender culture that affect all women only *intensify*. So if you tailor your marketing to PrimeTime Women™, you are very likely to attract the attention of their younger counterparts. Meanwhile, the differences in gender culture that affect men and women in their younger years actually *decrease* in importance as they pass the age of 50. Human biology and human social development combine to make 50-plus men, in crucial ways, more like 50-plus women than like men in their 20s and 30s.

Too many marketers, I believe, continue to approach their work from the wrong direction altogether. If the point is to "covet" one group both for its purchasing power and for its role as a "leading indicator" market—as the market that draws other markets behind it—then the time has come to focus on PrimeTime Women™. Target that market and you lay claim to three out of four corners of the marketplace.

Prime Mover: The Demographic Bull's-Eye

In previous chapters, I've explained how the precepts of marketing came to be oriented around the principle of male gender culture. The skew toward youthful consumers is just as strong—and just as misguided. Some of that bias results from a general tendency (one that's especially common in the United States) to value youth for its own sake and to be fearful of aging. We equate being young with being sexy, lively, adventurous, optimistic, and all sorts of other good things. By contrast, we often equate growing old with the inevitable loss of those qualities. There's a glamour and excitement to youth and a cultural aversion to aging that undermine our ability to see the consumer population as it really is. Marketers, who themselves skew toward the younger side of the age curve, simply assume that the youth market is the market that truly counts—because youth is what they've seen in every ad created since the 1960s.

Battle for the Bulge

But marketers need to go a step further and look into the reason for that: the impact of the baby boom generation. Boomers, those born between 1946 and 1964, are the largest generation in history. When they entered their teenage and young adult years in the 1960s and 1970s, they took the consumer world by storm—and revolutionized marketing in the process. As they began buying and furnishing houses and forming and feeding families, their wants and needs naturally became a point of obsession for marketers. Further, this influx of new consumers coincided with a period when the marketing field was developing an initial understanding of how to direct specific messages to specific target audiences. Moving beyond brilliant copywriting and simple ad placement, marketers began to build campaigns around one or another slice of the population. But boomers weren't just a slice, they amounted to *a huge bulge,* one that has moved through recent history like the proverbial "pig in a python."

How do you capture the magnitude of the baby boom generation, now that its members are moving into midlife? No single figure does the matter justice. (Complicating the issue somewhat is that authorities don't all agree on a starting point for the "mature" market. Some start at age 40, others at age 50, and still others at age 55. While I peg the beginning of PrimeTime at age 50, I also note other data that shed light on the overall long-term trend.) Here are a few choice facts concerning the 50-plus demographic—and the boomers who are steadily joining its ranks.

- *Hitting the half-century mark.* Every seven seconds, someone in the United States turns 50. In 2000, 37 percent of the adult U.S. population was 50 or older, and by 2010 that percentage will rise to 43 percent.[2]
- *Driving "55."* From 1992 to 2020, the number of people age 50-plus is expected to *increase 76 percent,* while the number under age 50 will decrease 1 percent.[3]
- *Going "boom."* In all, there are about 78 million baby boomers. In 1995, they began to turn 50, and the process of their turning 50 is now halfway complete. In 2011—just a few years from now—they will start to pass the traditional retirement age of 65.
- *Tilting older.* By 2030, the boomers' proportion to the total population will increase to 20 percent, up from 13 percent today. Meanwhile, the total elderly population will increase vastly: From 2010 to 2030, the 65-plus population will spike by 75 percent, reaching 69 million people.[4]

In the Vanguard: Boomer Women

Now consider 50-plus women in particular. Today, they account for 19 percent of the adult population and 15 percent of the total population. On its own, that figure should be enough to give marketers pause before deciding to ignore this group. But that's only part of the story. The other, bigger part is that women will make up an ever-larger share of the surviving (and thriving) baby boom generation. It's a demographic truism that as any population ages, it becomes more female. The reason is simple: On average, women live longer; their life expectancy is seven years higher than that of men.

According to recent figures, there are 116 women in the 55-plus group for every 100 men in that age segment. And the higher you go on the age scale, the sharper the imbalance. At age 75, there are 175 women for every 100 men.[5] So as boomers grow older, women—Prime-Time Women™—will be the more prominent gender within this histor-ically influential generation.

What's more, boomer women who are passing the age 50 mark are a different breed from earlier generations of older women. These boomer women came of age and spent their younger adult years in a period when their opportunity to excel in the economy reached an un-precedented level. As noted earlier, they have been equal earners with their husband, and they have had a far-greater-than-equal share in household consumer decision making. As confident breadwinners and as chief purchasing officers for their families, they enter their prime years with a degree of market clout that previously belonged al-most exclusively to older men.

Boomer women are the first female cohort in history to have these characteristics. But they won't be the last. To capitalize on the oppor-tunity that PrimeTime Women™ represent, marketers must follow the boomers—and then they must follow the money. They must follow it, from this day forward, as it moves in and out of the purses of 50-plus women.

"Old" Money: The Spending Bull's-Eye

The demographic numbers are absolutely inarguable. Yet advertis-ers remain astonishingly indifferent to them, and television networks continue to party like it's 1975, scrambling to develop shows that de-liver audiences in the "highly coveted" 18–34 demographic. What gives?

Ironically, as the boomer bulge has moved forward, the world of marketing has stayed put. Marketers have mistaken a temporary condi-tion—being young—for the real long-term significance of this genera-tion: Boomers are large in numbers, they control an immense amount of spending power, and they're used to inhabiting a marketplace that caters to their every whim. That irony is compounded by another irony. Marketers focused obsessively on boomers back in the 1960s and 1970s, when boomers were first making their way up the economic lad-der. But now that boomers have begun to amass considerable wealth, marketers practically treat them as invisible.

By hanging on to the delusion that young people are the big spenders in our economy, companies are losing sales. The generation that comes after the baby boomers was formerly called the "baby bust" to reflect a dramatic dip in the birth rate that occurred during the upheaval years of the Vietnam War and Watergate. Now more politely renamed Generation X, this age cohort certainly spends at a healthy clip on a per-household basis because right now they are incurring all the costs of a growing family—homes, cars, camps, bicycles, and blue jeans. But their overall power as a market does not warrant a continued focus on youth.

The subsequent generation, called Generation Y, is large again—but not nearly large enough to justify neglect of boomers. True, now that Generation Yers are starting to form families, they will be a sizeable market for companies that sell baby products and the like. Conversely, though, the disposable income that they have available for other goods and services will plummet. And that's in sharp contrast to boomers, who are reaching a point where their kids' college tuition is mostly paid off and they can begin to spend money on themselves for a change.

In a way, we have returned to the historical norm. During what other period in history have teens and 20-somethings been the driving force in commerce or culture? In revolutions, to be sure, young people are always the driving force. But not in commerce. They're kids, for crying out loud—they don't have any money! Despite a smattering of young dot-com millionaires, wealth distribution patterns today match the dominant pattern throughout history: *Older people control most of the money.*

Assets: The Wealth Factor

In the United States, consumers aged 50 and older make up "only" 27 percent of the total population[6]—yet they own between 70 percent and 79 percent of all financial assets.[7] In addition, they control 80 percent of all the money in savings accounts,[8] 62 percent of all large Wall Street investment accounts,[9] and 66 percent of all dollars invested in the stock market.[10]

That's not all. The trend lines for such data indicate that 50-plus Americans' slice of the financial pie is growing. In 2001, this group held $29.1 trillion in net worth, or 69 percent of the U.S. total—up from 56 percent in 1983. As of 2004, median financial assets (the value of assets, in inflation-adjusted dollars, held by a family in the exact middle of the wealth distribution) had increased among 50-plus Americans by more than 50 percent in the previous decade.[11]

Moreover, when you look specifically at the difference between older and younger consumers in the level of assets held, you see a yawning gap. In 2000, households headed by people in the 55–64 age group had a median net worth of $112,048—which is *15 times* as much as the $7,240 in median net worth reported for the under-35 age group.[12]

Income: The Stealth Factor

Older consumers also bring in considerable income, although certain factors make evaluating income figures a dicey business. In assessing spending power, marketers tend to go off-track by using "household income" as their statistic of choice. It may have made sense to focus on that category back when boomer-populated nuclear families—you know, a husband, a wife, and 2.4 kids—formed the core of a huge mass market. But these days, the "household income" rubric hides as much as it reveals. The reason is twofold.

First, many 50-plus households consist of just one person, often a widow. So a relatively low "household income" can disguise healthy-sized per capita spending. And second, because many members of older household are retired, they earn less income than younger people who remain in the workforce. Yet they have plenty of spending power. Often, they no longer have a mortgage to pay off, and their kids' college tuition bills have mercifully stopped. As a result, a greater share of their income counts as discretionary. Plus, as noted, they can draw on the assets they have accumulated over the years.

Look at data for 65-plus households, and you'll see this dynamic clearly at work. As of the late 1990s, median household *income* for people in this group was slightly less than $23,000, compared with a median income for all householders of nearly $41,000.[13] By contrast, the median *net worth* for 65-plus householders was more than $92,000, whereas the comparable figure for all householders was a mere $40,000.[14] It should be no surprise, then, that people in the 65–74 bracket have a higher percentage of household income that is classifiable as "discretionary" than any other age group.

Spending: The "Health" Factor

By *healthy,* I simply mean that 50-plus consumers spend their earnings and assets at a very robust pace. They account for more than 40 percent of total consumer demand[15] and control 50 percent of all discretionary spending—again, despite constituting just 27 percent of the total population.[16] They buy $2 trillion worth of goods and services each year,[17] and spend *2.5 times* as much as younger consumers on a per capita basis.[18]

That's how it stands today. But the balance is shifting still further toward older consumers. By 2010, according to one estimate, spending by consumers in the 45-plus group will exceed spending by people in the 18–39 group by a whopping margin of *$1 trillion* ($2.6 trillion vs. $1.6 trillion).[19]

The fact is, older consumers buy stuff—lots of stuff. Like younger consumers, they buy goods and services to maintain their day-to-day lifestyle. Those in the 45–65 bracket own and use credit cards at a higher rate than any other age group and also account for the highest percentage of frequent-flier memberships among all age groups. In addition, older consumers buy stuff to replace older stuff, often trading up in the process. For example, of all the 13 cars that a typical U.S. household buys over its "lifetime," 7—the majority—are bought after the head of the household passes the age of 50.[20] And to a greater degree than younger consumers, they buy gifts for others. Here, the big story is the grandparents' market. By 2010, there will be an estimated 80 million grandparents in the United States. Already, spending by older Americans on their grandkids amounts to about $30 billion annually, and as more boomers become grandparents, more grandkids will find themselves on the receiving end of that indulgent impulse.

Women: The "XX" Factor

PrimeTime Women™ are at the forefront of these developments—especially those that relate to spending. Remember: women in general control an estimated 80 percent of all household spending. There's no reason to think that their influence on buying decisions wanes in later years. (Quite the opposite, as we'll soon see.)

To measure the weight of the purchasing power of PrimeTime Women™, consider the apparel industry. A set of recent figures paints a very revealing picture of how spending varies from age group to age group—with a trendline that gives a clear advantage to older women. In the year ending August 2004, women's apparel sales came to $93 billion. Of that total, girls aged 13 to 17 spent $12 billion, which was *down* 7.6 percent from the previous year, while women in the 35–54 bracket spent $30.5 billion, *up* 1.2 percent.[21] As for 50-plus women, they spend an estimated $21 billion on clothes annually.[22]

Baby boomers are the first generation in which women have exerted a big financial impact on their household. In fact, as I discussed earlier, their massive movement into the workplace accounts for much of the increased wealth of boomer households: Simply put, two-income households can afford to buy more stuff. Meanwhile, boomer women have grown into their "purchasing officer" role in a decisive way. That role now extends far beyond the purchase of groceries, cleaning supplies, and kids' clothes. Women in their PrimeTime years are used to making and influencing big-ticket buying decisions as well. And marketing hasn't caught up with that change.

Marketers also haven't caught on to another point that I mentioned earlier: Over the next decade or two, boomers will be on the receiving end of the largest intergenerational transfer of wealth in history as they inherit money from their high-saving parents. And in the decade or two that follow, boomer women will in turn inherit a similarly large chunk of wealth from their husband. Again, women generally live longer than men, and they tend to marry men who are older than they are; on average, they become widows at the age of 67 and continue to live for another 15 to 18 years. So women boomers will inherit considerable assets, both from their parents and from their spouse, and they will have sole control of those assets for a long time.

Message to marketers, especially those of you who sell big-ticket items: learn to communicate with women. Get gender savvy—and do it fast. If your business is financial services, for example, or real estate (think "second homes," think "retirement communities"), then you will find that 50-plus women make up a bigger and bigger portion of your market. Follow the dollar signs, and they will point you to Prime-Time Women™.

Biological Jujitsu: Don't Be "Flip" about It

Becoming gender savvy about the 50-plus market means coming to understand that differences in gender culture aren't completely static. Men and women change attitudinally over the developmental stages of their life. In other words, gender culture *evolves*. Earlier, I wrote about the evolutionary, cognitive, and biochemical factors that lead men and women to approach consumer decision making differently. To a degree, those differences persist. But something else occurs in people's later years: The genders undergo a "fifth decade hormone flip"—a biochemical jujitsu in the way that they interact with each other.

To put the matter in its simplest terms: At some point after age 40, men relinquish many of the aggressive, combative characteristics that mark them in their youth, whereas women become more assertive. According to a study by Grey Advertising, far from fading away, the great majority of women—eight out of ten—feel *stronger and more confident* as they grow older.

Here's why. Between the ages of 40 and 80, men's T-levels (levels of testosterone in their blood) drop dramatically, by as much as 50 percent. Thus, after 30 years of focusing on work and on moving up in a hierarchy, they become more relaxed about interpersonal relationships and more interested in strengthening family ties. In short, they mellow out. Women's hormone levels also drop precipitously. Their estrogen levels fall off so much that by age 72 they actually have less estrogen in their blood than men do. A *lot* less: men's estrogen levels at that age are *three times* as high as women's. Moreover, because one function of estrogen is to dampen the effects of testosterone, the drop in estrogen levels in women results in an "unmasking" of the testosterone in their system. Women have testosterone, too, and without estrogen to suppress it, that hormone is free to manifest itself in the form of greater assertiveness and self-confidence.[23]

That has been the case from time immemorial. Yet in previous eras, the effects of this hormonal shift have usually been masked, so to speak, by women's lack of social and economic power. Older women, made newly assertive because of "biological jujitsu," might become an aggressive force when it came to the emotional life of their family. But tradition and social habit limited their role as big-ticket consumers. What's different now is that 50-plus women today undergo this attitudinal change after a long period of being out in the work world and developing their own sources of financial power. So the impact of biology actually reinforces an existing tendency within boomer women: Long accustomed to having money and to buying their own stuff, they now assume even greater sway over a couple's consumer decision making.

Take another look at the demographic quadrant analysis that I introduced a few pages back. That analysis should ring even truer now that we have seen how older men and older women differ attitudinally less than their younger counterparts do. And by recognizing that women become stronger personalities as they enter PrimeTime™, we should be able to appreciate the "mind flip" suggested by that analysis: It is 50-plus women, rather than younger men, who will wield the greatest influence over consumer behavior in the coming years.

Beyond Stereotypes: From "Sunset Years" to "High Noon!"

So why, in spite of all these data showing the power of 50-plus consumers—and the power of PrimeTime Women™ in particular—do companies still give short shrift to this market? The simple, sorry answer: Stereotypes die hard, and the language that conveys our stereotyped thinking lingers on, long past the point when it matched reality.

Images Deceive Us

In the United States, and in Western countries generally, people just assume that being older is a bad thing. A while back, I got a call from a marketing guy in Detroit who wanted some input from me on older women. "We need to take a look at the older population," he said, "because everybody is getting older. You know how it is . . . we're all getting a little slower, we're getting a little fatter, our eyesight is going . . ." (you know the rest). He's not alone. That sense of fatalism, and that emphasis on the physical differences between being older and being younger, are all too common. This stereotyped view of the aging process has become wired into all of our psyches—even among 50-plus people themselves. And, irony of ironies, the boomers are partly to blame. They grew up saying, "Never trust anybody over 30," and believing that people are "over the hill" at age 40.

For a great many people, though, the experience of midlife contradicts that stereotype. As Gail Sheehy documented years ago in her book *New Passages* (and as many other studies have confirmed), people report that their 50s and 60s are actually the happiest period of their life. I confess that when I first encountered that research, I was taken aback. It contradicted everything that everybody "knew" about what it was like to be "old." If it were true, how come it was such a big secret? But it *is* true! As long as they enjoy decent health—and more and more often, they do—people in the 50-plus group have a confidence in themselves and a sense of being settled in their life that younger people lack. Our obsession with physical infirmities has obscured the positive side of aging.

In the case of older women, the prevailing stereotypes are more specific, reflecting attitudes that range from indifference to hostility. One common image of the older woman is that she's a sad, passive emptynester: her children have left home, she feels useless—why, the poor old thing has practically no reason to live anymore. Or if she does, it's only to take care of her husband until he dies—at which point she becomes a still more pitiable figure. In short, she's a caregiver, and marketers write her off as a target of last resort.

Another stereotype is that of the horrid, meddling mother-in-law: she's overly assertive, she's a busybody, and so forth. (It's interesting that there is no comparable stereotype about fathers-in-law, negative or otherwise.) A more benign version of that image is the matriarchal figure. But even there, the focus is still on a woman's circumscribed role as a homebody. None of these images encourages us to see women as major consumers, capable of driving big-ticket buying decisions. And yet, as we have seen, that is indeed what 50-plus women are today.

Words Fail Us

Even as research lays bare the truth about the 50-plus group, and especially about 50-plus women, our language continues to get in the way. People are at a loss to describe the mature market in ways that don't conjure up negative associations. Let's start with the phrase that

I just used: Terms like *mature market* and *senior market* come freighted with auras and overtones that are inherently unattractive. "Mature" suggests something that is "past the point of ripeness." And while being a senior in high school or college is a status that underclassmen aspire to, perversely, "senior" in the context of older consumers connotes a sense of being "all done," "out to pasture"—in short, no longer relevant.

Or take the term *middle-aged.* Several years ago, I was interviewed by a reporter from a major business magazine who was doing an article on "middle-aged women." Even *I* flinched when he used that phrase—and I know better! Why does it sound so unappealing?

"Middle-aged" calls up images of frumpiness, of dowdiness; it makes you think of someone who is just plain tired and who no longer cares, for example, about her appearance. Who would want to market to such a woman?

That whole image of older women simply doesn't correspond to the new reality of midlife. It may have been accurate 30 or 50 years ago, but it's obsolete now: Today's 50-year-old woman is *not* your grand-mother's grandmother. So what is she? We need new language to help us get beyond the views that tradition has foisted on us. Which is why I use the term *PrimeTime.* It conveys vitality and primacy—the vitality and primacy not only of 50-plus women but also of the marketing opportunity that they present.

We need to revamp the entire vocabulary of aging. Too many terms that purport to be positive in tone are actually patronizing, misguided, or both: *golden years, golden moments, the silver age.* Worst of all—marketers should curse themselves if they ever utter these words—is *sunset years.* As if your life is all but over! (Equally bad are the images that go with these phrases. For some awful reason, ads aimed at older consumers always seem to feature an old couple sitting side by side in a matched pair of Adirondack chairs, content to watch the sun set over the dimming ocean.)

These days, being in your 50-plus years isn't about passively watching the light fade out. People are staying healthy and lively well into their 70s. Forget "sunset years." Instead, think "High Noon!" Older consumers, and PrimeTime Women™ especially, approach this phase of their life with a sense that their sun is at its highest point. They know who they are and what they want. They have a wealth of experience—and they have had a chance to build financial wealth over their lifetime. They have brought kids into the world and have seen those kids grow up. They've done a lot. They're at their peak. They're in their prime—*their PrimeTime.*

Perfect Storm: *Don't* Run for Cover

PrimeTime Women™ are large in numbers. *And* they have lots of money to spend. *And* they have long years of experience as confident consumers. *And* they are growing more assertive (thanks to biology). *And* they are entering a stage of life in which they are free from old responsibilities and eager to embrace new adventures.

It's what I call a perfect storm: several factors converge to create an incredibly concentrated and exciting climate of opportunity for savvy marketers.

For those caught in the old mindset that still dominates the marketing field, the emerging cohort of 50-plus women might as well be a different species. While the typical grandmother of yesteryear sat in a rocker and sipped tea while reading a book, today's boomer grandma is more likely to be sitting at her computer and sipping Evian, having just come from a tennis match. She is not pining for the good old days of her lost youth. When she thinks of her life, she doesn't think in terms of loss. She thinks in terms of experience gained. And she thinks enthusiastically about experiences yet to be enjoyed.

Quite simply, the women today who have passed the age-50 mark— or who will be passing it in the years to come—are the healthiest, wealthiest, most active, and independent generation of older women in history. In case I haven't made that point strongly enough yet, consider:

Healthiest. According to Diane Holman of Woman-Trends, if a woman reaches her 50th birthday without cancer or heart disease, she can expect to reach the age of 92. This generation of women—with their walking and running and swimming, with their yoga and their exercycling and their Pilates—will stay healthy and active for many years to come.

Wealthiest. Recall that women in general earn half or more of household income in the majority of U.S. households. Recall, too, the considerable assets that they are gathering in their 50-plus years, both through their own earning power and through inheritance. Now add in the fact that, having raised their kids, they can finally begin to spend time, energy, and, yes, money on themselves again. Talk about pent-up demand!

Most active and independent. Not only are 50-plus women more *physically* active today than ever before, but they are also remaining *economically* vital to an unprecedented degree. For all 50-plus Americans, the labor force participation rate in 2003 was 46.3 percent, up nearly 7 percentage points from a decade ago.[24] And according to the Bureau of Labor Statistics, the number of women aged 55 and older in the workforce will increase by a whopping 52 percent between 2000 and 2010—from 6.4 million 10.1 million. Whether they work out of choice or out of necessity, PrimeTime Women™ possess both self-reliance and purchasing power that their mothers and grandmothers could hardly dream of.

There's a PaineWebber ad that does a great job of capturing the spirit of this generation of women. It shows a woman, probably in her late 50s, sitting outside with her 30-something daughter, who appears on the left as you look at the page. The copy reads, "You're psyched about the future. You're full of new ideas. You're looking to start a business. You're the one on the right." What a perfect evocation of the oft-overlooked vitality and aspirations of 50-plus women!

Star System: Gender Culture Meets Human Development

Putting your company or your brand in the middle of this "perfect storm" of opportunity doesn't require a massive readjustment of your marketing operation. It means adapting yourself to a new way of thinking—but it's not brain surgery. In fact, because so few marketers have even begun to delve into this area, just a little effort on your part will take you a long way. Recognizing the size and the relevance of the PrimeTime Women™ market is the first step. The next step is to absorb a few key insights about what *motivates* those who make up this market.

Now we've covered the "Women" side of that equation quite thoroughly. What about the "PrimeTime" side?

To the extent that marketers have paid any attention to the so-called mature market, their focus has been on the *physical* aspects of aging. Noting that eyesight deteriorates in midlife and beyond, for example, they suggest increasing the type size in advertisements and other communications (a great piece of advice that has been honored more in the breach than by any kind of sustained execution). Similarly, retailers are told to improve the lighting in their stores because older people's eyes require more light to see. Managers in the food service and packaged goods industries are told to reduce portion sizes and container sizes as older people eat less and in general consume less per household than do younger people. In the automotive industry, designers are donning "old suits"—body gear that simulates stiffness of joints and other conditions of aging—in order to fashion car interiors for 50-plus drivers.

All of that is fine. It's dandy. But that's the easy stuff, the obvious stuff. In a culture that understands aging simply as a matter of physical infirmity, the tendency has been to go no further. In effect, too many of us are walking around in an old suit, when what's really necessary is to put on a PrimeTime thinking hat. How *do* PrimeTime Women™ think? What inspires them? What captures their imagination—and their attention? What drives them? What, in other words, are the attributes of PrimeTime culture?

What follows is an effort to merge my analysis of women as a whole (as described earlier in this book) with an analysis of people in the 50-plus age bracket. For the latter, I draw extensively on the groundbreaking work of David B.Wolfe, author of *Serving the Ageless Market* (McGraw-Hill, 1990) and *Ageless Marketing: Strategies for Reaching the Hearts and Minds of the New Customer Majority* (Dearborn Trade, 2003). David's books outline the profound changes in attitude and behavior that people undergo in their later years—changes that reflect fundamental patterns of human psychological development. These changes, and the attitudes that arise from them, are not generation-specific, they don't apply only to boomers. Yes, understanding the size and the financial circumstances of the baby boom generation is essential to ap-

preciating the current market opportunity. But the PrimeTime phenomenon extends far beyond a single age cohort. It runs deep, and it's
here to stay—just like the basic elements of gender culture.

In studying David's keen observations regarding what he calls the
New Customer Majority (those aged 40 and older), I have been struck
by one thing above all: Many of the factors that distinguish male and
female gender culture find a parallel in the factors that make older
consumers different from their younger counterparts. To put it another way, there is *a huge area of attitudinal convergence* between these
two demographic groups—women and older people.

I have touched on this point already, both in my discussion of cornering the marketplace and in my comments on biological jujitsu.
Now I can make the point in the simplest, boldest way possible: *Marketing to women and marketing to 50-plus consumers go hand in hand. You
don't have to choose between them!* Far from it. By learning how to market
to PrimeTime Women™, you develop a powerful array of insights that
will help you appeal to a broad swathe of the whole population.

To organize those insights, I turn again to the GenderTrends Star
model. Just as that four-pointed star aids in linking gender culture to
practical marketing lessons, so it also provides a structure for presenting several "best practice" principles related to PrimeTime Women™.

Star Point One: Social Values

PrimeTime Women™ value their connections to other people. (Remember: Women are *ensemble players;* they favor a *"warmer"* form of social interaction and orient their life toward *a peer group.* Those qualities
only intensify with age.) Their sense of themselves and their sense of
priorities draw them toward certain kinds of marketing appeals and
away from others. So . . .

Give them "real," not "ideal." Make sure that your communications depict people as they really are—or, more to the point, as your customers
really are. Show characters who are attractive, warm, and natural but
not perfect. Avoid using ridiculously beautiful models, as well as images that relate more to fantasy than to the way PrimeTime Women™
live. (One recent campaign for a line of kitchen appliances revolved

around a series of goddess figures: an ice princess symbolized a refrigerator, a fire queen showcased an oven—that sort of thing. The ads are lush and striking, but, well, *get real.*)

Stay away, for the most part, from celebrity endorsements. Prime-Time Women™ are past being inspired by people whom they're supposed to *want to be* like. Instead, they're drawn to people whom they already *are* like. In some cases, of course, endorsements can be very powerful. Oprah, for example, is one celebrity whom PrimeTime Women™ identify with. But that's because she's less a figure of *aspiration* than she is a figure of *authenticity*.

The appeal of authenticity affects women and 50-plus consumers alike (Figure 11.2). In the case of women, it is their sense of empathy—in contrast to men's sense of hierarchy—that drives this attitude. Unlike men, who feel a need to "look up to" heroes and higher-ups, women "look across" to their peers. They care first and foremost about what they have in common with others.

That outlook converges with an attitudinal shift that affects people of both genders in midlife. In their younger years, people work to establish a "social self"—a self that can hold its own in society. By age 50, that work is mostly done. People then begin to focus on what David Wolfe calls "the real self." They stop worrying about impressing others, and they redirect their energies toward being the best, truest person that they can be.

Marketing pitches that play upon an idealized figure (the impossibly gorgeous woman, the unstoppably victorious man) definitely have an impact on younger consumers, who are seeking models on which to base their social selves. With 50-plus consumers, especially the women among them, they fall completely flat.

Let them see your corporate halo. Women, as I've explained, greatly appreciate a company that does well by doing good. Their "people first, last, and always" orientation leads them to favor companies that approach society on a benevolent, win-win basis. With PrimeTime Women™, that admiration for good corporate citizenship becomes even stronger. So to reach them, publicize your company's involvement in the arts, its philanthropic contributions, its environmentally sensitive practices, and so on.

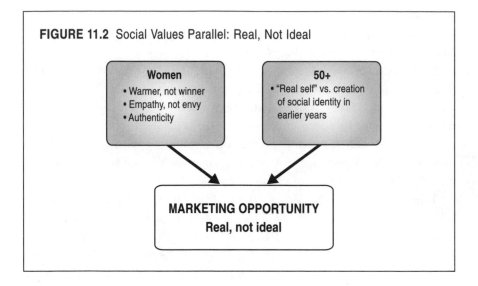

FIGURE 11.2 Social Values Parallel: Real, Not Ideal

That attitude correlates with an outlook that develops among people in the 50-plus group. For them, a corporate halo takes on a special radiance. As people grow older, they find that their priorities shift not only from the social self to the real self but also from self to others. David Wolfe, borrowing from the psychologist Abraham Maslow's theory of the "hierarchy of human needs," points out that once people satisfy their need for status and belonging, they turn their attention to the question of legacy. They ask, "What will I leave behind?" This transformation—from "success" to "significance"—draws people in midlife toward organizations that have a similarly generous and expansive understanding of their purpose.

Look at it this way: Women see the social world as a series of concentric circles that extend beyond themselves. A spirit of "passing it along" is part of their identity from the get-go. Then, in later years that attitude converges with the legacy impulse—the urge to "pass it down." (See Figure 11.3.) For PrimeTime Women™, the goal is not just to "grow old gracefully," but to grow old *gratefully*.

Star Point Two: Life/Time Factors

PrimeTime Women™ face challenges that stem from their busy, complex lives. (Remember: Women are used to getting through a

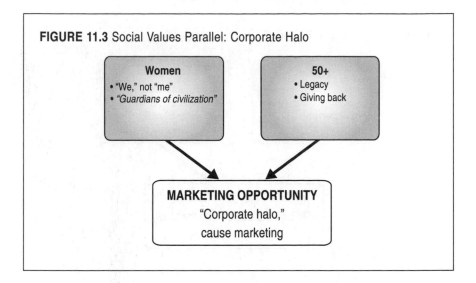

FIGURE 11.3 Social Values Parallel: Corporate Halo

"double day.") They also experience new stresses that come with growing older. In addition, though, they revel in the adventure of entering an entirely new stage of life. So . . .

Serve their critical needs. Why don't hardware stores offer a "winterizing" service in which they would bring rock salt and other necessary (and heavy!) supplies to your home at the start of cold-and-snow season? Why don't outdoor and garden retailers branch out into home delivery of potted plants and flowers, soil and mulch, and other products—cumbersome, heavy products—that people want as spring rolls around? Those are just a few examples of ways that companies could go beyond mere customer service (the price of entry onto the playing field) to "customer *services*" (the much appreciated competitive edge that will score you a goal). More and more consumers want and need *help* with managing all the *stuff* in their life, and they will gravitate to companies that provide it.

The emerging high demand for customer services results from the convergence of two factors. (See Figure 11.4.) First, as previously noted, women are perpetually starved for time, so any company that helps them make their day go just a little smoother earns their loyalty and keeps their custom. Second, as people of both genders grow older, they lose muscle mass and hence physical strength. Here again, companies that "give them a hand" will be handily rewarded. To be sure,

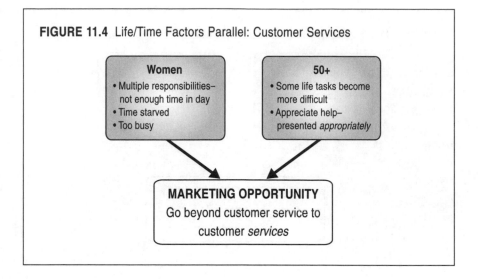

FIGURE 11.4 Life/Time Factors Parallel: Customer Services

Women
- Multiple responsibilities–not enough time in day
- Time starved
- Too busy

50+
- Some life tasks become more difficult
- Appreciate help–presented *appropriately*

MARKETING OPPORTUNITY
Go beyond customer service to customer *services*

responding to the physical infirmities of age is one area where companies have begun to address the 50-plus market. But they have focused on product design, overlooking *service design*–which may well be the greater opportunity.

PrimeTime Women™–indeed, all women and most 50-plus men as well–do not have the macho obsession with self-sufficiency that characterizes younger men. Once marketers recognize that most of their customers will gladly accept their help, they will discover a fantastic way to differentiate themselves from their competitors.

Play to their (new) strengths. The fact that older people lose strength physically blinds many of us to the strengths that people *gain* as they reach the age of 50. As Gail Sheehy first observed, the extension of longevity has created not "an extra decade at the end of life" (that's how it's usually formulated) but rather an extra decade in the *middle* of life. In other words, *50 is the new 40.* People are entering their middle years in a spirit of expansion, not of contraction–with a sense of possibility, not of limitation. In effect, they are launching into a phase of life that didn't previously exist, a phase between young adulthood and what we used of think of as middle age. As a marketer, you need to adjust your pitch accordingly.

For women, this redefinition of midlife is proving especially powerful. Consider menopause. Once a topic that was shrouded in secrecy–

people shunned the "M word" and spoke mysteriously about "change of life"—menopause is now openly discussed, widely studied, and even occasionally celebrated. No longer is it mainly a matter of being moody and erratic. On the contrary, it's associated with hormonal changes that have a positive effect (as in the case of the "biological jujitsu" that I discussed earlier).

PrimeTime Women™ are greeting the aging process on their own terms. That's not to say that they run, kicking and screaming, away from middle age. Instead, they take it as it comes, neither passively "giving in" to the effects of aging nor trying to hide them out of shame. Back in the 1970s, Clairol built an ad campaign for its hair-color product around the coy phrase "Does she or doesn't she?" The idea was that it would embarrass a woman if others knew that she dyed her hair. That attitude is simply irrelevant today, when women freely change their hair color from one week to the next—or proudly wear it gray.

To get a flavor of how PrimeTime Women™ view themselves at this new stage of their life, check out the Red Hat Society (http:// www.redhatsociety.org). It's a far-flung network of 50-plus women who come together to celebrate "fun after fifty . . . for women in all walks of life." They sponsor events, share stories through print and on-line publications, and in general promote their ideal of "greeting middle age with verve, humor, and élan." And they wear red hats and purple scarves and other flamboyant regalia as a way of expressing that commitment.

Recently, the AARP ran a series of ads that sought to jolt the marketing profession out of its persistent youth bias. Among the copy lines used in the campaign: "These days, doctors don't pronounce you dead. Marketers Do." And "To most marketers, consumers die the minute they turn 50." How (sadly) true! And how ridiculously off-base that perspective is—given that 50-plus consumers, especially women, are being virtually reborn!

Star Point Three: Focus Strategies

PrimeTime Women™ see every aspect of their life within the context of a greater whole. (Remember: Women seek to *integrate* as many *details* as possible into their understanding of a topic—and into their vision of the Perfect Answer.) They want, in their role as consumers, to transcend the narrow confines of a product spec sheet. So . . .

Immerse them in an experience. Provide a sense of *context* for your customers—a richly textured picture of what it's like to use your product or to enjoy your service. In their book *The Experience Economy: Work Is Theater and Every Business a Stage* (Harvard Business School Press, 1999), B. Joseph Pine and James H. Gilmore argue that we have entered an era when consumers expect companies to engage with them in a deep, all-encompassing way. That experience, more than the particular features of a good or service, is what builds strong brand identity and strong sales. (My colleague Tom Peters puts this idea at the very center of his vision of the new economy.) Well, that applies with special force to PrimeTime Women™. They base their purchase decisions on a less linear, more intuitive form of reasoning than that allowed by the traditional "just the facts, ma'am" style of marketing.

The convergence at work here is between women's "multiminded" way of thinking and the experiential form of thinking that people develop in midlife. Women, as we have seen, favor synthesis over analysis, weaving together numerous facts and insights to create an intuitive understanding. Unlike men (younger men, at least), they don't try to reduce a matter to a few "essential" details. Older people, meanwhile, favor wisdom over analysis. They draw on a lifetime of engagement with the world to create a gut-level sense of what matters and what's true. In short, they trust themselves, whereas younger people—who lack experience—place their trust in data and in standard logic. These points are illustrated by Figure 11.5.

One further lesson on this point: *Don't be a novelty act.* Novelty-based pitches work with men because of the male urge to be the "first on the block" with the latest and greatest product. And they work with younger consumers in general because, as David Wolfe points out, novelty is nature's way of encouraging people in their youth to learn about the world. But women are less thrill seeking than men and have less of a need to prove their superiority. Similarly, 50-plus people have a reservoir of experiential knowledge and don't need to go prospecting for what's new. Combine those attitudes in PrimeTime Women™, and you have a consumer who cares more about the fullness of experience than the flash of excitement.

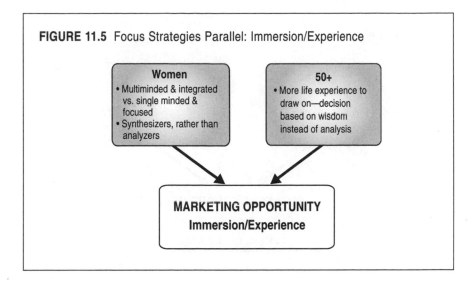

FIGURE 11.5 Focus Strategies Parallel: Immersion/Experience

Tell them a story. To create a sense of context for your product or service, embed information about its strengths and features within a story that people can relate to. Use telling anecdotes, appealing characters, and authentic-sounding dialogue to fashion a compelling narrative. In other words, as a marketer, see yourself as a *storyteller*—not as a geek who spouts out data for their own sake.

Again, for women, stories are a form of social currency. Women of all ages trade stories in order to forge relationships. And that habit finds a parallel in a similar practice that becomes salient as people grow older. For people in the 50-plus group, according to David Wolfe, stories are an absolutely essential means of processing the events of their life. Unlike younger people, they have *lived* a story—and so they view all of life from a storytelling perspective. With PrimeTime Women™, those attitudes come together in a big way. (See Figure 11.6.)

Star Point Four: Communication Keys

PrimeTime Women™ prize warm, honest relationships with others—and especially with their peers. (Remember: Women routinely engage in *"rapport talk"* and relate to people through *"same-same"* patterns of communication.) They also appreciate warm, honest depictions of who they really are and how they really live. So . . .

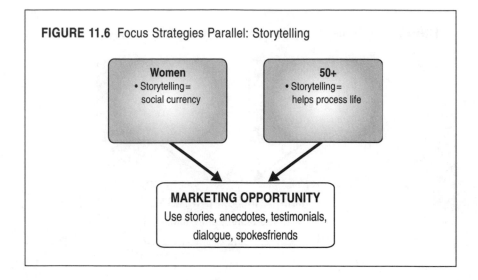

FIGURE 11.6 Focus Strategies Parallel: Storytelling

Use their connections to connect with them. In communicating with Prime Time Women™, let your mantra be "Tell a friend, bring a friend." (See Figure 11.7.) Use referral and incentive programs and other advanced word-of-mouth techniques—not only to reach more people but also to reinforce your bond with existing customers. PrimeTime Women™ love to share a good story or a good tip, so by giving them a reason to do so, you give them a reason to feel great about your brand. Event marketing works especially well in this regard. When you host an occasion where consumers can sample your product or service, while also developing their relationships with peers, you make their network *your* network.

Why are such practices so effective? Once more, it's a matter of convergence. For women, sharing information and building relationships are a way of life. With the 50-plus group, and especially the men in that category, aging brings a new perspective on what matters most in life. In ways that stem partly from the "biological jujitsu" process, men shift their focus away from work and material accumulation—and toward family and friends. They yearn to form (or re-form) connections that they fear may have been lost. PrimeTime Women™ don't have that need, but their penchant for relationship building is stronger than ever.

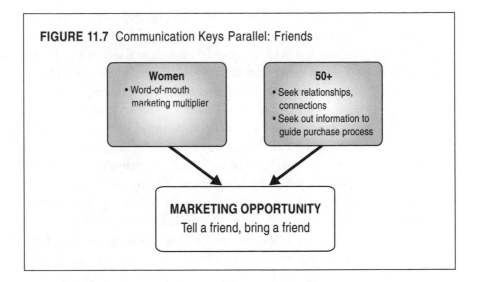

FIGURE 11.7 Communication Keys Parallel: Friends

Portray them in the way that they perceive themselves. Banish all the old stereotypes of the 50-plus woman! In conceiving of ways to represent older women in ads and other marketing materials, steer clear of anything that suggests "middle-aged woman, circa 1950" (or even circa 1980). PrimeTime Women™ are a different breed. More important, they see themselves that way. They see themselves in optimistic but realistic terms—as people who are growing older but not frailer and certainly not uglier. (A useful rule of thumb is that they, like most people, have a mental image of themselves as being about ten years younger than their actual age.)

Here a few quick tips on choosing images of PrimeTime Women™:

- Realize that beauty comes before, during, and *after* age. In ads, 50-plus women should be attractive but not absurdly so. Older women don't want to deny their age, nor do they want to give up their aspiration toward beauty. (Dove's recent Campaign for Real Beauty is an impressive move in the right direction.)
- Retire the standard image of retirement. Enough already with all those images of sunsets and Adirondack chairs and people playing golf! The fact is, large numbers of baby boomers don't plan to retire in the traditional sense of the term. (Eight out of ten baby boomers say they plan to work in retirement, according to AARP.) And when they do "retire," they will devote themselves

at least as much to philanthropic efforts and other kinds of purposive activity as they do to leisure pursuits. PrimeTime Women™, accustomed to making an impact in their work life, are not going to stand down just because they reach the age of 65.

- Think "on their own"—and "on the go." The usual practice is to depict older women as part of an older couple. Avoid that cliché. Again, many PrimeTime Women™ will spend part of their later years as widows. And they will spend all of their later years as active members of a circle of close friends. Getting out and about with those friends will be a huge part of their life. (By the way, one of the fastest-growing segments of the travel industry is called "soft adventure." It involves taking people—typically, a group of women on a "girlfriends' getaway"—on tours that combine creature comforts with exotic locales.) So portray 50-plus women as vibrantly independent or as part of a vibrant set of peers.

Who's the Dummy? Sizing Up the Opportunity

Several developments are converging to elevate PrimeTime Women™ to a position of high importance for marketers—if only marketers would take notice! These women belong to an age group whose numbers are swelling. They have a work and income history that no previous generation of women could claim, and the same goes for their status as owners of financial assets. And they bring to their prime years as consumers an assertive, confident attitude that says, "You ain't seen nothin' yet."

Unfortunately, it seems that most marketers still haven't seen *anything* yet. Or, at best, they see PrimeTime Women™ only through a distorted lens that applies to their industry or to the culture at large.

Take the retail apparel industry. For years, clothing manufacturers have designed their merchandise according to a rather diminutive conception of the female frame, generally using a size-8 mannequin to create the key pattern for each item. (Patterns for other sizes follow, of course, but the item is designed to look best on a size-8 woman.) That approach might work with younger women, who identify with a culturally defined ideal that associates beauty with thinness. But PrimeTime Women™ are so *over* that ideal. They're at peace with their real self, they're comfortable with their real body, and they want to wear clothing that's been made with real women in mind.

So how have the fashionistas in the apparel industry responded? One retailer, which will remain nameless, made a big fuss over its decision to switch to a size-10 mannequin for its line of clothes aimed at women aged 35 and older. But get this: The median dress size for women of *all* ages in the United States is a *size 12*—and we can safely assume that the median size for 35-plus (or 50-plus) women is higher still. In short, the gap between Seventh Avenue and the Main Street on which PrimeTime Women™ live could not be wider.

Hint: Just because they're still called baby boomers doesn't mean they'll put up with companies that take baby steps. Marketing to PrimeTime Women™ doesn't require you to get a wholesale brand makeover. But it does require you to get serious—and to *get real*. Get real about how 50-plus women see themselves. Get real about how they set their priorities. Get real about how they spend their money.

PrimeTime Women™ might well be the cornerstone market of the next few decades—the segment that forms the foundation for the consumer market as a whole. As with the broader women's market opportunity, companies stand to reap big rewards from relatively simple adjustments in how they think about it and how they market to it.

People in all parts of an organization should be setting their sights on the huge target that women consumers represent—and on the bull's-eye that PrimeTime Women™ represent. But there's one person above all others who needs to understand this great and growing area of opportunity: the CEO.

CHAPTER 12

Notes to the CEO

It's an interesting field, isn't it? At this point in the book, you should all feel you've gotten a good dose of new information, insights, and ideas: *information* about the market, *insights* about women, and *ideas* on how to capture the competitive edge for your company. Just about everybody can apply this learning productively in his or her current job. Sometimes, it doesn't take a lot. Anyone who has read *The Tipping Point* recalls the radical insight that very small causes can have very big effects. Still, to get the most out of marketing to women, to really seize the opportunity, and to secure all the incremental business that's there waiting for you, you're going to need the support of the corner office on the top floor. Some things only a CEO can sign off on—overall corporate strategic direction, major budget commitments, and, toughest of all sometimes, changes in organizational structure and attitudes.

But no self-respecting CEOs are going to sign off on anything unless they know what they're getting for their money. So this chapter is the executive summary: why CEOs should care and what they should do about it. If you have a male CEO (and most of them are), just give him this chapter and he'll get it. If your CEO is female, give her the whole book. She's just as busy as he is, of course, but chances are she demands a more thorough briefing. (You learned that in "Details, Details" in Chapter 4, remember?) I'm kidding of course. The point is, no matter the gender of your CEO, make sure she or he gets the information needed to help you go after this monster opportunity: the women's market.

News Flashes

Women Are Not a Niche

Women are not a "niche," so get this initiative out of the Specialty Markets group. Sometimes, ya gotta laugh. Time and time again, I'm invited to speak at a major corporation by the executive heading up a business group called something like Specialty Markets, Minority Markets, or Emerging Markets. This group has responsibility for marketing to Hispanics, African Americans, Asian populations—and women. All I can say is, "Wait a minute! You're supposed to motivate 80 percent of the population and you have, what, 4 percent of the corporate marketing budget?"

The big picture is that an organization, like any other culture, is defined and affected by the language it uses. Putting a diminutive label like "specialty" or "emerging" on the major growth sectors of the consumer population for the 21st century is guaranteed to result in failure, regardless of which of those sectors the organization is dismissing.

With respect to women specifically, there are two issues to consider. First, *women are not a niche.* A niche is a small specialty category: Amish farmers who listen to hip-hop or people who cross-stitch Star Trek theme pillows. At 51 percent of the population, women are the *majority*. Second, in most households women handle the finances—*they* spend the money. In other words, the real story is that even though they're "only" 51 percent of the population, women represent more like *80 percent* of the purchasing power.

So change your thinking. And to help your organization follow your lead, change your label. You have two options: Either you could tell your core "big brand" marketing group you want to see women built into every aspect of its planning process—market analysis, research, strategic decisions, and tactical choices—not as an addendum but as a target audience or, alternatively, you could keep your women's initiative focused in a separate group but rename it. How about something like Monster Opportunities group or Future of the Company group?

First In, First Win

The competition is starting to catch on. I can't explain why it has taken so long for American business to recognize and act on the tidal wave that is the women's market. What I can tell you is that the opportunity isn't a secret any longer. Companies from Nike to Nokia and from Wachovia to Wyndham, companies like General Motors, Volvo, Harley Davidson, and Jiffy Lube, as well as Charles Schwab, Citigroup, Best Buy, Kimpton Hotels, MinuteClinic, DeBeers, Lowe's, and The Home Depot, are all seeking their industry's lead in the women's market.

Paradoxically, there's still room to leap ahead. That's because many pioneers entered this new territory cautiously and tentatively. (See "Get Serious" below.) For whatever reason, their hearts aren't truly in the game, and that means good news for you. Their reticence means that you can benefit from what they've learned—and leapfrog to the front.

First in, first win—nowhere is this truer than in the women's market. There's not just the single benefit—a substantial one by itself—of being able to claim the high ground while it's uncluttered with competitors. The purse isn't equal for win, place, and show. Whoever is first to build a brand bond with women will be rewarded with a shield of brand loyalty that wards off future competitors. It's better to be a "warder" than a "wardee," so you'd better get started. *Get there fast and come in first.*

Get Serious

If you dip your toe in the water, what makes you think you'll get splashy results? Unlocking a gigantic new consumer segment warrants at least—at least!—as much commitment as launching a new product line. Why is it, then, that so many companies approach this immense market so tentatively? There are companies that spend millions to market a line extension without blinking an eye; others invest billions to open undeveloped foreign markets without a backward glance. Why? Because it's an "obvious" opportunity. Plus there's no time to test, because the competition is right on their heels. How is it that the same companies can decide that the women's market warrants a test launch in only a single market, and involving only a single tactic, to "see how it does"?

Let's say the competitors in your industry haven't caught on yet (a risky assumption, but let's make it for the sake of discussion). You want to run a test before you commit to a full-scale effort. In that case, keep in mind that only a multipronged marketing program conducted in *two or more markets* and supported by solid *communications* and *sales training* can deliver effective impact and readable results.

Effective impact. As every marketer knows, in our media-rich world each consumer is exposed to thousands of marketing impressions a day. For your message to generate awareness, convey information, and evoke action, it must have three characteristics: continuity, consistency, and multiple points of contact with the target prospect. You can't get that with an isolated tactic or two—*especially* not with women, who tend to crave a richer communication. You need a comprehensive program to ensure that you get through to the consumer you're trying to reach.

Readable results. Granted, these days few companies undertake the careful test-marketing protocols pioneered by leading marketers in the 1970s. These protocols involved using two or more sets of matched markets, test versus control panels of consumers, and quantitative tracking of every detail. Nonetheless, keep in mind the *reason* the ideal research design involves multiple markets: Solo markets are fraught with geographic, logistical, and competitive variables, any one of which could render the results unusable. So if your rationale for a limited effort is that you're "testing your way in," remember that any initiative that's dependent on a single venue is equally likely to give you a false positive *or* a false negative versus the control. And you'll never even know, because you have nothing to compare it to. If you can't trust the results, what's the point of spending the money and wasting your competitive lead? What a shame—all that test-marketing money down the drain.

Bottom line: Whether you're talking about a national initiative or an effective test market, get serious. For any marketing initiative to be successful, you have to act on the opportunity as if you believed in it. Toe dippers create little rings in the water that fade away in seconds. *If you want splashy results that will wash away your competitors, you have to jump in and get wet.*

Bust through the Walls of the Corporate Silo

The spirit is willing, but the budgets don't work. In working with companies that have decided to pursue the women's market, I often observe that the actual marketing is a breeze compared to dealing with the organizational challenges, which is more like leaning into a hurricane. It doesn't matter whether the company is structured by product (as it is with Ford Windstar or Ford Explorer) or by function (as in advertising, sales, Web site communications, etc.). The problem remains the same: Because the company is not organized by *customer*, it's almost impossible to get the whole team pulling in the same direction.

Everybody in the organization may agree that marketing to women is a great idea. "Absolutely, marketing to women; let's get right on it!" Unfortunately, everyone's budgets are already maxed out on other priorities this year, so it will have to wait until next year. Unless someone at the top builds "Opportunity Number One" (as Tom Peters has called the women's market for years) into the company's strategic priorities, you don't have a prayer at putting a concerted effort into the marketplace.

To get the maximum horsepower out of any strategic initiative, every department that touches the customer needs to participate. Moreover, every customer contact needs to be consistent and integrated with all the others so that the company delivers a *"one look, one voice"* message to the customer. This is *particularly* true with marketing-to-women initiatives because of a woman's greater propensity to respond to context and multiplicity, the sum total of the brand contacts she encounters from day to day.

What this means is that Moses (that would be *you*, Oh Chief Exec!) must come down from the mountain and communicate the company commitment in no uncertain terms. Right after you've put down the heavy stone tablets, you need to create a cross-functional team with the *same objectives, authority, and budget* as a new product launch team— and the same accountability for success.

Once again, both men and women should be equally represented on this team. Too many men and you won't have the female perspective you need to make the right judgment calls. Too many women and— rightly or wrongly, but in any case, realistically—the team will lose credibility, and its efforts will be discounted as "the women's project."

Keeping Customers Is Cheaper Than Buying New Ones

Once you've got her, don't let her slip away. In marketing, the rule of thumb is that it costs four to six times as much to acquire a new customer as to retain an existing one. Furthermore, a satisfied female customer has a "customer multiplier effect" far beyond her own purchases: she generates word of mouth and referrals—new customers that cost you virtually nothing.

Because of the cost of customer acquisition and the benefit of customer retention and referrals, product warranty, repair service, technical support programs, and customer relationship management are even more critical in marketing to women than to men. Don't be content with lip service from the departments responsible for making this happen; see firsthand what's happening. Ask your female employees and executives to help you keep your finger on the pulse of performance by "mystery shopping" the service centers and hot lines, and then to report in on how they're treated.

Be sure to be open to what they discover; for instance, don't discount any warning flags they bring you as "overly sensitive." Remember that this is a "sensitized population" we're talking about here. Quiet courtesies and slight snubs both have an impact disproportional to the response that either would engender in men, but that doesn't mean they're not worth your notice; far from it. Given how much you're spending to bring new customers in the front door, it seems a shame to let a little carelessness on the back end cost you your prospect and your profit.

Be Farsighted

Women are the long run. The irony of publicly held businesses is that their shareholders expect them to be successful in the long run yet hold them accountable for results on a quarterly basis. The burden of that accountability falls largely on the sales and marketing folks in the organization. Oh, *sure*—the multibillion-dollar new factory, the R&D for a major new production model, or the installation of expensive new technology get payback periods of 5 to 10 years! Any new marketing initiative, though, gets 6 to 12 months to live or die.

It's a pretty fast-paced world these days, and all of us feel the urge for instant results. With a serious marketing-to-women initiative—the kind we were talking about above—and the tracking systems to measure incremental changes, you *will* see instant results. The more you do, the more you'll get. But that's only one part of the story. There are two other considerations you need to build into your great expectations of a women's marketing program.

First, *women's immediate response to your marketing efforts is only the leading edge of the wedge.* Have the patience and persistence to evaluate the returns to you in subsequent purchase cycles, two to four years down the road. Find a way to capture data about the revenues you gain from women who may not even buy the product themselves, yet recommend it to their friends and family members. For example, a Generation X mom may not need a laptop in addition to her current desktop computer right now. However, knowing that her college-age sister is looking for a laptop to take to school, she's likely to tear out the ads for products she thinks are promising and pass them on. Ka-ching!

Think of it as compound interest—the sooner you start accumulating women customers, the more you get. And thanks to the multiplier effect, the faster it grows. The ROI on women is higher than on any other target-based alternative. They deliver *greater share of wallet,* as they consolidate more business with you; *greater loyalty,* as they stand by you in downturns; and a much *higher rate of referrals,* as they tell their friends how great you are.

Second, what we can *see*—the purchasing power women have *today*—doesn't account for what *will be.* Today's *purchasing power is only the tip of the iceberg in the women's market.* As pay levels continue to equalize, as women continue to increase their investment participation, and as baby boomer women start to inherit, first from their parents and then from their husbands, the wealth of the nation will become increasingly concentrated in women's wallets.

The moral of the story? Don't go into a marketing-to-women initiative constrained by short-term expectations. Give yourself a chance to see what you can really do for your business with a *long-term outlook.*

The Final Analysis: More Bang for Your Marketing Buck

Every year during the planning season, companies challenge themselves and their marketing groups to develop something new. *This year is going to be about innovation! Think out of the box! Let's have some breakthrough ideas!* For many of these companies, marketing to women is an idea that—if executed well—can translate to the most powerful positioning, innovative creative, and successful marketing investment they've seen in years.

It's only a matter of time. The situation is analogous to the conception and growth of marketing to kids. Only 15 years ago, marketing to kids was in its infancy (pun *intended*—you didn't miss it, did you?). Now, the field is all grown up, worth billions of dollars, and served by a corps of sophisticated practitioners. By delving into the mysterious minds of preschoolers, 'tweens, or Generation Y consumers—and consequently by understanding how kids spend not only their own money but their parents' money as well—marketers sought, discovered, and mapped new pathways in marketing. They took an iffy concept—for some companies it's always an iffy idea until someone else has made a million off it—and then ran with it, taking it to the competitive edge.

By contrast, companies that took a wait-and-see attitude found themselves desperately scrambling to catch up—and sometimes it was just too late. They were left behind, with market share surrendered to newer or savvier competitors. Today, companies that overlook the immensity of women's rapidly growing buying clout will find themselves losing ground fast to competitors who recognize the new force in an old phrase: *the power of the purse.*

Whether you work for an established market leader looking for additional prospect pools or for an innovative newcomer that thrives on fresh ideas, going after the women's market is a *big idea.* This book, *Mar-*

keting to Women: How to Increase Your Share of the World's Largest Market, is the written account of that big idea. It shows you why it's so big and what to do about it, introducing you to the concepts, strategies, and outcomes for doing so. All that remains now is for you to get out there and mix it up with your market, creating and activating a marketing-to-women initiative of your own. When you do, you'll take the "big" out of idea and put it into your business.

GenderTrends
Geniuses
Follow-Up from Sidebars

1. **Lisa Finn, Managing Editor, EPM Communications**
   What's New about the Women's Market?
2. **Dori Molitor, President, WatersMolitor**
   Turn Women Consumers into Brand Enthusiasts
3. **Joanne Thomas Yaccato, President, Women and Money, Inc.**
   Reading Her Signals Right Can Make or Break Your Sale

What's New about the Women's Market?
Lisa Finn, EPM Communications

The biggest hurdle in building effective marketing programs to tap the women's market is the illusion of familiarity. Most marketers have experience creating campaigns aimed at Mom. So there's a sense of being on familiar terrain. But the women's market is no longer so simple—and never will be again.

The current status of female-focused marketing has been compared to the status of youth marketing ten years ago. There is growing awareness of the need to create appropriate, targeted messages and of the enormous profit potential of the women's market, but this awareness has not yet seeped into all aspects of mainstream marketing.

As industries that formerly aimed messages at men begin to realize their market has shifted, those that have targeted women are also reassessing their strategies. Women's lives have undergone radical changes in the past few decades. Most women now work, and most working women also continue to shoulder the bulk of child care and household responsibilities. Where women and men share tasks, women are frequently the primary decision makers—winnowing down a series of options to a couple of final contenders, researching products through word of mouth and the Internet.

Not only does this make women a crucial target for purchases both major and minor, but it underlines the complexity of women's lives. These days, marketers wanting to get women's attention have to go much, much further than a simple spot on daytime television. Slipping in between the cracks, finding ways to tap informal networks, presenting a product or service as the solution to a problem right when and where the problem occurs—this is intricate, subtle marketing.

Added to that is the challenge of appealing to consumers who are experts—attuned to detail and nuance, savvy about marketing pitches, and concerned about getting the best quality for their money.

But the rewards are enormous—women's personal spending power has never been greater, and women's influence over family spending continues to peak. Women have become our country's expert consumers, and this ensures they will continue to hold those keys for a long time to come.

Lisa Finn, Editor, Marketing to Women *and* All about Women Consumers *(the* Marketing to Women *yearbook). Phone: (212) 941-1633, ext. 33; fax: (212) 941-1622; e-mail: lisa@epmcom.com. EPM Communications, 160 Mercer St., 3rd Fl., New York, NY 10012.* Marketing to Women *is a monthly newsletter that covers research on women's attitudes and behavior, tracks marketing efforts aimed at women, and identifies and analyzes trends in the women's market.*

Turn Women Consumers into Brand Enthusiasts
Dori Molitor, WatersMolitor

1. **Dig for the root motivators that drive her purchase!**

    Emotions drive most, if not all, purchase decisions. It's why we walk past our coffeemakers several times a week to stand in line at a coffee shop. Traditional research tools mostly focus on conscious motivators, yet emotion's influence over purchases is largely unconscious. What's needed are new tools that provide a more holistic view of women's life. It's the only way to discover the deeper, underlying root emotional needs that drive their purchases.

One of the tools available today is the "consumer archeologist," who observes consumers in their home to feel their stress, experience their fears, and share their aspirations. As professional psychologists/marketers, consumer archeologists use an intuitive, empathetic understanding to discover and articulate vivid consumer motivational insights. These insights can then be translated into go-to-market brand strategies.

2. **Play a broader, more meaningful role in her life!**

Women want brands to simplify and bring meaning to their life, but women don't trust marketers' claims. The key to winning her trust is to know her heart, mind, and life. The key to winning her purchase is to ignite an intense connection between her emotional need and your brand! It is within this connection that Brand Enthusiasm™ is born, the kind of enthusiasm that motivates women consumers to welcome your brand to play a broader, more meaningful role in their life. Brand Enthusiasm provides the power to lift your brand above the shifting sands of product and functional comparison. And it has the power to transform ordinary brands into power brands!

3. **Create Brand Enthusiasm™ to drive immediate and ongoing purchases.**

Brand Enthusiasm not only creates more powerful brands; it also makes them more profitable! It's why we pay as much for a bottle of water as we pay for a bottle of beer. Brand Enthusiasts become brand champions who won't stop talking about your brand—and other women listen! Women claim that recommendations from friends influence 54 percent of their purchase decisions and nearly 70 percent of their new product trials.

The women's market is enormous and as yet unrealized by today's marketers. Your opportunity of a lifetime is here! And it is as close as your ability to think beyond traditional marketing truths, to find that root emotional need your brand can satisfy, and to fan the flames of enthusiasm that will set cash registers ringing.

WatersMolitor is a full-service brand marketing agency with a passion to create Brand Enthusiasm™. The agency has won seven "Best in the World" Pro Awards of Excellence in the past four years alone, more than any other global agency in the history of the competition. Please contact Dori Molitor at (952) 797-5000; e-mail: dmolitor@watersmolitor.com; Web site: http://www.watersmolitor.com.

Reading Her Signals Right Can Make or Break Your Sale
Joanne Thomas Yaccato, Women and Money, Inc.

Even men who are excellent salespeople can be way off in terms of understanding women's readiness to close. They often misunderstand a classic feminine communication ritual. For all you guys reading this, heads up. This will be the most important piece of information about women that you will ever hear. When a woman nods her head up and down, it does not mean she is agreeing with you. This is merely a listening cue. In fact, it is entirely possible that a woman can be nodding her head and thinking at the same time, *You just might be the biggest goof I have ever met.*

For valid reasons, many men can interpret affirmative head nodding as a sign of prospect readiness to close. That may be what is happening when selling to men, but research proves this isn't necessarily the case with women. If you attempt to close before a proper sales or business relationship has been formed, especially with women, you've blown it. This also might be a contributing factor to why women constantly complain that many salespeople are too aggressive and "hard sell." Without understanding the different styles and rituals women and men have in communicating, this kind of sales miscue will continue to happen.

Joanne Thomas Yaccato, President, Women and Money, Inc., and author of The 80 Percent Minority: Reaching the Real World of Women Consumers. *Phone: (416) 367-3677. Web site: http://www.womenandmoneyinc.com.*

The Best Resources
in the Business

Here is a list of sources I've found valuable in my years of work and writing on the topic of marketing to women.

Essential Books

Baron-Cohen, Simon. *The Essential Difference: The Truth About the Male and Female Brain.* Perseus Books Group, 2003.

Blum, Deborah. *Sex on the Brain: The Biological Differences between Men and Women.* Viking Penguin, 1997.

Browne, Kingsley R. *Biology at Work: Rethinking Sexual Equality. The Rutgers Series in Human Evolution.* Rutgers University Press, 2002.

Fisher, Helen, PhD. *The First Sex–The Natural Talents of Women and How They Are Changing the World.* Ballantine Books, 1999.

Gurian, Michael. *Girls and Boys Learn Differently: A Guide for Teachers and Parents.* Jossey-Bass, 2002.

Moir, Anne, and Bill Moir. *Why Men Don't Iron: The Fascinating and Unalterable Differences between Men and Women.* Citadel Press, 1999.

Ridley, Matt. *The Red Queen: Sex and the Evolution of Human Nature.* Harper Penguin, 1995.

Sax, Leonard, PhD. *Why Gender Matters: What Parents and Teachers Need to Know About the Emerging Science of Sex Differences.* Doubleday, 2005.

Sheehy, Gail. *New Passages: Mapping Your Life across Time.* Ballantine Books, 1995.

Tanenbaum, Joe. *Male and Female Realities–Understanding the Opposite Sex.* Robert Erdmann Publishing, 1990.

Tannen, Deborah, PhD. *You Just Don't Understand.* Ballantine Books, 1990.

———. *Gender & Discourse.* Oxford University Press, 1996.

Tingley, Judith, PhD. *Genderflex: Men & Women Speaking Each Other's Language at Work.* AMACOM, 1993.

Comprehensive Study

Anderson, Deborah, PhD, and Christopher Hayes, PhD. *Gender, Identity and Self-Esteem: A New Look at Adult Development.* Springer Publishing Company, 1996.

Brothers, Joyce, PhD. *What Every Woman Should Know about Men.* Ballantine Books, 1981.

Driscoll, Richard, PhD. *The Stronger Sex: Understanding and Resolving the Eternal Power Struggles between Men and Women.* Prima Publishing, 1998.

Fausto-Sterling, Anne. *Sexing the Body: Gender Politics and the Construction of Sexuality.* Basic Books, 2000.

Gilligan, Carol. *In a Different Voice: Psychological Theory and Women's Development.* Harvard University Press, 1993.

Gray, John, PhD. *Men Are from Mars, Women Are from Venus.* HarperCollins, 1992.

Levinson, Daniel. *The Seasons of a Woman's Life–A Fascinating Exploration of the Events, Thoughts and Life Experiences That All Women Share.* Ballantine Books, 1996.

Moir, Anne, PhD, and David Jessel. *Brain Sex–The Real Difference between Men and Women.* Dell Books, 1991.

Pease, Barbara, and Allan Pease. *Why Men Don't Listen–and Women Can't Read Maps: How We're Different and What to Do about It.* Welcome Rain Publishers, 2000.

Weiner, Edith, and Arnold Brown. *Office Biology: Or Why Tuesday Is Your Most Productive Day and Other Relevant Facts for Survival in the Workplace.* Master Media, 1993. (See Chapters 3 and 4, "Gender: Bridging Brains, Babies, Bodies and Brawn" and "The Body Burden: The Inescapable (?) Facts of Aging.")

Weiss, Daniel Evan. *The Great Divide: How Females and Males Really Differ.* Poseidon Press, 1991.

Wilson, Glenn. *The Great Divide: A Study of Male–Female Differences.* Scott Townsend Publishers, 1992.

Marketing/Selling to Women

Bartos, Rena. *Marketing to Women around the World.* Harvard Business School Press, 1989.

Leeming, Janice E., and Cynthia F. Tripp. *Segmenting the Women's Market.* Probus Publishing Company, 1994.

Meyers, Gerry. *Targeting the New Professional Woman.* Probus Publishing Company, 1993.

Peters, Tom. *The Circle of Innovation.* Alfred A. Knopf, Inc., 1997. (See Chapter 12, "It's a Woman's World.")

Popcorn, Faith, and Lys Marigold. *EVEolution.* Hyperion, 2000.

Roberts, Sharon. *Selling to Women & Couples.* Cambium Press, 1999.

Tingley, Judith C., PhD, and Lee E. Robert. *GenderSell—How to Sell to the Opposite Sex.* Simon & Schuster, 1999.

Underhill, Paco. *Why We Buy: The Science of Shopping.* Simon & Schuster, 1999. (See Chapters 8 and 9, "Shop Like a Man" and "What Women Want.")

Stats, Facts, and Findings

Women and Diversity: WOW! Facts. The Business Women's Network in Washington, D.C., publishes this wide-ranging and interesting collection of independent facts from myriad sources on everything from the women's market to health, philanthropy, politics, and sports. Also available in print as a book of the same name.

Books

Dailey, Nancy. *When Baby Boom Women Retire.* Praeger Publishers, 2000. Impressive and scholarly; really good perspectives on retirement prognosis for boomer women.

EPM Communications. *Marketing Yearbook.* Year-end compendium of all the stats, facts, and findings published in the newsletter for the past 12 months. A streamlined way to access all their material for the past year, consolidated and organized by topic.

New Strategist editors. *American Women: Who They Are and How They Live.* New Strategist Publications, 1997. (Demographic charts and tables)

New Strategist editors. *American Men and Women.* New Strategist Publications, 2000. (Demographic charts and tables)

Women in Canada 2000. Pretty comprehensive information but focuses as much on social questions as on issues of relevance to marketers. Order from Statistics Canada, (800) 267-6677, or via e-mail, *order@statcan.ca.* Price is approximately U.S. $33, including shipping.

Newsletter

Marketing to Women. This is the only newsletter to focus exclusively on the women's market, and it does a superb job. Every month, the 12-page hard-copy newsletter is packed with snippets of research from sources all over the country—they seem to know everyone who's doing anything in this market. Editor Lisa Finn's commentary is always well informed and insightful. A truly wonderful aspect of the newsletter is that it gives you sources—not just organizations, but contact names, phone numbers, Web sites, and so on. For a streamlined way to access all their material for the past year organized by topic, be sure to buy their year-end compendium, the *Marketing Yearbook.*

Web Sites and Links

Blue Suit Moms. A Web site dedicated to helping executive working mothers find balance between work and family. *www.bluesuitmom.com*

Business and Professional Women USA—101 Facts on the Status of Working Women. It is just what it sounds like. *www.bpwusa.org/content/Workplace/ FactsandFigures/101Facts.htm*

Catalyst. Extraordinary resource on the evolving status of women in the workplace. Dozens of publications, very comprehensive (30–250 pages), and all very accessibly priced (most are $25–$90). *www.catalystwomen .org/Publications1.htm* Selected statistics from the studies are excerpted in the synopses under Research: *www.catalystwomen.org/Research1.htm*

Center for Women's Business Research; formerly the National Foundation for Women Business Owners (NFWBO). The definitive source for information on women business owners in the United States and a few other countries. Primary research is conducted in partnership with sponsor corporations and reported in very useful and reasonably priced reports (most are around $90–$100). Topics range from WBO volunteerism to use of technology, leadership style, and many others. *www.womensbusinessresearch.org/publications.html* Check out their Key Facts page: *www.womensbusinessresearch.org/key.html*

HNW. Fabulous compendium of facts on the high-net-worth market, encompassing estate planning, Internet use, philanthropy, and more. *www.hnw.com/newsresch/hnw_market/index.jsp* Also published a terrific study on HNW women, but for some reason it's nowhere to be seen on the site anymore. Worth giving them a call to ask about it, if you're a corporation in the financial services business with some decent resources.

ReachWomen. Andrea Learned and Lisa Johnson are cofounders of this savvy company specializing in marketing to women online. *www.reach women.com* Be sure to subscribe to their very informative, well-written, and well-produced e-newsletter.

Shell U.S. Poll. Winter 2000. Wide-ranging survey of men's and women's attitudes on a variety of subjects including work, politics, investing, and sports. *www.shellus.com/products/poll/pdf/Women_On_The_ Move.pdf*

Statistics Canada. The central source for all Canadian statistics. *www.stat can.ca/english/Pgdb* Has some fundamental information broken out by gender but is not an exhaustive resource. The site is a little difficult to use—the best way to get access to a concentration of data is to order their print publication, *Women in Canada 2000* (approximately U.S. $33, including shipping).

U.S. Trust Survey of Affluent Americans. Very useful information, including a separate breakout on affluent women business owners. *www.ustrust.com/ ustrust/html/knowledge/WealthManagementInsights/SurveyofAffluent Americans/index.html*

ENDNOTES

Chapter 1. The Power of the Purse

1. U.S. Department of Education, National Center for Education Statistics, *Digest of Education Statistics: 2002,* as quoted in the Department for Professional Employees AFL-CIO, Fact Sheet 2005, Professional Women: Vital Statistics.

2. "Trends in Educational Equity of Girls and Women: 2004" published by the National Center for Education Statistics, a division of the U.S. Dept of Education. http://nces.ed.gov/pubs2005/equity/Section8.asp.

3. U.S. Department of Education, National Center for Education Statistics, *Digest of Education Statistics: 2002,* as quoted in the Department for Professional Employees AFL-CIO, Fact Sheet 2005, Professional Women: Vital Statistics.

4. "Women and Pensions," *Risk Management and Insurance Review* 8, No. 1, 2005.

5. "She Works, He Doesn't," *Newsweek,* 12 May 2003, p. 44.

6. "Women and Pensions," *Risk Management and Insurance Review* 8, No. 1, 2005. *Adweek,* 27 May 2002, p.2.

7. "Look Who's Bringing Home More Bacon," *BusinessWeek Online,* 31 Jan 2003.

8. *Generation X,* 4th ed., *The Baby Boom,* 4th ed., *Older Americans,* 4th ed., all New Strategist Publications, 2004.

9. "Look Who's Bringing Home More Bacon," *BusinessWeek Online,* 31 Jan 2003.

10. Calculated from New Strategist editors' data, *American Men and Women,* New Strategist Publications, 2000, pp. 260–61.

11. *BusinessWeek Online,* 31 Jan 2003.

12. Calculated from 1999 federal population data by Richard B. Freeman, Harvard economist; cited in the *Washington Post.*

13. "Breadwinning Wives Alter Marriage Equation," *Washington Post,* 27 Feb 2000, A01.

14. New Strategist editors, *American Men and Women,* pp. 260–61.

15. *American Demographics* 19, No. 11 (Nov. 1997), p. 37.

16. *BusinessWeek Online,* 31 Jan 2003.

17. *Bank Investment Consultant,* Oct. 2004, p. 204.

18. U.S. Labor Department, reported in the *Wall Street Journal,* 24 Nov 1997.

19. Federal Reserve, cited in PBS Online, *To The Contrary*, Hot Topics, Women & Philanthropy.

20. IRS Publication, *Statistics of Income Bulletin*, Winter 1999–2000, cited in Women's Philanthropy Institute, *Facts about Women, Wealth, and Giving*, 16 Jan 2001.

21. *Bank Investment Consultant*, Oct. 2004, p. 204.

22. Nancy Dailey, *When Baby Boom Women Retire*, Praeger Publishers, 2000, p. 39.

23. Securities Industry Association, e.1998.

24. Consumer Electronics Assn, 2004.

25. Lowe's, per CEO Robert Tillman, cited on Forbes.com and quoted in Tom Peters presentation, 1 June 2003.

26. American Woman, *Road & Travel* magazine, on Roadandtravel.com 2005; "Ford aims at women's market as it lines up ad space for '98," *Automotive News*, 14 July 1997, by Jean Halliday.

27. Condé Nast/Intelliquest Survey, as quoted in *Ad Age*, 1997.

28. *American Women*, New Strategist Publications, 1997.

29. Time Inc.'s Women's Group, *Seven New Rules of the Road–Understanding Today's Woman*, 2004, pp. 50–51.

30. Center for Women's Business Research, formerly National Foundation for Women Business Owners, 1999.

31. Ibid.

32. Center for Women's Business Research, 2004.

33. Ibid.

34. Ibid.

Chapter 2. The Differences That Make a Difference

1. *Women on the Verge of the 21st Century*, published in *Grey Matter Alert*, a white paper from Grey Advertising, Fall 1995.

2. Gillian Turner, "Intelligence and the X chromosome," *The Lancet* 347, No. 9018 (29 June 1996), pp. 1814–15. Cited on http://www.igs.net/~cmorris/turner.html, revised by Clifford Morris, 16 July 2000.

3. Anne Moir, PhD, and David Jessel, *Brain Sex: The Real Difference between Men and Women*, Dell Books, 1991, p. 83.

4. June Reinsich, director of the Kinsey Institute, cited in Moir, *Brain Sex*, p. 79.

5. Moir and Jessel, *Brain Sex*, p. 93.

6. Barbara Pease and Allan Pease, *Why Men Don't Listen–and Women Can't Read Maps: How We're Different and What to Do about It*, Welcome Rain Publishers, 2000, p. 157.

7. Deborah Blum, *Sex on the Brain: The Biological Differences between Men and Women*, Viking Penguin, 1997, p. 114.

8. "Female Friendships Have a Salubrious Effect, Research Shows," by Melissa Healy, Tribune Newspapers: *Los Angeles Times,* 18 May 2005.

9. Marvin Zuckerman, cited in Anne Moir and Bill Moir, *Why Men Don't Iron: The Fascinating and Unalterable Differences between Men and Women,* Citadel Press, 1999, pp. 160–63.

10. Pease and Pease, p. 134. Based on research conducted by Canadian scientist Dr. Sandra Witelson.

11. Helen Fisher, PhD, *The First Sex–The Natural Talents of Women and How They Are Changing the World,* Ballantine Publishing Group, 1999, p. 90.

12. Blum, p. 67.

13. Pease and Pease, p. 35.

14. Diener, cited in Goleman, *Emotional Intelligence,* Bantam Books, 1997, p. 50; and Brody and Hall, cited in Goleman, p. 132.

15. Based on research by Galea and Kimura, cited in Fisher, p. 94.

16. Doreen Kimura, *Sex and Cognition,* MIT Press, 1999, p. 89.

17. Moir and Jessel, *Brain Sex,* p. 57.

18. Ibid.

19. Blum, p. 75.

20. Kimura, Chap. 8.

21. Blum, p. 58.

22. Ibid.

23. Kimura, p. 67.

24. Fisher, p. 15.

25. Pease and Pease, p. 111.

26. Blum, p. 58.

27. Fisher, p. 162.

28. Pease and Pease, p. 105.

Chapter 4. The Star Gender Culture

1. *Adweek,* 27 May 2002, p. 2.

2. *Marketing to Women* newsletter, February 2000.

3. Anne Moir, PhD, and David Jessel, *Brain Sex: The Real Difference between Men and Women,* Dell Books, 1991, p. 157.

4. Helen Fisher, PhD, *The First Sex–The Natural Talents of Women and How They Are Changing the World,* Ballantine Publishing Group, 1999, p. 188.

5. James Patterson and Peter Kim, *The Day America Told the Truth,* cited in *Women & Money* newsletter, April 1998, p. 13.

6. Deborah Blum, *Sex on the Brain: The Biological Differences between Men and Women,* Viking Penguin, 1997, p. 74.

7. Ibid., p. 179.

8. Psychologist Jim Sindanius, University of California–Los Angeles, cited in Janice E. Leeming and Cynthia F. Tripp, *Marketing by Gender,* About Women, Inc., 1997, p. 30.

9. Joe Tanenbaum, *Male and Female Realities–Understanding the Opposite Sex,* Robert Erdmann Publishing, p. 78.

10. Moir and Jessel, *Brain Sex,* p. 130; Barbara Pease and Allan Pease, *Why Men Don't Listen–and Women Can't Read Maps: How We're Different and What to Do about It,* Welcome Rain Publishers, 2000, p. 133.

11. Time Inc. Women's Group, *Seven New Rules of the Road,* p. 7, 2004.

12. 1998 U.S. Census Bureau data, cited in *Marketing to Women* newsletter, May 2001.

13. Denise Fedewa, Leo She, quoted in *Sales and Marketing Management,* January 2000.

14. Employment Policy Foundation analysis of March 2001 Current Population Survey, cited in *Marketing to Women* newsletter, May 2002.

15. Employment Policy Foundation analysis of 1997 PSID (Panel Study of Income Dynamics) data, cited on http://www.epf.org.

16. 101 Facts on the Status of Working Women, produced by Business and Professional Women's Foundation.

17. Time Inc. Women's Group, *Seven New Rules of the Road,* p. 7, 2004.

18. Tanenbaum, p. 160.

19. Time Inc. Women's Group, *Seven New Rules of the Road,* p. 18, 2004.

20. Fisher, p. 7.

21. *American Generations,* 2000, p. 342. Calculations by New Strategist, based on numbers from U.S. Bureau of the Census.

22. New Strategist editors, *Americans 55 and Older,* New Strategist Publications, 2001, p. 293. Calculations by New Strategist, based on numbers from U.S. Bureau of the Census.

23. Time Inc. Women's Group, *Seven New Rules of the Road,* p. 29, 2004.

24. http://www.geocities.com/Heartland/Lane/8771/chromosomes.html

25. Travelandleisure.com, "On the Move," by Kate Zernike, November 2004 issue.

26. *Travel & Leisure*'s Laura Begley quoted in Harvard Business School *Working Knowledge* newsletter, "The Hidden Market of Female Travelers," 7 Feb 2005.

27. Kimptonlife.com, article by travel expert Marybeth Bond (author of *Travelers' Tales: A Woman's World,* 1995), 2005.

28. *Travel & Leisure*'s Laura Begley quoted in Harvard Business School *Working Knowledge* newsletter, "The Hidden Market of Female Travelers," 7 Feb 2005.

29. Ibid.

30. Ibid.

31. Time Inc. Women's Group, *Seven New Rules of the Road–Understanding Today's Woman,* 2004, p. 58.

32. *Brandweek,* May 2002, p. 9.

33. National Opinion Research Center, University of Chicago, *1998 General Social Survey,* cited in *American Men and Women,* New Strategist Publications, 2000, p. 49.

Chapter 5. The Circle and the Compass: Response to Marketing Contacts

1. 2002 Pew Internet and American Life study as quoted in Time Inc. Women's Group, *Seven New Rules of the Road,* 2004, pp. 58–59.

2. "Women wear the pants online also," *Ad Age,* 25 April 2005.

3. *Health Magazine,* Women in Motion 2001.

4. Consumer Electronics Association, as noted in the article dated 27 May 2005, "Women Interested in Consumer Electronics Discover First Magazine Written Especially for Them," PRWeb; 6 Jan 2004 CEA press release.

5. Best Buy provided these figures.

6. *Ad Age,* 10 Nov 1997, pp. 24–26.

Chapter 6. The Spiral Path: How Women Make Purchase Decisions

1. Paco Underhill, *Why We Buy: The Science of Shopping,* Simon & Schuster, 1999, pp. 101–2.

2. Lifestyle Monitor, in *Marketing to Women* 14, No. 9 (Sept. 2001).

3. Condé Nast, *Working Woman,* July/August 2001, p. 25.

4. Time Inc. Women's Group, *Seven New Rules of the Road,* 2004, p. 35.

Chapter 7. On Your Mark: Market Assessment

1. Lowe's own internal research, as quoted in *Marketing to Women* Newsletter, October 2003; *DSN Retailing Today* magazine, 16 Dec 2002.

2. Lowe's research, per CEO Robert Tillman, cited on Forbes.com and quoted in Tom Peters presentation, 1 June 2003.

3. Ace Hardware, PDR, 7/03, p. 41.

4. Homebuilders Ass'n, reported in *Computerworld,* BWN, WOW! Facts, 2001.

5. Home Improvement Research Institute, as quoted in "Things Fall Apart: Here's How to Fix 'Em," by Robyn Blumner, *St. Petersburg Times,* 27 June 2004.

6. National Association of Realtors, as quoted in the *Wall Street Journal* real estate section, "Single Women Become a Force in Home-Buying," by Jennifer Lisle, 24 Nov 2004.

7. Sears survey titled "Her Home: How Women Homeowners View Home Maintenance," press release issued July 2004.

8. CTNow.com–produced by Hartford Courant, http://www.ctnow .com/business/hc-pitch0730.artjul30,0,1972970.column?coll=hc-head lines-business; Inside Pitch, Matthew Kauffman, "Showing Its Softer Side Home Depot Marketing Strategy Has Eye on Women," 30 July 2003.

9. "Yes, Women Spend (And Saw and Sand)," *New York Times*, 29 Feb 2004.

10. American Women, New Strategist Publications, 1997, p. 28.

11. Women.com, P&G, Harris Interactive Study, 1999.

12. MarketResearch.com; Simmons Market Research Bureau, All About Women Consumers, 2002 Yearbook, p. 70.

13. "Women now comprise 70 percent of the membership of the nonprofit National Association of Investors Corporation (NAIC)." National Association of Investors Corporation Web site: http://www.better-investing.org, press release 18 Oct 2001.

14. http://womensinvest.about.com/library/weekly/aa030500; Women's Financial Network quoted on WOW Facts, 2001.

15. Securities Industry Association, e.1998.

16. Prudential Securities poll, 1995.

17. Investment Company Institute, cited in Diane Harris, "How Women Have Wised Up," *Money* magazine, 1996.

18. Janice E. Leeming and Cynthia F. Tripp, *Marketing by Gender*, About Women, Inc., 1997, p. 57.

Chapter 8. Get Set: Strategy and Tactical Planning

1. American Woman, *Road & Travel* magazine, on roadandtravel.com 2005; "Ford aims at women's market as it lines up ad space for '98," Automotive News,14 July 1997, by Jean Halliday.

2. American Woman, *Road & Travel* magazine, on roadandtravel.com 2005.

3. American Woman, *Road & Travel* magazine, on roadandtravel.com 2005; WomensWallStreet.com, quoted in Spring Wheels, part of the Gazette Interactive Network, 2004; Detnews.com "Ford's 'Windstar Moms' re-vamp van," 4 Nov 2000; *Automotive News*, 11 Sept 2000.

4. American Woman, *Road & Travel* magazine, on roadandtravel.com 2005; quoted in General Motors news release "GM Goodwrench Provides Safety and Maintenance Tips for Busy Women," 6 April 2005.

5. Aftermarket Business, "Marketing lessons from out of the toolbox," 6 June 2005.

6. American Woman, *Road & Travel* magazine, on roadandtravel.com 2005.

7. *Automotive News*, 8 March 2004 "All-female Volvo gets mixed reviews; officials say design cues could be used in upcoming vehicles," by Mark Rechtin.

8. Paco Underhill, *Why We Buy: The Science of Shopping*, Simon & Schuster, 1999, p. 37.

9. National Institute for Automotive Service Excellence [ASE].

10. Cited in *Marketing to Women* newsletter, September 2001.

Chapter 9. Go! Communications That Connect

1. "Considering a Fifth C: Cheap: Revenue of Online Jewelers Swells with Consumer Confidence in the Internet," by Dina ElBoghdady, *Washington Post,* Thursday, 1 Jan 2004; "Right Hand Rings," ABC7chicago.com, by Linda Yu, 26 Feb 2004.

2. "Right Hand Rings" ABC7chicago.com, by Linda Yu, 26 Feb 2004.

3. "The Way We Live Now: The Right-Hand Diamond Ring," by Rob Walker, *New York Times,* 4 Jan 2004.

4. Ibid.

5. The Business Report, South Africa, "Women Take Charge of Their Own Sparkle," by Sherilee Bridge, 5 Oct 2003.

6. "'Right-hand' diamonds marketed to women as power sign—A subsidiary of DeBeers gets its message out with an aggressive ad drive," by Melanie Payne, *Sacramento Bee,* 2 Dec 2003.

Chapter 10. Face-to-Face: Sales and Service

1. Center for Business Women's Research, 2005.

2. Center for Business Women's Research, 2005.

Chapter 11. PrimeTime Women™: The Target Marketer's Golden Bull's-Eye

1. University of Georgia, Selig Center for Economic Growth, 2004, "Women of Color are on a Buying spree," DiversityInc.com, 1 July 2004, PR Newswire, 19 Jan 2004, 2000 U.S. Census, "African-American Women Gaining in Biz Starts," We News, 13 Feb 2005.

2. *New York Times,* 25 July 2001.

3. Source: American Demographics, December 1992, Women of a Certain Age; based on statistics from the U.S. Census Bureau.

4. 2005 White House Conference on Aging Policy Committee Hearing, 1 Oct 2004, Statement of Paul Hodge, Director, Harvard Generations Policy Program.

5. U.S. Census Bureau.

6. Ken Dychtwald, *Age Power,* page 20.

7. 70%: Ken Dychtwald, *Age Power,* page 20 . . . 73%: AARP . . . 79%: Gary Onks, SoldOnSeniors, Inc. Another (slightly lower, but authoritative-sounding) assets figure: The 78 million Americans who were 50 or older as of 2001 controlled 67 percent of the country's wealth, or $28 trillion, according to data collected by the U.S. Census and the Federal Reserve. Source: "Older Consumers Buy Stuff, Too," *Wall Street Journal,* 6 April 2004.

8. Gary Onks, SoldOnSeniors, Inc.

9. Ibid.

10. Dychtwald, p. 20.

11. Source: AARP State of 50+ in America report, 2004.

12. Source: "Older Consumers Buy Stuff, Too," *Wall Street Journal,* 6 April 2004.

13. http://www.census.gov/Press-Release/www/2000/cb00-158.html.

14. http://www.census.gov/Press-Release/www/2001/cb01-33.html.

15. Onks, SoldOnSeniors, Inc.

16. Dychtwald, *Age Power,* p. 20.

17. Onks, SoldOnSeniors, Inc.

18. Dychtwald, *Age Power,* p. 20.

19. David Wolfe's *Ageless Marketing.*

20. *Wall Street Journal,* "Older Consumers Buy Stuff, Too," 6 April 2004.

21. According to market research firm NPD Group.

22. Onks.

23. Dianne Hales, *Just Like a Woman: How Gender Science is Re-defining What Makes U.S. Female,* p. 75.

24. Source: AARP State of 50+ in America report, 2004.

INDEX

Share the message!

Bulk discounts
Discounts start at only 10 copies and range from 30% to 55% off retail price based on quantity.

Custom publishing
Private label a cover with your organization's name and logo. Or, tailor information to your needs with a custom pamphlet that highlights specific chapters.

Ancillaries
Workshop outlines, videos, and other products are available on select titles.

Dynamic speakers
Engaging authors are available to share their expertise and insight at your event.

Call Dearborn Trade Special Sales at 1-800-621-9621, ext. 4444, or e-mail trade@dearborn.com.

Dearborn™
Trade Publishing
A **Kaplan Professional** Company

658.804
B 257
2006

LINCOLN CHRISTIAN COLLEGE AND SEMINARY

118455

3 4711 00181 1860